Contents

FINANCIAL MANAGEMENT

Fourth Edition

T. M. KENNEDY, B.Comm., A.C.M.A.

M. J. MacCORMAC, M.A., M. Comm., D.Econ. Sc., F.A.C.C.A.

J. J. TEELING, B.Comm., M.Econ. Sc., M.B.A., D.B.A.

GILL AND MACMILLAN

Published in Ireland by
Gill and Macmillan Ltd
Goldenbridge
Dublin 8
with associated companies in
Auckland, Delhi, Gaborone, Hamburg, Harare,
Hong Kong, Johannesburg, Kuala Lumpur, Lagos, London,
Manzini, Melbourne, Mexico City, Nairobi,
New York, Singapore, Tokyo
© T. M. Kennedy, M. J. MacCormac and J. J. Teeling, 1988
First published 1971; second edition 1976; third edition 1980
© M. J. MacCormac and J. J. Teeling, 1971, 1976, 1980
Fourth edition 1988
Reprinted 1989
Print origination in Ireland by Graphic Plan, Dublin
Printed in Great Britain by
The Camelot Press, Southampton

British Library Cataloguing in Publication Data
Kennedy, Tom *1949-*
    Financial management.—4th ed.
    1. Ireland (Republic). Business firms.
    Financial management
    I. Title II. MacCormac, M. J. (Michael Joseph), *1926-* III. Teeling, J. J. (John James), *1946-*
658.1′5′09417
ISBN 0-7171-1591-7

Preface

It is almost two decades since the first edition of *Financial Management* was written. In the intervening period major convulsions have shaken the very foundations of the world's economy.

The 1970s had soaring oil prices, rampant inflation, world economic recession, floating currencies and declining stock exchanges. Financial managers had to learn new techniques to handle the challenges, the risks and to seek out opportunities.

The 1980s have been no less turbulent. Falling oil prices, deflation in certain countries, growth in Western economies, stagnant Third World economies leading to debt defaults and a stock market boom, offered new and exciting challenges. The collapse of share prices all over the world on 'Meltdown Monday' in October 1987, followed by the collapse in the value of the US dollar, threatened a serious economic recession. Once again money managers had to adapt to a changed economic environment.

The structure of *Financial Management* has not changed much in the fourth edition, but the content and emphasis has. Legislative and accounting changes have led to major revisions in the early chapters. The changed competitive scene for financial institutions in Ireland is reflected in a change of emphasis in the chapter on financial institutions. The Stock Exchange has experienced major innovations in the recent past. This is reflected in a greatly revised chapter.

The chapters on sources of finance have been updated and emphasis changed to reflect the increased importance of leasing and factoring. The impact of the Business Expansion Scheme incentives on raising of new equity is an important addition to the chapter on 'Ownership Sources of Finance'. The chapter on 'Mergers and Takeovers' has been rewritten and expanded greatly to reflect the financial activities of Irish companies. Finally, the chapter on 'International Finance' has been expanded to deal with the greater internationalisation of modern business.

In this fourth edition we are joined as authors by Tom Kennedy of the National Institute for Higher Education in Limerick.

J. J. T.
M. J. M.
T. M. K.
Dublin, June, 1988.

Introduction

For many years financial management played a secondary role to business finance. Business finance concentrated on financial institutions such as banks and on the financial instruments provided by these institutions, such as term loans and overdrafts. Financial management was regarded as a function of the manager of a business. In reality, the business manager often assigned the task of managing finance to the business accountant. It was only during the 1960s and 1970s that a central role was assigned to the management aspect of finance. New technologies and inflation combined to make new investments very expensive or, in the language of finance, capital intensive. Sound capital budgeting procedures including accurate measurements of the cost of capital became the accepted norm. It was quickly realised that a poor investment decision could bankrupt a business. Apart from the threat posed by the size of investments, further problems were identified in handling uncertainty. Projects with extended lives often depended for their profitability on cash inflows arising some years in the future. Experience, often bitter, sometimes fatal, taught managers to view distant cash flows with a jaundiced eye. To put the problem in perspective, consider the major upheavals which have occurred in the past decade. Many of those upheavals ultimately produced huge distortions in the incomes arising from many projects and made nonsense of the original investment decision.

Due to pressure from external forces such as inflation, currency volatility, technological innovation and the growing substitution of capital for labour, financial management has developed new and more sophisticated techniques for analysing and handling change and the uncertainties which surround change.

Inflation had not only a major impact on capital investments but also produced significant problems in the day-to-day management of business. In more settled times with easy access to money, low annual rates of both inflation and interest, business could often afford the luxury of relatively lax management of working capital—that is, managing the investment in accounts receivable, inventory and cash. Higher rates of inflation meant that many profitable businesses did not earn enough each year to finance the consequent increase in the amounts invested in inventory and accounts receivable. One result is that many businesses borrowed heavily to finance growth. The term 'overtrading' was coined to describe the situation of a business that had too little ownership funds invested. Using other people's money is fine in good times but can be disastrous in bad times. The columns of Stubbs Gazette pay weekly tribute to the profitable businesses which have gone bankrupt due to the mis-management of working capital. Techniques have evolved which can assist the financial manager in deciding how best to manage investments in accounts receivable, inventory and cash. The renewed interest in merger activity, with an increase in the process of conglomeration allied to the blurring of the distinction between the private and the public sector, also contributed to the changing role of financial management in the past decade.

The traditional roles of finance—financial institutions and financial instruments—have continued to evolve. Ireland has seen a rapid development in financial institutions. The associated banks continue to dominate lending in Ireland but they now face competition from overseas banks and from specialist lending houses such as merchant and industrial banks and from the fast growing leasing companies. The state, through the medium of the Industrial Development Authority, the Industrial Credit Company and numerous other agencies, plays a central role in providing money to business. The Central Bank of Ireland has gradually exerted control over all the financial institutions in the country.

In response to the growing scale and diversity of investment, financial instruments have changed. Gone are the days of using bank overdraft to finance the building of a factory. Demands for finance have created new sophisticated instruments. Term loans, leasing, sale and leaseback and project finance are relatively new financial instruments in which Irish financial institutions have played a major development role.

THE NATURE OF FINANCIAL MANAGEMENT

Financial management can be defined as:

Assisting in the achievement of the overall objectives of the firm through:

(a) The provision of finance when and where required in a manner and at a cost which provides an acceptable level of risk to the business.

(b) The investigation and evaluation of investment opportunities open to the business.

Financial techniques generally assume that the overall objective of the business is the maximisation of the owners' wealth. Note that wealth rather than profit is being maximised. Maximisation of profit is not very applicable to an ongoing business in that the concept is short term, that is, it is possible to maximise current profits at the expense of long term success. Maximisation of wealth is a useful objective in that it requires a set of corporate policies which maximise the present worth of the owners' investment.

For many years now, a learned debate has been proceeding over the relative merits of profit maximisation, wealth maximisation or—to introduce a recent contribution—wealth satisficing, that is, the objective of a satisfactory level of profit. Many individuals with little or no understanding of business, capital or economics have denounced wealth maximisation as immoral, unethical, anti-social or worse. To do so ignores the basic fact that wealth maximisation as an objective ensures that management will attempt to use all available resources in a manner which promotes the long-run efficient use of such resources. Should other policies be followed then either the business will cease to exist or it will be taken over by others who can use better the resources involved. This text assumes that the objective of business is the long-run maximisation of the value of the owners' investment.

Decisions within companies are taken by managers who are not always involved in ownership. Frequently, managers objectives differ from those of shareholders as well as a number of other interested groups such as the workers, customers and finally society as a whole. Management may seek to maximise sales, profit growth or market share given that their level of remuneration may be linked to one or more of these indicators. The greater the dispersion of shares among the owners of a company, the easier it is for management to ignore the shareholders wishes and pursue motives and goals of their own. Significant changes have taken place in the past fifteen years in the pattern of share ownership due to the growth and interest of financial institutions in equity holdings. This makes it much more difficult for managers to ignore the wishes of these large shareholders, whose interest is most likely to be exerted privately rather than overtly. These sophisticated financial investors are themselves under intense pressure to produce portfolios which perform better than the market average.

Returning to the definition of financial management it concerns two central and related questions: How firms should choose the investments they make, that is, the investment decision, and how they should raise the necessary finance, that is, the financing decision. Allied to these is the question of dividend policy, if applicable. The investment decision concerns both the long-term appraisal of many types of capital projects or investments and the efficient management of existing assets. Decisions on large-scale projects are usually designed to maintain the long-run profitability of the business while the day-to-day decisions control the current profitability.

The financing decision is concerned with determining the best financing mix or capital structure. In a perfect capital market the capital structure of the firm would be irrelevant to its value but in reality the market imperfections of taxation, bankruptcy costs and information costs have a major impact. The other important decision that must be made from time to time is the firm's dividend policy. This involves striking a balance between the dividend payout ratio, that is, the percentage of earnings paid out in dividends and the need to retain earnings for future growth financing. Considerable judgement is required in evaluating the firm's financing needs and the investor's preference for dividend income or capital gains.

Financial management therefore, involves the solution of these major decisions. Together they determine the value of the firm to its shareholders.

THE JOB OF FINANCIAL MANAGER

Because finance is a critical function of business the financial manager is almost always a senior member of management. The primary functions of the financial manager are:

(1) To advise on the investments which the business should make.
(2) To procure the finance necessary to fund the investments.
(3) To record and report on the activities of the business.

Major investment decisions will rarely be made solely by the financial manager. Certainly day-to-day decisions on cash or credit are routine and may be only subject to periodic review, but larger decisions to acquire assets are usually made by the directors and/or owners of a business. Providing finance is often called the 'treasury function'. The treasurer is usually responsible for relationships with financial institutions and for handling cash.

Recording and reporting on the activities of the business is the accounting or controllership function of finance. The simplest method of controlling the activities of a business is to reduce every activity to a set of financial statistics. Usually the objective of a business is stated in financial terms: therefore the performance of the business must ultimately be translated into financial statistics. Many developments have taken place in the technology area of control. New quantitative techniques have offered opportunities for greatly improved reporting and control. The systems established to produce management control data are known as Management Information Systems (M.I.S.). Reporting to management has the generic name of Management Accounting. External reporting to shareholders and to the state is known as Financial Accounting or Auditing.

AN OUTLINE OF THE TEXT

The text can be divided into a number of different sections. Chapter 1 deals with the different ways in which businesses can be established ranging from the sole trader to co-operatives. Chapters 2, 3 and 4 cover financial analysis and planning. Chapter 2 presents and examines a set of financial accounts for an engineering company, Ardmore Limited. Various analytical techniques are defined and applied in Chapter 3. Short-term financial planning is covered in Chapter 4.

Current asset management or, as it is better known, working capital management, is covered in detail in Chapter 5. Asset management is extended to fixed assets in Chapter 6, which examines the capital budgeting process.

Chapters 7 to 14 deal with the raising of finance. Chapters 7 and 8 examine Irish financial institutions. Chapters 9, 10 and 11 examine respectively the short, medium and long-term sources of finance available to Irish business. A separate chapter, Chapter 13, analyses the extensive financial assistance provided to Irish business by the state. Chapter 14 examines the cost of the various sources of finance and demonstrates their effects on the capital structure of a business. Chapter 15 outlines the financial implications of mergers and acquisitions. The growing internationalisation of business and the increasing role of foreign activities in Irish business is reflected in Chapter 16 which provides an introduction to international financial management.

Further Reading
E. F. Brigham and J. F. Weston: *Managerial Finance*, Holt, Rinehart and Winston, New York 1979.
Arthur J. Keown et al.: *Basic Financial Management*, Prentice Hall, Englewood Cliffs, New Jersey 1985.

Chapter 1

Legal Forms of Business Organisation

Business may take on a number of different forms of legal entity. Throughout this book the company is used as the standard organisation but in fact other forms are more numerous. The type of legal organisation assumed by a business is often a function of the amount of finance available. Once established, the legal form affects the taxation, financial and auditing requirements as well as the sources of finance which are available to the business. The following legal forms of business organisation are considered below: sole trader or sole proprietorship; partnerships; limited liability companies; co-operatives; state-owned enterprises.

SOLE TRADER

The sole trader is the dominant form of business organisation in Ireland. Exact numbers are not available but practically every farmer, small shop-keeper and tradesman operates this form of legal organisation.

A sole trader or sole proprietorship is formed each time an individual trades in his or her own name. That is the major advantage of this form of organisation: simplicity. The sold trader is totally independent. Independence means that the owner usually makes all the important decisions.

Until recently sole traders were relatively free to maintain or discard detailed financial records. This is no longer true. Now Value Added Tax, Income Tax and Social Welfare regulations require the sole trader to keep detailed financial records which must be available for state inspection.

The general features of a sole proprietorship are that:

(1) The owner has unlimited liability. A recent change in Irish law makes it difficult to foreclose on the family home.

(2) Profits are taxed at the rate of personal income tax appropriate to the owner.

(3) There are almost no legislative constraints on the establishment of a sole proprietorship. An exception exists where the owner wants to register

a business name. The name must be registered under the Business Names Act 1963. Table 1 gives details of recent business name registrations.

Table 1	Registered Business Names					
	1979	1980	1981	1982	1983	1984
New registrations	2,266	2,583	2,804	3,089	3,758	4,321
Statement of changes in the registered particulars	147	112	79	61	152	186
Number of names removed from the register	176	269	159	134	147	224

Total number of Registrations on Register at 31 December 1984: 55,898.
Source: Dept of Industry and Commerce

(4) The owner, with total control, can operate, invest and divest as he or she sees fit.

(5) Sole traders are not required to register details of loans secured by mortgages.

(6) One person may have difficulty in managing all of the functions of the business. This, of course, does not mean that functional specialists cannot be hired.

(7) In cases of the absence or illness of the owner, mis-management can and does occur.

(8) Death effectively dissolves the legal form of organisation and often causes succession problems.

(9) Sole traders find difficulty in raising finance other than their own funds and personal borrowing powers.

Despite the many problems the sole trader form of organisation is useful for small businesses.

PARTNERSHIP

A partnership is legally defined as an association of persons carrying on a business in common with a view to profit. It may be formed by a verbal agreement among partners but it is usual to draft a Deed of Partnership. The number of partners may not exceed twenty, or ten in the case of a banking partnership. As in the case of the sole trader, the liability of the partners for the debts and obligations of the partnership is unlimited. The Deed of Partnership would normally contain details of the following:

(a) The name of the partnership.
(b) The date of commencement of the venture.
(c) The duration of the venture.

(d) The retirement or admittance of partners.

(e) Capital subscription and division of profits.

(f) Signing powers for cheques.

Without a Deed of Partnership no new partner can be introduced without the unanimous approval of all existing partners and in the event of the death or bankruptcy of a partner, the partnership is dissolved. Partnerships are legally controlled by the Partnership Act, 1890 and the Limited Partnership Act, 1907. There are two types of partnership:

(1) A general partnership where each partner contributes an agreed amount, is an agent of the partnership and has full liability for all debts. General partnerships are common in Ireland, particularly among the professions, for example lawyers and accountants.

(2) A limited partnership. Under the terms of the 1907 Act a limited partnership must consist of:

> One or more persons, called general partners, who shall be liable for all debts and obligations of the firm, and one or more limited partners, who shall at the time of entering into such partnership contribute thereto a sum or sums of capital or property valued at a stated amount, and who shall not be liable for the debts or obligations of the firm beyond the amount so contributed.

A limited partnership is a medium whereby an investor can share profits without assuming the risk of unlimited liability. Limited partners may not take an active part in the business.

Note that a sleeping partner is not a limited partner. A sleeping partner is one who takes no active part in the management of the partnership but who retains unlimited liability for the debts of the venture. The number of limited partnerships registered in Ireland is small as can be seen from Table 2.

Table 2   Limited Partnerships Registered in Ireland

Year of registration	Number	Amount contributed by the limited partners
		IR£
1979	8	598,805
1980	7	606,100
1981	12	30,867
1982	10	234,705
1983	11	69,839
1984	19	899,702

Source: Dept of Industry and Commerce

Partnerships have greater access to capital than sole traders but the limitations set by the availability of additional partners (for example, limited capital and borrowing powers) still exist. The sharing of responsibility for the firm among a number of partners allows a larger type of firm to emerge under this form of organisation than under that of the sole trader.

Partners often have a blend of dissimilar skills and it is quite usual to find three partners, one of whom is a marketing man, one a production or technical expert and one a financial specialist. There is a high possibility, however, of disagreement developing between partners and the possible break-up of the firm. The Deed of Partnership may offer some insurance against this danger but it cannot cover all possible contingencies.

In law each partner carries full powers to commit the partnership, for example, in the purchase of goods, and even though partners may agree that these powers might be limited, there is no way in which this could be notified validly to third parties. Since all partners are liable for the debts of the firm each partner must have complete trust in the way the other partner conducts business. In summary, the general features of the partnership form of legal organisation are:

(1) Unlimited liability of all partners. In rare instances partners with limited liability may be admitted but they cannot take an active part in the business: if they do they become liable as general partners.

(2) Profits are taxed at the appropriate income tax rate of the partners.

(3) A partnership is an association of individuals and not a separate legal person.

(4) A partnership can obtain a wider range of skills and access to greater capital resources than is available to the average sole trader.

(5) Partnerships need not register details of loans secured by mortgages.

(6) Partnerships by their very nature are unstable and often dissolve over simple disputes.

(7) The instability of the legal form of organisation restricts the ability of the partnership to raise capital.

LIMITED LIABILITY COMPANY

In the seventeenth and early eighteenth century a new form of business organisation developed in England—the so-called joint stock company. Individuals were offered, at a price, shares in a particular venture. In this period English merchants were extending their trading routes all over the world and many new ventures needed finance. The joint stock company was an excellent way of financing these ventures.

The advantage of the joint stock company was that each investor was entitled to share the proceeds of the trade in proportion to his investment. A period of wild speculation in the stock of the South Sea Company took place in early 1720. This led to the Bubble Act of 1720 which effectively made illegal the formation of all joint stock companies. The only way to establish a company was through royal charter or Act of Parliament. The Bank of Ireland was established by charter and the Alliance and Dublin Gas Company was established by Act of Parliament. In 1768, the Warmsley Company petitioned parliament for a charter to establish a company. What was unique about this application was that the petitioners sought to have the liability of shareholders limited to the money which they had subscribed. The petition was granted. During the following seventy-five years many companies were incorporated by parliament. Most of them sought, and obtained, limited liability. The Joint Stock Companies Act of 1856 was a major step forward in the organisation of business. Now a business could be legally organised by means of a joint stock limited liability company. Investors were liable only for the amount of capital which they agreed to invest. Since this Act, and others similar, were passed during the early stages of the English Industrial Revolution there was a rapid and sustained increase in the number of companies formed. The new technologies which spurred industrial growth were often both high risk and capital intensive. Many investors were needed to raise the required capital but unless their risk could be quantified they would have been unlikely to invest. The limited liability joint stock company was the perfect answer. Over time numerous refinements were introduced so that now joint stock companies have become the dominant form of legally organising large businesses.

A company is a corporate body which has a legal existence quite distinct from the persons who are the shareholders. A company can have a perpetual life since ownership is represented by transferable shares.

Formation of Limited Companies
The formation of a limited company is normally handled by a lawyer who drafts the necessary documents for registration with the Registrar of Companies. The main documents required are:

(a) Memorandum of Association.
(b) Articles of Association.
(c) Statutory declaration of compliance with all of the requirements of the relevant Companies Act.
(d) Statement of nominal share capital.
(e) List of persons who have consented to be directors.
(f) Form of consent to act as director from those who have agreed to be directors.

The first two documents are of particular importance as they affect the company not only on incorporation but also throughout its existence. Only these two are examined in detail.

Memorandum of Association. This document sets out, for the information of the public, the basic facts relating to the company. It governs the relationship of the company with others. The contents must include:

(a) The company name with 'Limited' as the last word in the title in the case of a private company and 'public limited company' (PLC) in the case of a public company.

(b) The location of the registered office.

(c) The objects of the company, for example, the areas of activity in which the group operates or intends to operate; it is usual to make the objects cover as wide a range of activities as possible.

(d) A statement that the liability of the members is limited.

(e) The authorised or nominal capital of the company.

(f) The signature of two subscribers, generally directors, with their addresses and the number of shares they are initially taking in the company. The signatures must be witnessed. A public company must have a minimum of seven subscribers.

Articles of Association. The 'Articles' govern the internal workings or management of the company. In effect they are a set of rules and regulations which the company may draw up on its own or it may adopt a model set as given in Table A of the Companies Act 1963. This table applies to any company which does not draw up its own articles. The Articles of Association form a contract between the company and the shareholders, defining their respective and relative rights and duties.

The model set of articles as set out in Table A of the Companies Act includes the following:

(a) A statement of the authorised share capital of the company and its division into shares.

(b) The rights attaching to these shares and their voting rights.

(c) Provisions relating to share issues, calls, transfers, forfeiture, alteration of share capital etc.

(d) Appointment, retirement and powers of directors.

(e) Meetings of the shareholders and procedures at such meetings.

The Articles are subject to the memorandum and cannot confer or include any powers beyond those contained in the memorandum. They are signed by those who signed the memorandum. They must also be witnessed. The Articles can be altered at any time by special resolution of the shareholders, that is, with the approval of 75 per cent of those voting.

The six documents outlined above are lodged with the Registrar of Companies. Within a short period, if everything is in order, the Registrar will issue a Certificate of Incorporation. The company is now registered and if private can commence business. A public limited company, must wait until £30,000 of share capital has been subscribed. The fact that liability is limited means that investors are liable only for the amount of capital which they have agreed to subscribe. Once the capital subscription is fully paid no further liability arises, irrespective of how much money a company loses.

Types of Joint Stock Companies:
There are four types: private limited companies; public limited companies; companies limited by guarantee; and unlimited companies.

Private Limited Companies. Private companies have the following characteristics:

(1) Between two and fifty shareholders. A minimum of two shareholders is necessary for incorporation.

(2) The right of transfer of shares is restricted.

(3) Business can commence immediately on incorporation.

(4) Up to the passing of the Companies (Amendment) Act 1986, private companies did not have to make copies of their accounts available for public inspection. Since the passing of that act, incorporating the European Communities Fourth Council Directive of 1978, all limited companies with certain exceptions, must file their financial statements with the Registrar of Companies.

(5) The company is prohibited from inviting the public to subscribe for its shares or debentures. Consequently a Stock Exchange quotation is not possible.

In 1984 there were almost 80,000 private companies registered in Ireland with a nominal paid up capital of £950,000,000, an average of £11,875 per company.

Public Limited Companies (PLCs). The main features of a public company are that:

(1) A minimum of seven persons is required for incorporation. The maximum number is governed by the number of shares the company proposes to issue.

(2) Shares are, generally speaking, freely transferable.

(3) Though incorporated, a public company cannot commence business until the Registrar of Companies issues a certificate to commence business. This is known as the Trading Certificate.

(4) Accounts must be audited each year and then filed with the Registrar of Companies. These accounts are available for inspection by the public.

(5) The shares and debentures of public companies may be quoted on the Stock Exchange subject to permission being granted by the Stock Exchange authorities. (Chapter 8).

In 1988 there were 344 public companies registered in the twenty-six counties, less than seventy of whom were quoted on the Dublin Stock Exchange. These 344 public companies had a nominal paid up capital of £335,000,000, an average of £973,000 per company. As can be seen public companies are normally much larger than private companies.

Companies Limited by Guarantee. A very unusual type of registered company is one where members or shareholders agree to subscribe an agreed sum towards the assets of the company in the event of liquidation. Usually the sum is a nominal amount.

This method of incorporation is used by non-profit organisations such as clubs, associations, societies etc. There are over 1,000 companies limited by guarantee.

Unlimited Companies. An unlimited company is formed if shareholders decide that any or all of the following advantages offset the disadvantages of unlimited liability:

(a) The right to produce issued capital without court permission.
(b) The right to purchase shares.
(c) Exemption from filing accounts.

Features of Limited Companies

The main features of limited joint stock companies are that:

(1) Investors' liability is limited.
(2) There is greater access to capital.
(3) The business survives the death or incapacity of the investors.
(4) Skilled managers prefer to work for companies which are regarded as more stable than either partnerships or sole proprietorships.
(5) Income is taxed at a specific corporation tax rate. This is usually lower than the top rate of personal tax but if profits are paid out as dividends then income tax must be paid in addition to the corporation tax.
(6) Large organisations tend to become bureaucratic. Organisational entropy is the technical description of increasing organisational inefficiency.
(7) The owners of the business may lose control to directors and/or managers who may not adequately safeguard shareholders' interests.

(8) Limited companies are more regulated than either partnerships or sole proprietorships.

The Companies (Amendment) Act 1983

The Companies (Amendment) Act 1983 which became law on 13 October 1983 implemented the Second EEC Directive on company law. The directive was adopted by the Council of Ministers in 1976 and applies only to public limited companies. The 1983 Companies (Amendment) Act extends some of the rules to private companies.

The main provisions of the act relate to the following matters:

(1) *Name of a public limited company* ·

Public companies will have to be clearly distinguished in their name, from other types of companies. This will mean that 'limited' will no longer be sufficient for both private and public companies with public companies to be known as public limited companies (PLC) or the Irish equivalent, *cuideachta phoibli theoranta* (CPT).

(2) *Registration and re-registration for companies*

In the case of old public companies, the directors of the company may apply to the Registrar of Companies to be re-registered as a public limited company. If, however, its allotted share capital is less than the authorised minimum for a public company (£30,000), then the company must either increase its share capital or re-register as another form of company or wind up voluntarily. There are also optional provisions for all companies to re-register in another form, for example, private company as public limited company and *vice versa*; unlimited company as limited company and *vice versa*.

A new public limited company may not commence business until it has registered and obtained a certificate from the Registrar of Companies certifying that it has complied with the rules governing public limited companies.

(3) *Minimum share capital and the issue of shares*

A public limited company must have a minimum of £30,000 share capital issued though it need only be partly paid. The Act restricts the rights of the directors of a public or private company to issue shares in that company. The directors are prohibited from issuing shares in the company unless they have been specifically authorised to do so by the members of the company in general meeting or by the Articles of Association. Members may remove, alter or renew such authority by ordinary resolution.

The offer of shares to the public by a private company is a criminal offence although any issue of shares arising from such an offer is valid.

If a public company wishes to increase its share capital, it may not issue shares unless the capital offered for subscription is fully subscribed, or the terms of the offer allow an issue, notwithstanding a shortfall in subscription.

(4) *Pre-emption rights*

This part of the act protects the right of existing shareholders to retain their percentage share in the company. Shares to be issued must be offered first to the shareholders *pro rata* to their existing holdings. These rights to first refusal are known as pre-emption rights and they apply to both public and private companies.

Pre-emption rights do not apply where shares are issued other than for cash (for example, takeover of another company). Also they do not apply to shares taken out by subscribers to the memorandum and shares in employee share schemes.

(5) *Payment for share capital*

The act introduces extensive provisions to prevent shares being issued without adequate consideration and in this respect, must be regarded as an improvement on previous legislation.

Public limited companies are prevented from accepting as payment for shares a promise to work or perform services in the future. If they do so, the holder of the shares will be liable to pay cash for the shares. The provision does not extend to private companies nor does it restrict the issue of shares for past services.

The issue of shares at a discount is prohibited, thereby repealing Section 63 of the 1963 Act which permitted issue at a discount subject to certain conditions.

In the case of public limited companies no share may be issued unless 25 per cent of the nominal value of the share and the whole of the premium, if any, has been paid.

Shares may be issued for a consideration that consists of non-cash assets. If so, in the case of public limited companies, the assets must be transferred to the company within five years of the date of issue. Otherwise the shareholders are liable to pay in cash. It is also a requirement in such circumstances that a report be prepared by an independent person on the value of the consideration. The act gives the independent person power to seek information and explanations from officers of the company.

(6) *Maintenance of capital*

The act introduces safeguards for the maintenance of its capital by requiring that directors call an extraordinary general meeting of the company if they become aware that the value of the net assets have fallen to half or less than half of the called-up share capital. The meeting is called to consider whether any, and if so what, measures should be taken to deal with the situation. The act goes beyond the requirements of the Second Directive in that it imposes on auditors the duty of ensuring that directors comply with the above. Auditors should base their opinion solely on the amount of assets and liabilities included in the balance sheet on which they are reporting.

Further, the act provides that no limited company may acquire its own shares as this would effectively be a reduction of capital. Certain exceptions to this rule are, however, permitted: (a) the redemption of preference shares; (b) acquisition of shares in a reduction of capital; (c) where the court orders the company to purchase its own shares; (d) forfeiture of shares for non-payment.

(7) *Distribution of profits and assets*

It is a fundamental rule of capital maintenance that dividends are paid only out of profits. Apart from the Companies Act 1963 which provides that dividends may not be paid out of unrealised surpluses arising from the revaluation of fixed assets, there was no statutory rules as to what profits may be distributed. As a consequence the major rules governing distribution of profits were to be found in a number of judicial decisions, some dating from the late nineteenth century. The 1983 Act goes some way towards rectifying this situation by re-affirming the 1963 Act and by laying down rules which supersede many of the judicial decisions which have, in the past, guided interpretation of the law. The rules which apply to public and private companies state that a company may only make a distribution out of profits available for dividend which are defined as 'its accumulated realised profits, so far as not previously utilised by distribution or capitalisation, less its accumulated realised losses, so far as not previously written off in a reduction or re-organisation of capital'. It will, therefore, no longer be possible for a company to pay dividends out of current profits unless past losses have been made good. Also accumulated unrealised profits will not be available for distribution.

The act contains further restrictions in that a public company may only make a distribution if the amount of its net assets exceeds the aggregate of its called-up share capital and undistributable reserves, and any distribution must not be greater than the excess. Distributable profits for a public limited company will, therefore, be net realised profits less net unrealised losses, if any. In effect, if a company's unrealised profits are less than its unrealised losses, the deficit must be covered by realised profits before a distribution can be made.

Apart from EEC derived legislation, the state is examining the workings of the 1963 Act and the subsequent Amendments. Serious abuses of limited liability have arisen and a new Companies Act is being drafted to remove such abuses.

CO-OPERATIVES

A co-operative society is formed by people who come together to undertake a venture which they could not undertake as individuals. Co-operatives are established for the benefit of all members. The co-operative movement in Ireland dates from 1889 when the first co-operative creamery was established in Drumcollogher, Co. Limerick. The Irish co-operative movement has remained almost exclusively an agriculturally based movement relying almost totally on producers. This is in marked contrast to worker co-operation in running of retail shops in other countries. Retail grocery co-operatives in Ireland are practically non-existent.

The initial efforts of the co-operative movement were mainly directed towards supplying farm raw materials. Early growth arose through the establishment of small creameries to ensure outlets for milk and markets for butter. Over 1,000 societies were later established for store trading, butter making and egg trading. In the 1920s and 1930s there was considerable growth in Agricultural Credit Societies. In the 1960s the number of societies dropped dramatically as many of the smaller societies went out of business, all the Credit Societies were wound up and most of the Creamery Societies amalgamated. There are 143 co-operatives in Ireland at present.

Irish co-operatives are registered under the Industrial and Provident Societies Acts of 1893 and 1934. They are required to make annual returns of their accounts to the Registrar of Friendly Societies. The maximum shareholding in a co-operative is £1,000 but there is no limit to the holding of one co-operative in another.

The features which distinguish co-operatives from other types of business units are that:

(1) Membership of a co-operative society is voluntary and open to anyone, subject to his being willing to accept the responsibilities of membership. Shares purchased are not transferable, but they are withdrawable.

(2) Voting depends on the number of members, not the number of shares held, that is, one man, one vote.

(3) Share capital receives a strictly limited rate of interest.

(4) At the year's end, after all payments and provisions for the future development of the business have been made, surpluses may be distributed among members in proportion to the business carried on by the individual members with the co-operative society.

(5) Provision is generally made for the education of the community in the principles and techniques of co-operation.

There should be co-operation among co-operatives at local, national and international levels. The co-ordinating body of the co-operative movement in Ireland, the Irish Co-operative Organisation Society Limited (ICOS), the successor to the Irish Agricultural Organisation Society (IAOS), has done great work for the Irish co-operative movement in this respect. Founded in 1894 by Horace Plunkett, it exists to help Irish farmers and fishermen and their families to enjoy higher living standards through better use of co-operatives.

The rapid growth in agribusiness in Ireland led to the development of co-operatives with sales larger than practically any other form of business in Ireland. Unfortunately not every co-operative had the skilled business management necessary to handle the business. Rapid improvements in management are now being made.

Table 3 gives a breakdown of the scope of co-operatives' sales in 1976 and 1985. Almost 200,000 people are members of co-operatives. This figure is undoubtedly higher than the total number of shareholders in Irish companies.

Table 3   Statistics on the Irish Co-operative Movement, 1976–1985

Type	Number of Co-operatives	1976 Turnover £m.	1985 Turnover £m.	1985 Turnover %	1985 Number of Members 000's	1985 Number of Employees 000's
Multi-purpose Dairies	48	807.3	2,779.3	76.1	99.6	11.3
Livestock	32	319.4	695.7	19.0	58.8	1.2
Meat Processing	1	156.1	15.1	0.4	3.0	0.3
Wholesales	3	39.3	103.6	2.8	0.2	0.4
Agricultural Stores	9	25.6	14.3	0.4	4.6	0.2
Others	50	29.7	46.3	1.3	30.7	1.2
Total	143	1,377.4	3,654.3	100.0	196.9	14.6

Source: ICOS Annual Report 1986

STATE-SPONSORED ENTERPRISE

In practically every developed country the state plays a vital role in business. In Ireland slightly less than 50 per cent of national expenditure is accounted for by the state. The largest business enterprises in the country are state-owned. Coras Iompair Eireann is one of the largest employers in the country while the Electricity Supply Board has more invested capital than almost any other Irish business venture.

State enterprise in Ireland rarely competes with private business. Usually the state invests in areas where private enterprise is either unwilling or unable to provide the service. There are two methods used to establish a state enterprise:

(1) For a commercial operation, a state-financed company is registered under the 1963 Companies Act, for example, Comhlucht Siuicre Eireann Teo, Nitrigin Eireann Teo.

(2) Where a non-competitive social service is involved a statutory corporation is established by the passing of a specific Dail statute, for example Bord na Mona, Bord Iascaigh Mhara. State bodies receive funds in any or all of the following ways:

(a) Invested share capital.
(b) Loans from the state.
(c) Loans from commercial sources.
(d) State subsidies.
(e) Indirect subsidies such as low interest loans or access to cheap raw materials.

Surprisingly, the owners of state bodies, that is, the public, cannot under existing laws question the activities of their organisations. Control rests with the government minister within whose range of activities the functions lie.

There are a number of serious structural problems associated with state-owned business organisations. They frequently lack objectives, are usually bureaucratic and often inefficient. There are over 100 state enterprises in Ireland. It is likely that the 1990s will see a movement toward the privatisation of certain state-sponsored enterprises.

CONCLUSION

It is possible to relate the legal form of organisation to the size of business involved. Small one-man businesses are usually organised as sole proprietorships. As business expands capital needs to increase and the business usually becomes a limited liability private company. Some private companies grow and develop into publicly-owned corporations. Partnerships, co-operatives and state-sponsored businesses are relatively rare. Where they exist they usually reflect the specific requirements of a particular situation.

Further Reading

Report of the Registrar of Companies, Stationery Office, Dublin, annual.
Report of the Registrar of Friendly Societies, Stationery Office, Dublin, annual.
Report of the Irish Agricultural Organisation Society, Dublin, annual.
G. Clegg and C. Barrow: *How to Start and Run Your Own Business,* Macmillan, London 1984.
Companies Act, 1963.
Companies (Amendment) Act, 1983.
Companies (Amendment) Act, 1986.

Chapter 2

Financial Statements

Control over the activities of a business venture is critical to success. In a small easily-managed operation the owner/manager will usually be able to maintain adequate control by simply keeping an eye on things. Informal controls continue to play an important part in many organisations but they are inadequate for the needs of most modern businesses. Over centuries a system of controls has grown and developed. These controls are known as financial statements. They are some of the basic tools used by accountants to measure the health of a business.

The basic requirements necessary to indicate financial performance are:

(a) The Balance Sheet.

(b) The Profit and Loss Account (Income Statement).

(c) Sources and Uses of Funds Statement.

These three statements, properly prepared and audited by reputable accountants, are the minimum legal requirements which must be met by all registered companies and co-operatives. Partnerships and sole proprietorships are not legally bound to prepare such accounts, but the Revenue Commissioners, in order to assess taxation, require data which make the preparation of basic accounts essential.

The primary purpose of providing financial statements is to show the owners of the business how their capital has been utilised. But other objectives also exist. Lenders to a business usually wish to examine financial statements. Often suppliers set credit limits based on an analysis of the financial statements of a customer. Traditionally, Irish businessmen have shied away from producing accounts. Though all limited companies have to produce audited statements, only public companies had to file such statements prior to the passing of the Companies (Amendment) Act 1986.

Businesses have not realised that publishing sound healthy accounts can do nothing but good. The often quoted reason for secrecy is 'the danger of injuring the business by disclosure of information to competitors'. In most cases the danger does not exist. With the passing of the Companies (Amendment) Act 1986, the purpose of which was to implement the European Communities Fourth Council Directive of 1978, all Irish registered public and private limited companies, with certain minor exceptions, are obliged to file statements with their annual returns to the Registrar of Companies. The most significant exemption is that which allows small private companies to file a balance sheet with relevant notes only—neither profit and loss account nor director's report has to be filed. However the financial statements must meet the overriding requirement to give a true and fair view of the state of affairs.

Medium-sized and small private companies are defined by the following criteria:

Companies which do not exceed two of the following limits for both current and previous year:

	Medium Sized	Small
Balance Sheet total at end of year	IR£5,000,000	IR£1,250,000
Turnover	IR£10,000,000	IR£2,500,000
Average number of employees	250	50

It is worth mentioning here that one disclosure required by the 1986 Act that goes beyond the requirements of the European Communities Fourth Directive is a detailed analysis of liabilities for taxation.

THE BALANCE SHEET
A Balance Sheet is a list of the assets and liabilities of a business grouped into relevant categories. It is a statement of the condition of a firm at a particular date and usually shows the comparative position for a previous date. A balance sheet may be compared to a still photograph showing the financial condition of the firm at a given moment: it reflects the past rather than the future. By comparing two balance sheets, at different dates, it is possible to provide some picture of the changes which have taken place. This provides information for future decision making. Although a firm's balance sheet might be prepared within guidelines of generally accepted accounting practice, that is, Standard Statements of Accounting Practice (SSAPs), the analyst must be aware of certain limitations in the statement. The following are some of the more important ones:

(1) The balance sheet does not reflect current values, as historical cost has been adopted as the basis for valuing and reporting assets and liabilities.

(2) Value judgements must be made in order to determine the level of several accounts. Examples include debtors estimated in terms of collectibility, inventories based on saleability and fixed assets based on useful life.

(3) Appreciation or enhancement in most values is generally ignored with depreciation of long-term assets being the accepted norm. This is particularly crucial in the case of property development companies and mining properties.

(4) Some items are omitted from the Balance Sheet because they involve extreme problems of objective evaluation. The most obvious example is the human resources of the firm.

Items which appear in a balance sheet can be grouped as follows: assets; liabilities; net worth or owner's equity.

Assets

The assets are the resources of the business. They can be classified as:

(1) Current assets, meaning assets which are convertible into cash within twelve months; such assets are also known as liquid assets.

(2) Fixed assets, meaning the permanent facilities of the business which are used to produce the product or services of the firm; fixed assets may be *tangible*, that is land, buildings, equipment etc., or *intangible*, such as goodwill, patents, trademarks, copyright, etc.

Fixed assets usually wear out over a period of time and so each year a part of the income of a business is set aside to account for this wear and tear. The amount set aside is known as depreciation. The objective of depreciation is to spread the cost of an asset over the useful life of the asset. In inflationary times depreciation does not provide adequate sums for replacement.

Liabilities

Liabilities are sums owed to entities other than the owners of the business. They are generally grouped into the following categories:

(1) Current liabilities such as creditors, short-term loans, overdrafts and other sums due for payment within twelve months.

(2) Long-term or deferred liabilities, which cover all liabilities payable in more than twelve months.

(3) Contingent liabilities—these do not yet exist but may come into being as a result of circumstances obtaining at the date of the balance sheet. Examples of contingent liabilities include guarantees given and consequences arising from legal actions.

Net Worth or Owner's Equity

Net worth is the owner's interest in the firm. It can be defined as follows:

$$Net\ Worth = Assets\ minus\ Liabilities.$$

In a limited company the net worth is usually presented in the following manner:

(1) Issued Share Capital, which means the funds raised from the owners.

(2) Share Premium Account, which shows the premium—if any—paid by investors to purchase new shares in the business.

(3) Reserves. Usually this covers profits not paid out to shareholders and/or surpluses produced from revaluing the assets of the business.

THE PROFIT AND LOSS ACCOUNT

The Profit and Loss Account (Income Statement) measures the progress of a business over a period of time, usually twelve months. The Profit and Loss Account is usually made up of three distinct accounts. The Manufacturing Account estimates the total cost of manufacture during the period in question; the Trading Account deducts the cost of manufacture from sales revenue to establish a gross profit; the Profit and Loss Account which deducts expenses to show the net profit or loss figure. Taken together the three statements are known as an Income Statement. The statements can be divided into five broad categories:

(1) Gross and net sales for the period. Any difference between the gross and net figures arises from discounts, allowances and returns.

(2) Cost of goods sold. Here, the cost of producing the sales is determined. The balancing figure between (1) and (2) is the Gross Profit.

(3) Selling and distribution expenses estimated and deducted.

(4) Itemised administrative, general and interest costs.

(5) Adjustments to profits, made for taxation and dividend purposes.

The Income Statement is compiled on an accrual rather than a cash basis. This means an attempt is made to match the firm's revenues for the period in question with the costs incurred in generating those revenues (SSAP 2). This gives rise to a difference between reported revenues and costs for the period and actual cash flows.

This conceptual difference, profit being a concept, cash a reality, gave rise to the need for a third financial statement called Sources and Uses of Funds statement or otherwise called The Statement of Changes in

Financial Position. The difference between profit and cash arises for two basic reasons:

(a) revenues and costs recognised in the Income Statement reflect all transactions applicable to the period in question and not just cash transactions, that is, credit and cash sales, wages actually paid and owing;

(b) certain expenses included in the Income Statement are non-cash items, that is, depreciation, goodwill.

THE SOURCES AND USES OF FUNDS STATEMENT

A Sources and Uses of Funds Statement means exactly what it says. All sources of cash such as new cash injections by owners, reductions of inventories, stretching of creditors are totalled. This is followed by an explanation of where this cash has gone.

The limitations of a profit and loss account and balance sheet are known to most practising accountants. Having discussed the year's results in detail, and told his client of the large net profit he has succeeded in making, the client will frequently ask 'where is it gone?' It is not often one can simply turn to the bank account and see the profit sitting there, waiting to be used.

The description 'funds statement' is unlike some accounting terms, purely factual. The statement shows the funds, that is, moneys which have been introduced into the business during an accounting period and how these funds have been applied or utilised. More detail is given in the next chapter.

THE ACCOUNTS OF ARDMORE LIMITED

The best way to illustrate the mechanics of financial statements is to work through an example. The accounts of Ardmore for 1986, with comparative figures for 1985 are presented in Table 4. Modern forms of presentation are used both for the balance sheet and income statement. The balance sheet is presented in columnar form instead of the more traditional listing of assets on the right-hand side and liabilities and net worth on the left. The income statement is presented in narrative form instead of the traditional listing of expenses on the left-hand side and sales and profit on the right. The sources and uses of funds statement is shown in traditional form without comparative figures.

Table 4

ARDMORE LIMITED
Balance Sheet as at 31 December 1986
(Amounts expressed as £'000.)

	1986		1985	
Fixed Assets (Note 7)				
Land and Buildings	135.0		135.0	
Plant and Machinery	138.1		139.2	
Fixtures and Fittings	25.2		27.3	
Motor Vehicles	29.1	327.4	12.9	314.4
Current Assets				
Inventory (Note 9)	326.4		268.5	
Accounts Receivable	405.6		362.7	
Cash	0.4		0.7	
	732.4		631.9	
Current Liabilities				
Accounts Payable	305.3		239.6	
Bank Overdraft	67.8		86.1	
Short-Term Loan	83.0		76.5	
Current Taxation	13.4		8.1	
	469.5		410.3	
Net Current Assets		262.9		221.6
		£590.3		£536.0
Financed By				
Authorised Ordinary £1 Shares				
Issued 335,000 Ordinary £1 Shares	335.0		335.0	
Reserves	—		—	
Share Premium a/c	25.0		25.0	
Profit and Loss a/c	122.6		41.4	
Government Grants (Note 6)	4.1		3.2	
Debentures (Note 8)	98.5		125.0	
Future Taxation	5.1		6.4	
		£590.3		£536.0

ARDMORE LIMITED
Manufacturing, Trading and Profit and Loss Account
For The Twelve Months Ended 31 December
(Amounts expressed as £'000.)

	1986	1985
Net Sales	1,419.3	1,300.8
Stocks of Finished Goods: 1 Jan 1986	121.5	112.3
Cost of manufacture (Note 1)	1,180.6	1,075.5
	1,302.1	1,187.8
Less Stocks of Finished Goods 31 December 1986	180.0	121.5
Cost of Sales	1,122.1	1,066.3
Gross Profit	297.2	234.5
Less Expenses		
Selling and Distribution (Note 2)	97.3	63.8
Interest Charges (Note 3)	35.7	38.9
Administration (Note 4)	80.5	67.7
Add Profit on Sale of Asset	2.7	—
Net Profit	86.4	64.1
Taxation (Note 5)	7.7	4.9
Net Profit after Tax	78.7	59.2
Government Grant (Note 6)	2.5	4.7
Transfer to Profit and Loss Account c/fwd	81.2	63.9
Balance in Profit and Loss c/fwd	41.4	(22.5)
Balance Carried Forward	£122.6	£41.4

ARDMORE LIMITED
Sources and Uses of Funds for the year ended 31 December 1986
(Amounts expressed as £'000.)

Sources:		*Uses:*	
Profit Before Tax	86.4	Inventory	57.9
Depreciation	12.8	Accounts Receivable	42.9
Mortgage Debenture	—	Fixed Assets	25.8
Grants Received	3.4	Retiral of Debenture	26.5
Accounts Payable	65.7	Bank Overdraft	18.3
Short Term Loans	6.5	Taxation	3.7
Cash	0.3		
	£175.1		£175.1

Explanation: Notes Forming Part of the Accounts

Note 1   Cost of Manufacture. The details behind the cost of manufacture are provided here. All items directly connected with production are included, for example, wages, raw materials and direct costs associated with the factory. The movements in the value of inventory and work in progress are monitored to identify those costs, and only those costs, associated with sales during the calendar year 1986.

ARDMORE LIMITED
Manufacturing Account for the Twelve Months ending 31 December
(Amounts expressed as £'000.)

	1986		1985	
Stocks of Raw Material 1 January		84.6		71.3
Purchases		741.1		712.5
Carriage Inwards		15.9		13.4
		841.6		797.2
Less Stocks of Raw Material				
31 December 1986		86.9		84.6
Raw Materials Consumed		754.7		712.6
Factory Wages		360.6		324.3
Prime Cost of Manufacture		1,115.3		1,036.9
Works Overhead				
Repairs and Renewals	19.0		14.6	
Rates	2.8		2.6	
Light, Heat and Power	21.4		18.2	
Laundry and Cleaning	6.4		4.1	
Depreciation: Machinery	12.8	62.4	11.9	51.4
Works Cost of Manufacture		1,177.7		1,088.3
Add Opening Work-in-Progress				
1 January		62.4		49.6
Less Closing Work-in-Progress				
31 December		(59.5)		(62.4)
Cost of Manufacture		£1,180.6		£1,075.5

Note 2   Selling and Distribution Expenses. It is common to give details of the sums spent in obtaining sales. For many Irish companies, particularly those exporting, this is a very significant item. In the case of Ardmore one of the owners acts as sales manager.

	1986	1985
Salaries	34.1	20.5
Travel Expenses	35.5	23.2
Advertising	17.2	8.7
Discounts Allowed	10.5	11.4
	£97.3	£63.8

Note 3   Interest Charges. The company has a variety of loans on which interest is paid as follows:

	1986	1985
Debenture Interest	15.3	17.1
Term Loan Interest	10.3	11.4
Overdraft	10.1	10.4
	£35.7	£38.9

Note 4   Administration Expenses. Modern business has many overheads such as rent, communications etc. Such costs are often grouped as administration or establishment expenses.

	1986	1985
Directors' Fees	24.5	19.7
Office Salaries	29.4	26.1
Rates	1.4	1.4
Insurance	10.4	9.3
Telephone	6.0	4.3
Postage	2.5	1.5
Light and Heat	2.8	2.3
Miscellaneous	3.5	3.1
	£80.5	£67.7

Note 5   Taxation. Irish companies are liable to Corporation Tax, Capital Gains Tax and Value Added Tax on sales. The rate of Corporation Tax is 50 per cent with a reduced rate of 40 per cent where profits do not exceed £25,000.

Value Added Tax (VAT) was introduced in 1972. Every taxable unit must be registered and must charge the proper amount of VAT. The taxable period is two months and returns must be filed with the Collector General of Taxes within nineteen days of the end of the taxable period.

In the case of Ardmore the taxation provisions have been estimated as follows:

	1986	1985
Corporation Tax	6.4	5.6
Adjustments in respect of prior year	1.3	(0.7)
	£7.7	£4.9

The rate of taxation is further reduced in Ireland by liberal depreciation allowances and by export tax relief. A 10 per cent rate of Corporation Tax —manufacturing relief—was introduced on 1 January 1981 and expires on 31 December 2000. This applies to companies manufacturing in the state and certain non-manufacturing services conducted at Shannon Airport. The relief also applies to fish farming activities, cultivated mushrooms and certain computer services carried on in the state in the course of a service undertaking which has obtained an IDA employment grant. The 1987 Finance Bill extended the relief to the profits from:

(a) The carriage of cargo and passengers on sea-going ships which are Irish owned and registered.

(b) A trade which consists exclusively of the sale by wholesale on the export market of Irish manufactured goods.

(c) Certain financial services carried on at the Customs House Dock Site.

Export Sales Relief is available to companies which had commenced to export prior to 1 January 1981 or to whom an assurance in writing had been granted by the IDA before that date. Relief is for a period of fifteen years and a further five years at partial relief with the benefit terminating for all companies on 5 April 1990. The rate of Capital Gains Tax in operation within one year of acquisition and after the 5 April 1986 is 60 per cent with reduced rates for assets held for longer periods of time. In addition, indexation applies, whereby the cost of any asset, including expenditure which enhances its value, is adjusted for inflation by reference to increases in the consumer price index.

Ardmore has depreciation allowances against profit and a limited amount of sales to Northern Ireland.

Note 6   Grants. The state, through the IDA, is one of the largest providers of finance in Ireland. Up to 50 per cent of capital expenditure may be recovered from the state. In exceptional circumstances the grant is repayable, so accounting conventions require it to be written into the Profit and Loss Account over the life of the asset to which it refers. In 1986 some £2,500 of grants was taken into the accounts. At the same time additional grants of £3,400 were received so the balance sheet figures have risen by £900.

Note 7   Fixed Assets. The figures in the balance sheet for assets are net of depreciation. It is usual to give the gross cost figures and accumulated depreciation figures in a separate note.

	Cost	Accumulated Depreciation	1986 Nett Book Value	1985 Nett Book Value
Land and Buildings	135.0	—	135.0	135.0
Plant and Machinery	251.6	113.5	138.1	139.2
Fixtures and Fittings	41.4	16.2	25.2	27.3
Motor Vehicles	33.4	4.3	29.1	12.9
	£461.4	£134.0	£327.4	£314.4

It is important to be aware of what these figures tell and what they do not tell. There is no mention of the current realisable market value of the assets. In a period of inflation this can be particularly important. For instance, it has been estimated that the market value of the 10,000 square foot Ardmore premises was £265,000 in 1986. In like manner highly specialised plant may have only a break-up market value.

Note 8   Debentures. It is usual to explain the nature of debentures, particularly if they are secured by mortgages. In this case Ardmore owes £75,000 to the Bank of Ireland on foot of a ten-year debenture which is secured by a floating charge over all of the assets of the business together with a specific charge on the premises. In addition a loan of £23,500 from the Industrial Credit Corporation is secured by mortgage ranking *pari passu* or equally with that of the Bank of Ireland. These mortgages in effect restrict the business in that the assets cannot be disposed of, except within the terms of the mortgage agreements. For example, it is most unlikely that Ardmore Limited could sell their premises and distribute part or all of the proceeds to the owners. The banks would insist on first being repaid.

Note 9   Inventory. This is made up as follows:

	1986	1985
Raw Material	86.9	84.6
Work in Progress	59.5	62.4
Finished Goods	180.0	121.5
	£326.4	£268.5

CONCLUSION

Financial statements are a fundamental requirement in every business. The three basic statements presented here: the balance sheet, the income statement, and the sources and uses of funds statement represent only the most basic of statements. Modern financial and management accounting has developed a wide variety of statements designed to assist in controlling business.

A note of caution must be sounded. Accounting conventions and a cautious approach to valuation means that a balance sheet rarely gives an accurate picture of the worth of the business. A businessman must evaluate carefully the real worth of fixed, current and intangible assets. Likewise, new methods of financing such as leasing and project finance may not be reflected on a balance sheet.

The income statement is often thought of as a better measure but it too suffers from serious defects. Often profits arise from changes in the value of inventory. Such profits may never appear. Depreciation figures are notional and usually bear little relationship to the actual decline in the value of an asset or to the sum required to be set aside to enable replacement.

Once a businessman is aware of the limitations of financial statements he can begin to use them. The uses to which financial data can be put are examined in the following chapter.

Further Reading

R. J. Bull: *Accounting in Business,* (5th ed.), Butterworths, London 1984.
L. E. Rockley: *The Meaning of Balance Sheets and Company Reports*, Business Books, London 1975.

Chapter 3

Financial Analysis

Having received a set of financial statements the next step is to elicit and interpret the information stored in them. The type of information being sought depends on the particular person or firm involved. A debenture holder wishes to know the long-term risk of the business not paying his interest or capital. A trade creditor or bank manager wants to know the availability of cash to meet short-term liabilities. An investor wants to know how profitable an investment in the company is likely to be. Put more crudely the financial *well-being* of the firm could be judged by answering some or all of the following:

(1) How liquid is the firm?

(2) How does the firm's management finance its investments and/or capital expenditure?

(3) Is management generating sufficient profits from the firm's assets?

(4) Are the common stockholders receiving sufficient returns on their investment?

The interested parties are summarised in Figure 1.

Analysis of financial statements uses data in a relative sense. An absolute figure may have little value whereas a relationship between two or more figures can tell a story. Likewise changes in a figure over time may be more important than the figure itself, that is, trend analysis.

There are six methods of analysing financial statements:

(1) Comparative Analysis of financial statements from different periods. Each item in the balance sheet and income statement is compared across statements and differences are then explained. This little used and simple method of analysis shows whether a firm is making or losing money and highlights changes in the way money is invested in assets and the way in which the investments are financed.

Figure 1

LIMITED COMPANIES
Financial Statement Analysis and Interpretation
Interested Parties

External

Debenture holders
Ability of company to pay interest promptly. Their security if the company gets into difficulty.

Trade Creditors
Current assets to pay current liabilities. Make-up of current assets.
Earnings record of possible expansion/contraction of the business. Priority of claim in event of Company failure, if any.

Bankers
Purpose of loan/plan for repayment. Prospects of firm—trend of profit as disclosed in past years statements. Prior rights on liquidation.

Potential Investor
Trends of profit and sales over recent years. Forecasts of expansion in the industry. Yield on proposed investments.

Others
Inland Revenue, Competitors, Customers, Finance Companies

Internal

Shareholders
Performance, Dividends, Expansion, Future prospects.

Employees
Profits/wage demands. Profit-sharing scheme.

Directors
Performance/survival. Earn optimum profits.

Trade Unions
See Employees above.

---

(2) Working Capital analysis examines changes in the current assets and liabilities of a business. Working capital management is examined in detail in Chapter 5.

(3) Internal Analysis. This form of analysis is used mainly to assess credit risks. The relative size of each balance sheet item is examined and compared to some 'norm' or average, for example, if you know that a business has had increasing sales by means of easy credit terms then you would expect a large figure for Accounts Receivable. Should the figures be different from those expected then further investigation is required.

(4) Analysis by Sales. Here data in the income statement is compared with items in the balance sheet and a series of operating ratios developed.

(5) Ratio Analysis. A series of ratios are constructed which analyse trends and relationships in a business.

(6) Sources and Uses of Funds Statements. This simple technique examines the ways in which investments have been made and discovers how these investments have been financed.

Ratio Analysis and *Sources and Uses of Funds Statements* are by far and away the most common forms of financial analysis. These two methods are applied to the Ardmore accounts.

RATIO ANALYSIS

The financial health of a business is often measured by means of financial ratios. A ratio is a measure which relates two pieces of financial information.

Financial ratios are used in two separate ways. Firstly, in comparison across periods of time, changes in ratios will help to explain trends in areas such as the profitability and/or financial stability of a business. Secondly, inter-firm comparisons can be applied either by comparing firms within the same industry or by comparing firms from different industries. In both the United States and United Kingdom, firms such as Dun & Bradstreet publish financial ratios for different industries. These enable companies to compare their performances with other firms. In Ireland only the small number of publicly quoted firms publish financial data: therefore comparisons are difficult. A table of ratios published by the Financial Executives Association is included later in this chapter.

The limitations of ratios must be stressed. Do not become a slave to ratios. The mathematical nature of ratios often gives a precision to the analysis which is simply untrue. Often the data on which ratios are based are estimates or are unrealistic valuations. In comparing ratios across companies the danger of false interpretations increase, so caution must be exercised.

Financial ratios fall into four broad categories: liquidity ratios; profitability ratios; activity ratios; debt ratios (also known as stability ratios).

Liquidity Ratios

Liquidity ratios rely on balance sheet data. The liquidity of a firm means the ability of the firm to meet its short-term liabilities without having to liquidate its long-term assets or cease operations. The two principal liquidity ratios are:

(a) Current Ratio.
(b) Acid Test or Quick Ratio.

Current Ratio. This measures the relationship of Current Assets to Current Liabilities. For Ardmore Limited the ratios for 1985 and 1986 were

(Expressed as £'000.)	1986		1985	
$\dfrac{\text{Current Assets}}{\text{Current Liabilities}}$	$\dfrac{£732.4}{£469.5}$	$= 1.56$	$\dfrac{£631.9}{£410.3}$	$= 1.54$

The higher the Current Ratio the greater the supposed ability of a firm to meet current payments.

Although it used to be held that a firm should aim for a current ratio of 2:1 it is now considered that the particular circumstances of each industry or company determine the optimum current ratio. Different industries have characteristics which seriously affect the current ratio. It is composed not only of cash but also of assets such as inventory and debtors, neither of which may be sold quickly for their balance sheet value. There have been instances of firms going bankrupt with high current ratios, that is many times more current assets than current liabilities. This could occur if the firm had a very low cash balance, a high proportion of unsaleable inventory and a large amount of bad debts. Despite these deficiencies, the ratio is widely used by managers, bankers and financial journalists with its major strength being that it presents the analyst with an absolute yardstick for measuring the liquidity of the firm. In the case of Ardmore Limited there has been very little change over the year. The company appears to be in a fairly tight current position, but has not deteriorated during the year.

Acid Test or Quick Ratio. The current ratio includes the effect of inventory. This may not be readily realisable and so does not meet the liquidity criterion, that is, easily convertible into cash. The acid test ratio is a more severe and stringent test of the firm's ability to meet current obligations but has its critics. They point out that receivables are stretching out in age and declining in quality of collectability, whereas inventory management has ensured greater stability, and control of what was once a significant value on the balance sheet of many companies.

That being said, the Acid Test or Quick Ratio like the current ratio is of some significance provided they are subjected to qualitative as well as quantitative tests and are compared to the industry norm or standard. This ratio is similar to the current ratio except that it includes inventory. Applying the ratio to Ardmore Limited for 1985 and 1986, the following information was discovered:

(Expressed as £'000.)	1986		1985	
$\dfrac{\text{Current Assets less Inventory}}{\text{Current Liabilities}}$	$\dfrac{£406.0}{£469.5}$	$= 0.86$	$\dfrac{£363.4}{£410.3}$	$= 0.89$

In theory Ardmore Limited has insufficient liquid assets to cover obligations. If all of the current liabilities were immediately pressed Ardmore would indeed be unable to pay, but this is most unlikely. A rule of thumb is a ratio of 1:1, though certain businesses, for example, supermarkets, would have a lower ratio. Ardmore is not in bad shape and is not deteriorating over time. However, a close eye should be kept on trends and comparative industry data.

Profitability Ratios

These ratios use both the balance sheet and income statement. They are used to discover how efficiently and effectively assets have contributed to the profits of the firm and can be divided into two groups: profitability in relation to sales and profitability in relation to investment. It is only possible to examine the most widely used ratios. They are:

(a) Gross profit margin.
(b) Net profit margin.
(c) Total asset turnover.
(d) Return on investment.

Gross Profit Margin. The Gross Profit Margin is calculated by expressing gross profit as a percentage of net sales. It indicates the percentage of sales remaining after paying for the cost of goods sold. The higher the margin the better.

	1986	1985
Gross margin of Ardmore	20.9%	18.0%

The gross margin is fairly low reflecting the fact that Ardmore is in a competitive industry. Gross margins of 25 to 30 per cent are not uncommon. The increase in gross margin is a welcome development.

Net Profit Margin. This is calculated by expressing net profit as a percentage of net sales, and is the margin of profit remaining after all costs have been deducted. Taxation may or may not be deducted. Here it is not deducted.

	1986	1985
Net profit margin	6.1%	4.9%

The low ratio further emphasises the difficulty of making profits in Irish manufacturing industry. The margin, though rising, is too low for comfort. If one allowed a realistic charge for the replacement of plant and equipment used during the year then the profit percentage would be minimal.

Total Asset Turnover. This examines the efficiency with which the resources of the business are being used. It is a measure of productivity as much as profitability. Extreme care must be taken in using this ratio for comparative purposes. For Ardmore,

$$\text{Total Asset Turnover} = \frac{\text{Annual Sales}}{\text{Net Assets}} = \overset{1986}{\frac{£1419.3}{£590.3}} = 2.40 \qquad \overset{1985}{\frac{£1300.8}{£536.0}} = 2.42$$

The slight drop in the ratio means that more assets are having to be used to generate every unit of sales. Ardmore's asset turnover figures reflect the nature of the business—relatively labour-intensive engineering.

Asset turnover ratios range from a high in the 20s for supermarkets and the like to a low of about 0.5 for capital-intensive projects such as steel mills.

Return on Investment (ROI). Ultimately, the success or failure of the business depends on whether or not the investment shows a profit. There are many methods of calculating ROI the most common of which is

$$\text{Return on Investment} = \frac{\text{Net Profit After Taxes}}{\text{Net Assets}}$$

The ratio for Ardmore is (Expressed as £'000.)

$$\overset{1986}{\frac{£78.7}{£590.3}} = 13.2\% \qquad\qquad \overset{1985}{\frac{£59.2}{£536.0}} = 11.1\%$$

The ratio by itself is of little value. A better version is the Return on Owner's Equity, that is, the return which the owners receive for investing their own funds (Expressed as £'000.):

$$\text{Return on Owner's Investment} = \frac{\text{Net Profit After Taxes}}{\text{Net Worth}}$$

$$\overset{1986}{\frac{£78.7}{£482.6}} = 16.3\% \qquad\qquad \overset{1985}{\frac{£59.2}{£401.4}} = 14.8\%$$

An after tax rate of return of 16 per cent is high by Irish standards and needs to be compared with the average inflation rate to establish if the owners of Ardmore are better off at the end of 1986 than they were at the end of 1985. The perils that go with investing in business demand an adequate and continuing reward in the form of profit, a small portion of which must be set aside for future growth. Nor can the firm attract more or new investment funds without a substantial return to show for present and past investments or at least the prospect of future profit attainment.

The 'Du Pont Formula' for calculating the Return on Investment is widely used. It breaks down ROI into two parts, net margin on sales and asset turnover. It is calculated as follows:

$$\text{ROI} = \text{Net Profit Margin} \times \text{Asset Turnover}$$

$$= \frac{\text{Net Profit After Taxes}}{\text{Sales}} \times \frac{\text{Sales}}{\text{Total Assets}}$$

For Ardmore the figures are,

		Margin		Asset turnover		
1986 ROI	=	5.5%	×	2.40	=	13.2%
1985 ROI	=	4.6%	×	2.42	=	11.1%

From these calculations it is evident that Ardmore management changed their strategy in 1986. Margins were improved. If, as is likely, the improved margins were due to price increases then the marginal decrease in the asset turnover ratio is explained. Ardmore is balanced on a knife edge. It is possible that lower margins and decreased turnover rates will come together. The effect on return would then be substantial. Careful management is essential.

Activity Ratios

Activity ratios measure the speed with which the money, which is invested in current assets, passes through the system and reappears as cash. The main activity ratios are:
(a) Inventory Turnover;
(b) Accounts Receivable Turnover;
(c) Accounts Payable Turnover.

Inventory Turnover. This is measured as follows:

$$\text{Inventory Turnover} = \frac{\text{Cost of Goods Sold}}{\text{Average Inventory}}$$

For Ardmore the ratio is:

(Expressed as £'000.)   1986   1985

$$\text{Inventory Turnover} = \frac{£1122.1}{£297.5} = 3.8 \qquad \frac{£1066.3}{£250.9} = 4.3$$

The opening figure for inventory on 1 January 1985 was £233,300. Clearly there was a significant increase in inventory in 1986 not matched by a corresponding increase in sales activity. This resulted in a reduction in the number of times inventory was turned over from 4.3 times in 1985 to 3.8 times in 1986. The slow down in turnover is not welcome but to be meaningful the ratio should be compared with similar ratios in like businesses. In the light engineering business in Ireland a turnover of 3.8 would be low. Note that supermarkets might have a turnover of 30 or more while a shipbuilding business could have a turnover of less than 2. This ratio could serve as an early warning signal of a firm's financial difficulties with a decline or slowing down in sales leading to a piling up of unsold and/or unsaleable inventory. There is some cause for concern in this regard for Ardmore Limited.

A derivation of inventory turnover is the average age of inventory in which the number of days in a year is divided by the turnover figures.

	1986	1985
Age of Inventory	$\frac{365}{3.8} = 96$ days	$\frac{365}{4.3} = 85$ days

The shorter the days in inventory the greater corporate liquidity.

Accounts Receivable Turnover. This ratio serves as the basis for determining how rapidly the firm's credit accounts are being collected and is defined as follows:

$$\text{Accounts Receivable Turnover} = \frac{\text{Annual Credit Sales}}{\text{Average Accounts Receivable}}$$

For the sake of clarity assume that all of the sales of Ardmore are on credit. The Accounts Receivable Turnover for Ardmore is as follows (Expressed as £'000.):

1986	1985
$\frac{£1419.3}{(£405.6 + £362.7) \div 2} = 3.7$	$\frac{£1300.8}{(£362.7 + £318.9) \div 2} = 3.8$

The figure for accounts receivable on 1 January 1985 was £318,900. The average age of receivables is normally then computed.

$$\text{Average Age of Accounts Receivable} = \frac{365}{\text{Accounts Receivable Turnover}}$$

	1986	1985
Ardmore Age of Receivables	$\frac{365}{3.7} = 99$ days	$\frac{365}{3.8} = 96$ days

The above figure of ninety-nine days for Ardmore is the average period for collecting a debt. Many people may be surprised at the apparently long collection period. Unfortunately, Irish customers are notorious for taking extended credit. In periods of tight bank credit, the collection period tends to extend. The collection period must be related to the credit terms offered by the firm. Ardmore nominally gives forty-five days credit. Whatever the cause, the slippage in this ratio indicates greater risk with the chances of default or late payment by customers increased with the resultant impact on the firm's cash flow.

Accounts Payable Turnover. This ratio is defined in a manner similar to the accounts receivable turnover. It is:

$$\text{Accounts Payable Turnover} = \frac{\text{Annual Purchases}}{\text{Average Accounts Payable}}$$

For Ardmore Limited this works out as (Expressed as £'000.):

1986		1985	
$\dfrac{£741.1}{(£305.3 + £239.6) \div 2}$	$= 2.8$	$\dfrac{£712.5}{(£239.6 + £210.9) \div 2}$	$= 3.2$

The opening figure for accounts payable on 1 January 1985 was £210,900. Computing the payment period for payables produces the following.

	1986		1985	
Average Payment Period =	$\dfrac{365}{2.8}$	= 130 days	$\dfrac{365}{3.2}$	= 114 days

Ardmore is 'stretching' its trade creditors to an unacceptable level. In 1986 Ardmore Limited has stretched the payable period by sixteen days. This was matched by Ardmore allowing the collection period to rise by three days and the inventory holding time to rise by eleven days, giving rise to an almost neutral cash/liquidity impact. The creditors have financed the build-up of inventory and the slippage in collections from debtors. While credit from suppliers is a valuable source of finance some concern could be noted at the possibility of 'stretching their goodwill' to an unacceptable level.

Debt Ratios (Leverage/Gearing Ratios)

Debt Ratios measure the ability of the firm to meet future obligations such as interest and repayments on both debentures and term loans.

Investors, suppliers, and bankers pay close attention to the amount of debt owed by a business. The three ratios commonly used are:

(a) The Debt Ratio.
(b) Debt to Equity.
(c) Times Interest Earned.

These ratios attempt to measure the long term stability of the business.

Debt Ratio. This ratio measures the extent to which the total assets of the firm have been financed using borrowed funds.

$$\text{Debt Ratio} = \frac{\text{Total Liabilities}}{\text{Total Assets}} = \frac{\text{Current Liabilities} + \text{Debenture} + \text{Taxation}}{\text{Fixed} + \text{Current Assets}}$$

For Ardmore Limited the figures were:

(Expressed as £'000.)   1986   1985

$$\text{Debt Ratio} = \frac{£573.1}{£1059.8} = 54\% \qquad \frac{£541.7}{£946.3} = 57\%$$

Ardmore has managed to finance over 50 per cent of its business by using borrowed funds. Using borrowed funds is known as financial leverage or gearing. Chapter 14 returns to the concept of leverage. The Ardmore figure is relatively high.

Debt/Equity Ratio. This commonly used ratio measures the relationship between long-term debt and the owners' investment. It highlights the cushion of owners' funds available to the debt holders. For Ardmore Limited the ratios were:

(Expressed as £'000.)   1986   1985

$$\text{Debt/Equity Ratio} = \frac{\text{Long Term Debt}}{\text{Issued Capital} + \text{Reserves}} = \frac{£98.5}{£482.6} = 20\% \qquad \frac{£125.0}{£401.4} = 31\%$$

The ratio is meaningful only when traced over time and/or when related to the business of the firm. Companies in capital intensive stable businesses tend to have high ratios. The ratio for Ardmore Limited is well within the acceptable range for Irish engineering firms.

Times Interest Earned. This measures the ability of a firm to meet interest payments out of its annual operating earnings. The ratio is defined as follows:

$$\text{Times Interest Earned} = \frac{\text{Net Profit before Interest and Taxes}}{\text{Interest Payments (including overdraft interest)}}$$

For Ardmore Limited the ratios were:

(Expressed as £'000.)	1986	1985
Times Interest Earned	$\dfrac{£122.1}{£35.7} = 3.4$	$\dfrac{£103.0}{£38.9} = 2.7$

The ratio enables one to see how far profits can fall before interest payments are not covered. For Ardmore profits would need to decline by over 75 per cent before this would occur. A 'cushion' of 5 times is often put forward as a useful rule of thumb. Where there are specific repayment or sinking fund provisions attaching to long-term debt a variant of this ratio is often computed, that is, Times Burden Covered. This measures the activity of the firm to fund both the interest and capital repayments. Chapter 11 further examines this issue.

Comparative Ratio Analysis

So far, this chapter has identified and computed a number of ratios which cover a wide range of financial activities. It was pointed out that ratios must be handled with care. If comparisons are made then be sure that apples are being matched with apples.

Users of financial statements should recognise that management can affect the timeliness and integrity of the information provided. For instance, minimal information about their off-balance sheet financing, that is, lease payments may be disclosed in an attempt to have external parties underestimate the underlying risk exposure of the firm.

To assist Irish business, the Financial Executives Association has analysed the financial data available on forty-four publicly quoted Irish manufacturing firms. The results of the analysis are presented in Table 5.

For comparative purposes the Ardmore ratios are included in the table. There are a number of points worth noting. The Ardmore liquidity ratios are average to good. The debt ratio is a little high but this would not be unusual since Ardmore is smaller than the average firm included in the data. As a result of the high debt ratio and low net margin on sales, Ardmore has a relatively poor interest cover. The activity ratios show that Ardmore Limited is much less capital intensive than the larger publicly quoted firms. It appears that debt collection could be improved as could profit margins.

Table 5   Ratio Analysis of Publicly Quoted Manufacturing Firms

Year ended 31 January 1986	Paper and Packaging	Building	Textiles	Engineering	Food, Drink and Tobacco	Misc.	Ardmore (1986)
LIQUIDITY							
Current Ratio	1.83	2.23	2.13	1.76	2.51	2.03	1.56
Quick Ratio	1.07	0.80	0.83	1.14	0.84	1.12	0.86
LEVERAGE							
Debt Ratio %	46.0	42.0	71.0	36.0	42.0	44.0	54.0
Times Interest Earned	5.3	3.3	0.8	- 5.7	5.8	6.1	3.4
ACTIVITY							
Inventory Turnover	10.5	6.8	5.2	7.1	5.5	5.1	3.8
Total Asset Turnover	1.8	1.2	1.9	1.9	2.1	1.6	2.4
Net Asset Turnover	2.6	1.6	2.8	3.2	3.0	2.3	—
Fixed Asset Turnover	3.3	2.3	5.9	5.5	6.6	4.8	—
Age of Receivables (days)	44	60	63	69	45	72	99
PROFITABILITY							
Net Profit Margin %	5.3	6.4	2.2	4.6	4.4	7.8	6.1
Return on Investment %	9.7	7.6	4.0	7.3	9.1	10.4	13.2
Return on Owners' Investment %	14.5	9.1	- 4.5	14.2	13.0	17.3	16.3

Source: Financial Executives Association

SOURCES AND USES OF FUNDS STATEMENTS AS ANALYTICAL TOOL

By examining the changes that have taken place, management can decide whether or not the policies followed were in the best interests of the firm. The first step is to examine the balance sheet changes between the periods. The changes in the various assets and liabilities are then sorted as to whether they provided or used finance.

Sources of funds, which make cash available, arise in the following ways:

(a) Profits from Operations.
(b) Proceeds from the Sale of Shares.
(c) Grants Received.
(d) An Increase in any Liability.
(e) A Decrease in any Asset.

Uses of funds are:

(a) An Increase in any Asset Other than Cash.
(b) A Decrease in any Liability.
(c) Dividends.
(d) Redeeming Preference Shares.
(e) Reducing Equity Capital. This requires the permission of a court.

At first glance, some of the categories appear misplaced. How can an increase in liabilities be a source of funds? Reflection should quickly provide the answer. If a supplier gives you credit then he is providing you with the use of his funds for a period. Depreciation is often included as a source of funds though it is not. This is because depreciation is a non-cash item, so when cash flows are being traced depreciation must be either added back to profits or included as a separate figure in the Sources of Funds Column. A Sources and Uses of Funds Statement for Ardmore Limited for the year ended 31 December 1986 is shown in Table 6.

The movement of funds during the year was reasonably consistent. The expansion of sales led to an increase in activity which required new investment in inventory and accounts receivable. The expansion was financed from trading profits and accounts payable as was the purchase of additional fixed assets. It can be concluded that the financial management of Ardmore was reasonable during the period in question. Sources and Uses were not seriously mismatched, that is, fixed assets were not acquired with current liabilities. It is well to remember than the Sources and Uses Statement shows movements and changes between the ends of two accounting periods. Transactions within the period do not appear.

Table 6

ARDMORE LIMITED
Sources and Uses of Funds for the year ended 31 December 1986
(Expressed as £'000)

Sources:		*Uses:*	
Profit Before Tax	£86.4	Inventory	£57.9
Depreciation	12.8	Accounts Receivable	42.9
Mortgage Debenture	—	Fixed Assets	25.8
Grants Received	3.4	Retiral of Debenture	26.5
Accounts Payable	65.7	Bank Overdraft	18.3
Short Term Loans	6.5	Taxation	3.7
Cash	0.3		
	£175.1		£175.1

CONCLUSION

This chapter has provided a framework for financial analysis. A series of ratios, liquidity, profitability, activity and debt were presented and examined. The objective in selecting the ratios was to maximise the information obtained from the minimum of analysis.

While it is important to know what the above techniques can do, it is vital to be aware of what they cannot do. Ratio analysis is based on the assumption that the financial statements present a reasonable picture of what is happening in the business. This is not always the case. The information in the financial statements relates to one particular period of time only. Rarely do businesses stand still, so it is advisable when applying ratio analysis to examine the analysis in the light of developments which have occurred since the statements were drawn up.

The significance of the results of an analysis lies in the future.

There is little point in undertaking the analysis if no action is to be taken. The difficulty here is that ratios are applied to past events and so may not truly represent the present or the future. In interpreting the trends or results in a business a skilled analyst will expect the analysis to provide a guide rather than a solution to present problems and future plans.

Users of financial statements over a long period of time have evolved rules of thumb for minimising the effect of the weaknesses of these statements. They may be summarised as follows:

(1) Analyse a series of statements rather than those of one year.

(2) Study carefully the notes and explanations attached to the statements.

(3) Check the veracity of the items by comparing them with those of previous years and treating any sudden change with suspicion.

(4) Adjust the data for inflation, if significant.

No attempt has been made to suggest absolute ratios for a firm. The most suitable ratio will depend on the industry, the competition, the financial resources of the firm and company objectives. A firm would be inviting danger by attempting to apply rigid or inflexible rules to ratio analysis.

The second method of analysis, Sources and Uses Statements, is a simple but effective technique for identifying the flow of funds through a business during a particular period. The next chapter extends funds flow analysis into future projections.

Further Reading

George Foster: *Financial Statement Analysis,* Prentice-Hall, Englewood Cliffs, New Jersey, 1978.

R. A. Foulke: *Practical Financial Statement Analysis,* McGraw Hill, London 1975.

Chapter 4

Financial Forecasting

The analysis in Chapter 3 relied on historical data. This can provide useful information to management but by itself it is insufficient. Business success lies in future outcomes. To assist overall corporate planning most managers attempt to forecast the future. This is normally part of corporate planning.

There are few firms operating today without a plan of some description. The plan may be in the mind of the owner or it may be an elaborate bound volume describing in detail the short- and long-run objectives of the business and of each section within it. Every plan and all the policies introduced to further the plan have financial implications. Every decision made will ultimately be reflected in the financial statements of the firm.

Just as overall planning is divided into two distinct stages, long-run/strategic planning and short-run/tactical planning, so too is financial planning. Short-run or current financial planning deals primarily with the effect of plans on the liquidity position of the business. This is sometimes known as financial forecasting. Long-run financial planning examines the effect of proposed capital investments and is known as capital budgeting or investment appraisal. Methods of capital budgeting are examined in Chapter 6. As in corporate planning, there is no clear-cut distinction between the short and long term. Financial plans undertaken for the immediate future often have long-term implications while long-term planning has implications for every short-term projection.

In planning, a co-ordinated, integrated effort is required to ensure that the firm has the necessary resources to undertake the projected plan, and that the objectives of the plan are reached. A firm cannot plan any aspect of business in isolation. A marketing plan may have implications for both production and personnel departments, but it most certainly will have implications for the financial department. Further, the replanning function is extremely important, since effective management cannot wait until the firm has experienced failure to take corrective action.

Management must engage in continuous analysis for the earliest detection of causes of financial embarrassment, in order to realise the highest return on investment and avoid insolvency.

A firm contemplating a financial management system will want to know the answers to the following questions: Why is financial planning necessary? What are the advantages of proper financial planning? What techniques should be used in financial planning?

If properly carried out the financial plan should give rise to a number of benefits such as:

(a) A readily available criterion for decision-making.
(b) A communication link between the owners, managers and employees.
(c) A motivational device for the firm's employees.
(d) An invaluable tool in analysing risk, that it, a sensitivity analysis.

It is the function of the financial manager to produce the financial plan based principally on company policy and on the forecasts of his marketing and production colleagues. In a small firm the general manager may undertake all these functions. It is his responsibility to co-ordinate the plans of each area. Once financial forecasts have been produced, management can review the projected plans and tailor them to match the financial resources of the firm. This will utilise available funds most efficiently and should avoid placing the firm in the embarrassing position of making commitments which it cannot meet. The advantages of financial planning are clear cut: it indicates to management the funds required, when, and for how long they will be required if specific plans and programmes are to be carried out.

It provides a method of control whereby deviations from expected performance are quickly brought to light, thus allowing management to take corrective action in time.

Two basic methods are used in forecasting the short-term financial requirements of a firm:

(a) Cash flow forecasts,
(b) Projected balance sheets (pro forma statements).

The cash flow forecast takes account of expected cash receipts and payments over a period of time. It provides detailed information on the projected cash position for the period under examination. If a firm is preparing a cash forecast for the coming year, it may develop the forecast on a monthly or even on a weekly basis.

A projected balance sheet is a normal extension of a cash flow forecast since the information required to prepare the cash flow forecast provides the information necessary for the balance sheet.

The projected balance sheet method is used to indicate a broad picture of the firm's expected position at the end of a particular period, for example, every three or six months or at the end of the next financial year. This method has the disadvantage that it represents only one point in time and gives no indication of results or requirements within the period. A further disadvantage is that it does not indicate when the maximum amount of funds will be required or the size of the amount required. This disadvantage can be overcome by projecting a balance sheet for the date when the maximum demand for funds is expected.

CASH FLOW FORECASTING

Cash flow forecasting is also known as 'Cash Budgeting'. It allows a business to plan short-term cash requirements. It should provide a picture of the timing and amount of cash inflows and outflows. This method compares the expected cash receipts with the expected cash payments. Only cash flows are considered. No allowance is made for items such as depreciation which affect profitability but not cash. Cash received is generally known as cash inflow while cash paid out is called cash outflow.

Cash forecasting is usually done on a monthly basis. Receipts and payments are estimated and compared month by month over, say, a period of twelve months. For periods longer than a year ahead, forecasts are drawn up quarterly, semi-annually and finally annually. Inability to forecast cash flows accurately in the distant future is the major reason for broadening the forecast period. Some firms with large discrepancies between inflows and outflows of cash find it necessary to prepare weekly cash flow forecasts.

Preparation of a cash flow forecast has three elements:
(a) Preparing the cash inflow forecast.
(b) Preparing cash outflow forecast.
(c) Comparing the two forecasts to discover whether there is a surplus or deficit of cash during each period.

Cash Inflow Forecast

The accuracy of the cash forecast depends totally on the reliability of the sales estimates. But sales forecasts are notoriously difficult to estimate accurately. They are generated in two ways. An internal forecast builds a sales estimate from the bottom up: each salesperson is asked to give his or her estimate of sales for the relevant period. External forecasts are based on known relationships between sales and economic indicators, for example, a period of tight credit is known to have an adverse effect on car sales. Usually a compromise must be reached between the two forecasts.

The importance of an accurate sales forecast cannot be overstressed. The sales schedule is the cornerstone of all the remaining calculations.

Having estimated sales the next step is to identify the percentage of credit sales and the likely credit terms.

Table 7 contains a projected Sales Estimate/Cash Inflow Statement for Ardmore Limited for the calendar year 1987. The following variables were considered in preparing the schedule.

(1) Ardmore Limited has a seasonal sales pattern. Peak demand generally occurs between January and June.

(2) An internal sales forecast expected a $12\frac{1}{2}$ per cent increase in sales in 1987.

(3) Economic forecasters predicted a relatively poor year in some of the sectors in which Ardmore Limited sells, for example, domestic central heating and agricultural machinery. Management is confident that an economic slowdown will not affect them too seriously. They have decided to allow for an 8 per cent increase in sales volume and a 4 per cent increase in prices giving an overall $12\frac{1}{2}$ per cent increase in sales revenue.

(4) Credit terms are net 45 days but few pay on time. Management expect to reduce the average period of credit to 90 days from a 1986 average of 99 days.

(5) There are no cash sales.

Lines 1 to 4 in the Cash Budget shown in Table 7 deal with the inflows of cash. Note that sales in October 1986 will be paid for in January 1987 while the January sales will be paid for in April. Obviously sales and inflows will not match perfectly but this assumption is a useful starting point.

Having compiled a cash inflow statement resulting from sales, any additional cash inflows from sales of assets etc. are then included. Ardmore management have no intentions of selling assets at present. A major capital expansion project is being considered. This is a separate item and is considered in detail in Chapter 6.

Cash Outflows

Given the sales estimates management can also produce a statement of all cash outflows. All cash payments must be included in the outflow statement, for example payments for wages, supplies, interest, taxation and capital expenditure. The critical item is often the production schedule. Management must decide whether to produce in line with the estimates of sales or whether to produce for inventory, thereby facilitating a smooth production pattern.

Once the production schedule is agreed then estimates of supplies, materials and labour can be made. It should be noted that suppliers give

Table 7

ARDMORE LIMITED
Cash Budget 1987 (Expressed as £'000.)

	1986 Oct.	Nov.	Dec.	1987 Jan.	Feb.	Mar.	April	May	June	July	Aug.	Sept.	Oct.	Nov.	Dec.	Total 12 months
INFLOWS																
1. Sales	135.2	135.2	135.2	159.0	159.0	159.0	168.5	168.5	144.0	96.7	105.4	105.4	110.4	110.4	110.4	—
2. Cash Inflow				135.2	135.2	135.2	159.0	159.0	159.0	168.5	168.5	144.0	96.7	105.4	105.4	1,671.1
3. Other Cash Receipts																
4. TOTAL CASH INFLOWS				135.2	135.2	135.2	159.0	159.0	159.0	168.5	168.5	144.0	96.7	105.4	105.4	1,671.1
OUTFLOWS																
5. Purchases	86.5	86.5	62.9	69.2	69.2	69.2	69.2	69.2	69.2	69.2	69.2	69.2	69.2	69.2	69.2	
6. Payments to Suppliers				86.5	86.5	63.1	69.2	69.2	138.4	69.2	69.2	69.2	69.2	69.2	69.2	928.1
7. Wages				31.6	31.6	31.6	31.6	31.6	31.6	31.6	31.6	31.6	31.6	31.6	31.0	378.6
8. Factory Overheads				4.4	4.4	4.4	4.4	4.4	4.4	4.4	4.4	4.4	4.4	4.4	4.4	52.8
9. Expenses				15.0	15.0	15.0	15.0	15.0	15.0	15.0	15.0	15.0	15.0	15.0	15.0	180.0
10. Interest						23.8						23.8				47.6
11. Taxation						6.0						7.4				13.4
12. Loan Repayment					5.0						5.0					10.0
13. Fixed Assets													30.0			30.0
14. TOTAL CASH OUTFLOWS (6–13)				137.5	142.5	143.9	120.2	120.2	189.4	120.2	125.2	151.4	150.2	120.2	119.6	1,640.5
15. CASH BALANCE (4 minus 14)				[2.3]	[7.3]	[8.7]	38.8	38.8	[30.4]	48.3	43.3	[7.4]	[53.5]	[14.8]	[14.2]	
16. CASH ON HAND 1 Jan.				[67.8]												
17. CUMULATIVE CASH BALANCE				[70.1]	[77.4]	[86.1]	[47.3]	[8.5]	[38.9]	9.4	52.7	45.3	[8.2]	[23.0]	[37.2]	

credit and so the payment for purchases often occurs in a different period to that in which the goods are received. The management of Ardmore have made the following assumptions in preparing their cash outflow statement:

(1) Production will be spread evenly over the whole year.

(2) Under pressure from suppliers only twelve weeks credit will be taken during 1987, compared with over eighteen weeks in 1986. This, of course, means that during the year cash will have to be provided to pay off the creditors. Presumably suppliers have begun to squeeze Ardmore because of their slow payment pattern. Payments to creditors will be increased in June to reduce the period of credit outstanding to twelve weeks.

(3) There are no cash purchases, that is, all suppliers give credit.

(4) The number of employees will not change but wage and salary increases will push up the wage bill by 5 per cent as of 1 January.

(5) Purchases will rise by only 10 per cent due mainly to a recession in the steel industry which means keen prices to purchasers.

(6) Expenses will be tightly controlled but are likely to increase by 6 per cent.

(7) A new piece of machinery will be acquired in August, costing £30,000 installed. It will be paid for in October. A 40 per cent IDA grant on the machine will not be received until 1988.

(8) It is expected that the taxation figure of £13,400 in the 1986 Balance Sheet will be paid in two instalments of £6,000 in March and £7,400 in September.

The anticipated commitments are calculated as follows:

	1986 Figure (£'000)	Growth	1987 Figure (£'000)	Monthly Average
Cost of Materials (inc. Carriage Inwards)	754.7	10%	830.4	69.2
Wages	360.6	5%	378.6	31.6
Factory Overheads (net of Depreciation)	49.6	6%	52.8	4.4
Expenses (Administration and Selling)	170.0	6%	180.0	15.0
Interest	35.7	Assume 23.8 in March and Sept. to cover increased short-term borrowing		
Taxation	13.4	6.0 paid March, 7.4 paid in Sept.		

Loan Repayments of £10,000 will be made to the Industrial Credit Corporation.

The figures used are rounded to the nearest hundred. Exact figures would imply a spurious accuracy in the data. Note that changes in Work in Progress are ignored, which may underestimate slightly the Cost of Manufacture. The schedule includes an estimate of interest charges arising from an increase in overdraft requirements during the first quarter of 1987. Lines 6-14 in Table 7 present the Cash Outflow Statement.

Net Cash Flow and Cash Balance

Having estimated the cash inflows and outflows a net cash position is calculated. This is line 15 in Table 7. To the net position is added the opening overdraft position at the beginning of the period, that is, 1 January 1987, £67,800.

At first glance the cash position in Ardmore appears frightening. The bank overdraft is expected to rise to £85,700 by the end of March. However, follow through the statement and it becomes clear that the peak financing requirements are rapidly repaid. It is interesting to speculate on how the various liquidity and activity ratios would differ from those in Chapter 3 if the Ardmore year end was 31 March instead of 31 December.

Management must decide policy on the basis of the above data. In addition to the expected cash needs it is usual to keep a 'cash cushion' to allow for emergencies. Therefore, management may seek an overdraft limit of say, £90,000. Such a figure, combined with the long-term debt, represents a large burden on a company the size of Ardmore Limited. It is possible that the banks may hesitate to grant the finance.

Other issues to be considered by management are:

(1) The wide fluctuation in the net monthly cash position with the positive cash flows of April, May, July and August giving rise to large cumulative cash balances in August and September. Should earlier payments be made to suppliers and/or consideration be given to possible early payment discounts during this period? Should the loan repayment schedule be looked at for possible net savings?

(2) Is the accounts receivable reduction from 99 to 90 days realistic and achievable? Can even further improvements be made given that a day's reduction in peak season would realise nearly £2,000 cash.

A combination of the above suggestions will reduce the cash requirements and make life much easier for both the Ardmore financial controller and the local Ardmore bankers.

The prime purpose of a cash budget is to determine the size and timing of cash flows. The use of the budget is very clear in the Ardmore situation where the year end cash figures hide major fluctuations. In the absence of a cash budget, and the resultant decisions taken, it is possible that

Ardmore would find itself technically insolvent in March 1987, that is, profitable but lacking cash to pay current liabilities.

PRO FORMA STATEMENTS

Apart from projecting cash flows it is also possible, and indeed advisable, to prepare projected financial statements. Such statements are known as Pro Forma Statements. Usually an Income Statement and a Balance Sheet is prepared, typically for a period of one year. The Pro Forma Income Statement analyses expected profitabiity while the Pro Forma Balance Sheet shows the expected financial position. Pro Forma statements forecast assets and liabilities as well as the future cash position.

Pro Forma Income Statement

The simplest way to develop this statement is to forecast sales and then take estimated values for the cost of goods sold, expenses and interest charges. All of the data required has already been produced for the cash budget. A 1987 Pro Forma Income Statement for Ardmore Limited is shown in Table 8.

Table 8

ARDMORE LIMITED
Pro Forma Income Statement for the Year ended 31 December 1987
(Expressed as £'000.)

	Sales		1,596.7
Less	Raw Material Consumed (Purchases & Raw		
	Material Inventory Movement)	865.5	
	Wages	378.6	
	Factory Overheads	67.5	1,311.6
	Gross Profit		285.1
Less	Operating Expenses	189.0	
	Interest	47.6	236.6
	Net Profit before Tax		48.5
Less	10% Corporate Tax Rate		4.8
	Net Profit after Tax		43.7
Plus	Tax Liability Written Back		5.1
	Amount Transferred to Profit and Loss Account		48.8

If management can increase sales by 12½ per cent and hold costs to the budgeted level then net profits in 1987 will be maintained at 1986 levels.

Pro Forma Balance Sheet

There are two ways to estimate a balance sheet. Where a cash budget and detailed production schedule exists it is possible to identify the sums invested in inventory, accounts receivable, and accounts payable. An alternative method is to estimate directly figures not readily available. In

Table 9

ARDMORE LIMITED
Pro Forma Balance Sheet for the year ended 31 December 1987
(Expressed as £'000.)

Fixed Assets			
Land and Buildings			135.0
Plant and Machinery			153.4
Fixtures and Fittings			21.2
Motor Vehicles			24.1
			333.7
Current Assets			
Inventory		291.3	
Accounts Receivable		331.2	
Cash		0.4	
		622.9	
Current Liabilities			
Accounts Payable	207.6		
Short-Term Loan	83.0		
Current Taxation	4.8		
Bank Overdraft	37.2	332.6	
Net Current Assets (Working Capital)			290.3
			£624.0
Financed By			
Authorised 1,000,000 £1 Ordinary Shares			
Issued 335,000 £1 Ordinary Shares			335.0
Reserves			
Share Premium Account			25.0
Profit and Loss Account			171.4
Government Grants			4.1
Debentures			88.5
			£624.0

the example below this latter method is used. The assumptions used in preparing the 1987 Ardmore Balance Sheet (Table 9) are:

(a) Accounts Payable to be £207,600. This figure is taken from the cash budget and represents the taking of twelve weeks credit.

(b) Accounts Receivable of £331,200 representing total sales in the last three months of the year, that is, giving 90 days credit. This figure differs from that obtainable by using an accounts receivable turnover figure because sales are not even throughout the year.

(c) Capital expenditure of £30,000, less depreciations of £23,700.

(d) Long term loan repayments debentures of £10,000.

(e) Taxation is reduced to 10 per cent of taxable profits. The figure for the future taxation in the 1986 Balance Sheet is to be written off.

(f) Grants received will remain the same.

(g) Issued share capital to remain the same.

(h) The net increase in the Profit and Loss Account will be £48,800.

(i) Cash of £400 will be maintained.

(j) The depreciation allowances are as follows:

Plant and Machinery	£12,800 + 15% = £14,700
Furniture and Fittings	3,500 + 15% = 4,000
Motor Vehicles	4,300 + 15% = 5,000
	£23,700

(k) Inventory is the unknown amount which acts as the balance for Assets and Liabilities. It is difficult to estimate as a detailed production schedule is not available. The balancing figure is £291,300 which is a significant improvement on the 1986 figure of £326,400 and represents an increase in the inventory turnover ratio of 3.8 times in 1986 to a budgeted ratio of 4.2 times in 1987.

These figures are those used in 1986 plus the increases in costs allowed for in the pro forma income statement.

The Pro Forma Balance Sheet highlights the effects of management policies. Comparing 1986 with 1987 it can be seen that a significant reduction in the credit available from suppliers is compensated in part by a small improvement in the credit given to customers and an increase in the inventory turnover ratio. In addition, the cash budget highlights that this proposed policy will stretch the cash resources of the company in the first quarter of 1987 with a short-term surplus arising mid year and normality restored by year-end 1987. Any slippage in one or other of these policy initiatives could have serious liquidity and operational problems for Ardmore in 1987.

CONCLUSION

This chapter extended the financial analysis of a firm's operations into the short-term future. Two separate techniques, a cash budget and pro forma statements, were developed to assist management in planning. The cash budget is an essential tool to forecast cash inflows and, more importantly, the net cash position on a monthly basis. Too many profitable firms go bankrupt because they lack cash. As managers become more expert in using cash budgets they can change the many variables to allow for deviations from the expected outcomes.

The pro forma statements provide incremental information to management. The income statement shows the effect on profits if projections prove accurate. The balance sheet shows the effect on assets and liabilities. Armed with the information provided by the above techniques, management can now decide what is to be done. The above analysis has raised question marks over Ardmore's accounts payable, inventory, accounts receivable and bank position. The following chapter examines in detail the issues raised.

Further Reading
J. A. Viscione & G. S. Roberts: *Contemporary Financial Management,* Merrill, Ohio 1987.
A. J. Keown *et al.: Basic Financial Management,* Prentice-Hall Inc., New Jersey 1985.
J. R. Franks & H. H. Scholefield: *Corporate Financial Management,* (2nd Ed.) Gower Press, London 1977.

Chapter 5

Managing Working Capital

Managing working capital means deciding on a level of current assets and current liabilities. Working capital itself is defined as the excess of current assets over current liabilities. The adequacy of a firm's working capital has a direct bearing on the ability of a business to pay bills. The level of working capital and the relationship between current assets and liabilities provides measures of financial risk, that is, the probability that the business will become illiquid or what is known as technically insolvent. The purpose of working capital management is to control the level of investment in each current asset so that an acceptable level of 'cover' is provided for the sources of current funds. Each individual source of short-term funds must be managed to minimise cost and risks. The easiest way to reduce the riskiness attaching to the working capital would be to finance all current assets with long-term funds. The possibility of lack of liquidity would be remote because there would be no short-term obligations. Many businesses do this, paying cash for purchases and having no bank borrowings. To use the vernacular, 'they owe no one'. No matter how long items remain in stock or how slow sales are such businesses will not be pressurised by short-term obligations.

Therefore the answer to working capital management appears to be long-term finance and no current liabilities. Unfortunately, as risk reduces so too does profitability. Long-term money tends to be expensive. The cheapest sources of finance are generally the shorter-term sources. The logic behind this is simple. A lender who loans his funds for a period of years needs a higher payment to cover the various risks attaching to his investment. Banks charge people simply for the use of money. A debenture holder charges for the use of the money and also for the possibility that over a period of years something may go wrong and the money will not be repaid.

To understand the need for careful working capital management consider for a moment the operation of a business. Owners and long-term lenders have provided funds to acquire fixed assets and to get the business operating through the purchase of supplies, the creation of inventory to meet the needs of sales, and the provision of credit to persuade customers to buy. The profitability of the business can be raised by increasing sales. One way of doing this is to extend credit terms. Greater sales generally means more inventory of raw materials and work in progress. The cash to finance these expansions is usually not available from profits. Certainly profits are being made but they are already tied up in the extra Accounts Receivable and Inventory. Bank Overdraft and Accounts Payable are the usual sources of finance used.

Many firms contrive to expand in this manner. Some survive but others discover the dreaded reality of 'overtrading'—having too small a base of long-term funds to finance an increase in operations. Suppose credit is restricted by government order. Business may slow up, leaving the firm with large inventories of unsold goods; customers slow up on payments; the bank insists on the overdraft being reduced; and suppliers threaten to cut off supplies unless they are paid. The crunch comes one Friday when management cannot pay the wage bill. Bankruptcy often follows.

This chapter concentrates on methods of controlling investment in the following current assets: inventory; accounts receivable; cash and marketable securities.

INVENTORY MANAGEMENT

Inventories represent a significant investment for most firms. For example, the Ardmore Balance Sheet for 1986 shows an investment in inventory almost equal to the total investment in land, buildings, plant, machinery, fittings and vehicles.

It is important to understand the role of inventory. It provides a coupling between production and sales. Only in very rare instances can a sales order be produced immediately. Usually inventories of parts are kept. Equally most manufacturing firms have at any one time a range of products at various stages of manufacture. These are known as 'Work in Progress'. Finally, management rarely produces to order. Instead, to minimise production costs and to facilitate efficient management, goods are produced for inventory. That means that products are produced and then stored until sold. Inventory allows flexibility.

The level of inventory maintained is subject to conflict between the various functional managers.

The marketing manager wishes to see a high level of finished goods inventory so that orders can be filled immediately. This is particularly important in industries where competition is tough, for example, a buyer of canned beans in a supermarket might seek a particular brand but if it is not available then another brand will be chosen. From the viewpoint of profits, incremental sales can be very profitable. Consider the effect on the profits of an ice cream company of having plenty of inventory during a long hot spell in August.

The production manager has different priorities to the marketing manager. He wants to minimise the unit cost of manufacture. He wants high raw materials inventories so that production is not disrupted by shortages, and long production runs to maximise efficiency. This produces high finished goods inventories but usually of only a few products.

The financial manager has yet another perspective; he regards inventory as an investment. He generally seeks to minimise levels of inventory at each particular level of sales, that is, he wants to maximise inventory turnover. Carrying inventory is expensive. Storage, handling, insurance, wastage, breakage, obsolescence and the cost of money tied up in inventory can result in annual carrying costs in excess of 30 per cent of inventory value. The objective of inventory management is simple to state, but very complex to achieve. Inventory levels should be increased until the additional costs equal the profits resulting from higher levels.

Inventory Valuation

Inventory is normally valued on the basis of cost or market value, whichever is the lower. Unfortunately, numerous methods of costing are used, which means that the value of inventory on a balance sheet is dependent on the particular method of valuation used.

The methods used are:

(1) *Unit Cost* Each item is valued individually. This method is rarely used.

(2) *FIFO* First In First Out. This assumes that materials purchased first are used first. Inventory is valued on the basis of the cost of the most recent purchases. In a period of rising prices inventory has a high value, and cost of goods is reduced. Therefore this method tends to produce high profits.

(3) *LIFO* Last In First Out. This assumes that the most recently acquired goods are used first. Therefore, inventory is valued at the cost of the oldest goods held. The cost of goods sold is high and profits low when this method is used.

Other methods such as average cost, standard cost and adjusted selling price are used. Standard cost is particularly relevant in medium to large manufacturing organisations with multiple raw material parts in each product.

It is important to know the inventory valuation method in use. The inventory figure of £326,400 in the 1986 Ardmore Balance Sheet might vary by as much as £40,000 if the method of valuation changed. Considering that 1986 after-tax profits were only £78,700 it is evident that financial analysts must be aware of the method in use.

Inventory Control

Most businesses find themselves with an inventory composed of many thousands of items. It is economically impossible to have tight control over all items. Rather than attempt the impossible, managers apply the '80/20' rule. This useful rule of thumb states that 80 per cent of inventory value is accounted for by 20 per cent of the items in store. Management concentrates effort on controlling the 20 per cent. To assist business an inventory control system known as the Economic Order Quantity model (EOQ) has been developed. This model helps management to identify not only the time to order but also the ideal order quantity. To develop an EOQ model the following information is needed:

(a) The time required from order to delivery.

(b) The rate of usage of the product.

(c) The cost of ordering.

(d) The cost of carrying a unit in inventory. This is composed of interest plus storage plus an allowance for wastage, breakage and obsolescence.

(e) The discount structure for bulk orders.

(f) The penalties for being out of inventory.

The simplest version of the EOQ model is as follows:

$$EOQ = \sqrt{\frac{2\,DS}{Ic}}$$

where

EOQ	= order quantity
D	= usage in units of the product per period
S	= order cost per order
Ic	= carrying cost per period per unit.

This formula and the logic involved can be clearly seen in Figure 2.

Figure 2

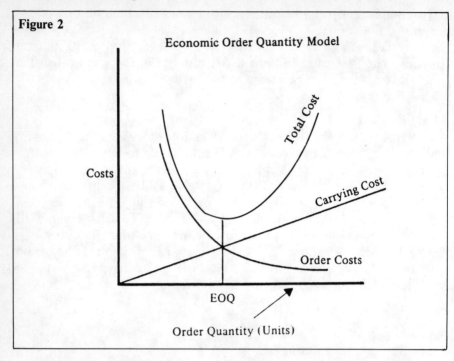

Economic Order Quantity Model

An example will help. Ardmore Limited expects to use 8,000 steel plates (D) during 1987. The estimated costs of placing an order verifying it and following up with written confirmation is £20 (S). The carrying cost of each plate costing £10 is 30 per cent per annum, that is, £3 (Ic). The economic order quantity for this item is:

$$EOQ = \sqrt{\frac{2 \times 8,000 \times 20}{3}}$$

$$= \quad 327$$

This means that Ardmore Limited should place an order twenty-four times a year. Note that by increasing the carrying cost the EOQ declines while it rises if the ordering cost declines.

There are many assumptions in this simple model, mainly those of constant usage and instantaneous delivery. For Irish firms importing much of their raw materials the latter assumption is a critical weakness, but one which can be removed by the use of a *re-order point*. The re-order point is defined as:

Re-order point = Days from order to delivery, that is, lead time
multiplied by daily usage.

In the case of Ardmore Limited it takes, on average, five days to obtain delivery. Daily usage is 22 (8,000 ÷ 365) so the following emerges:

$$\text{Steel Plate Re-Order Point} = 5 \times 22$$
$$= 110$$

When the number of steel plates in inventory falls to 110 an order for 327 is placed.

The second weakness, that of assuming constant usage, is alleviated by the holding of *buffer inventory* or *safety stock*. A buffer inventory is a quantity of inventory held to allow the fluctuations in the demand for the product. Instead of waiting to order until inventory had fallen to 110, management may agree to hold a buffer of fifty. In these circumstances an order is placed when the quantity in inventory falls to 160. This allows for variations in demand and also for delays in receipt of the re-ordered goods. The greater the level of uncertainty in demand and delivery times the greater required size of the buffer inventory.

A further problem associated with the simple EOQ model is that it does not allow for quantity discounts. Suppose that Ardmore Limited could obtain a discount of 10 pence per plate for orders of 500 or more. The maximum saving to the firm is £800 (10 pence × 8,000). The costs would be the additional carrying costs less the lower ordering costs of increasing the order size to 500 from 327.

The additional carrying cost is calculated as follows:

$$\frac{(500 - 327)\ \pounds 3}{2} = \frac{\pounds 519}{2} = \pounds 259.5$$

where

$$500 = \text{minimum order size for discount}$$
$$327 = \text{economic order quantity}$$
$$\pounds 3 = \text{unit carrying cost.}$$

The order cost savings are:

$$\frac{8,000 \times \pounds 20}{327} - \frac{8,000 \times \pounds 20}{500} = \pounds 489.3 - \pounds 320 = \pounds 169.3$$

The net effect on profits of taking a quantity discount is:

Cost savings + order cost savings – additional carrying costs

$$\pounds 800 + \pounds 169.3 - \pounds 259.5 = \pounds 709.8$$

Therefore the firm should move to an order quantity of 500.

Though the EOQ model has numerous weaknesses it does provide information for management. Over time some of the weaknesses can be eliminated and the inputs into the model can be refined. There can be no doubt that this method of inventory control is far superior to subjective methods. Greater availability of computers and operations research techniques make the application of sophisticated techniques easier.

'Just in Time' Inventory Control

This control system was originally developed in Japan by Taiichi Okno, a vice-president of Toyota, and is, in effect, a production and management system. The concept is that a firm should keep a minimum level of inventory on hand, thereby relying on suppliers to furnish parts 'just in time' for them to be assembled. This is in direct contrast with the traditional inventory philosophy of most firms, sometimes referred to as a 'just in case' system, where healthy levels of safety stocks are kept to ensure that production will not be interrupted. When interest rates are high, this philosophy can become costly.

While the 'just in time' inventory system is intuitively appealing, it has not proven an easy system to implement. Strong and close relationships with suppliers located in the same geographical area take time to develop, and ease of access and handling systems need to be installed. Yet in spite of the difficulties of implementation, many firms are committed to moving towards a 'just in time' inventory system. In doing so, they are effectively adapting a new approach to the EOQ model by reducing and/or eliminating the need for safety stock and recognising the need to reduce the cost of ordering inventory.

ACCOUNTS RECEIVABLE MANAGEMENT

In order to obtain sales it is normal to offer credit to customers. Credit sales lead to the establishment of accounts receivable, usually on terms which require payment within a number of weeks. Credit terms are an important element in marketing. A firm offering tighter credit terms than those available from competitors will find sales more difficult to obtain. Accounts receivable represent a major investment for most business. For Irish business in particular, the taking of extended credit means that accounts receivable often represent the largest single investment on the part of the business.

Credit Terms

Credit terms are generally determined by the custom of the trade and similar terms are usually adapted by firms within an industry. Credit terms are the result of many factors including:

(a) The period for which the purchaser will have the goods before he pays cash.

(b) Competitive conditions. The more competitive the industry usually the longer the credit extended.

(c) The delivery period involved. It may take up to six weeks to ship to overseas buyers. They will not wish to pay prior to receiving the goods.

Table 10 gives some details on credit terms current in a number of Irish industries.

Table 10	Irish Credit Terms
Industry	*Terms*
Hosiery	Net 30 days, 3 per cent for payment within seven days of invoice.
Clothing	2½ per cent discount 30 days; 3¾ per cent 7 days.
Footwear	Cash 5 per cent discount. Net 15th of the month following delivery.
Confectionery	Net 30 days, 2 per cent discount 10 days.
Grain Merchants	Net 30 days from date of invoice.
Textiles	Net 30 days, 1½ per cent discount 10 days.
Engineering Suppliers	Net 30 days.

Selling terms should state clearly the period of credit, the cash discount if any, and the length of time allowed for making the deduction from the invoice. The costs of offering cash discounts must be noted. Taking the example of the terms granted in the confectionery trade, 2/10 net 30 days that is, a 2 per cent cash discount if paid within ten days, otherwise the full amount within 30 days. The cost of offering this discount is 2 per cent to obtain money 20 days before it is due. On an annual basis this works out to be

$$\text{Annual Cost of Discount} = 2\% \times \frac{365}{20} = 36.5\%$$

The cost looks prohibitive and indeed it would be. However, a quick reference back to Table 5 shows that the food, drink and tobacco sector, which includes confectionery, had an average credit outstanding of 6.4 weeks or 45 days. Therefore, the cost is now for the average customer

$$\text{Annual Cost of Discount} = 2\% \times \frac{365}{35} = 20.9\%$$

The 35 days is the 45 days less the 10 days in which the discount can be taken. It can be seen that, relative to the average payment period, a 2 per cent discount for prompt payment is not unduly expensive. What must be very carefully monitored is a tendency among Irish customers to pay after a few weeks while still deducting the cash discount.

In specific industries particular credit terms may be granted. Agricultural suppliers operate a system of *seasonal dating,* whereby customers agree to pay their bills on a date in autumn when their crops have been harvested. Cash terms are used in some trades. They may be Cash with Order (CWO), Cash on Delivery (COD) or Cash in Advance (CIA). The timber importing industry uses Cash on Arrival (COA) where payment is due when the timber arrives at the Irish port. International trade uses Letters of Credit where a specific date of payment is stipulated. Often this method is guaranteed by a bank so there is no danger of bad debts.

Managing Existing Accounts Receivable

A later section of this chapter deals with credit policy towards new customers but the efficient management of existing accounts receivable is at least as important to the success of the business. Managers often consider their job done when they have approved the initial credit application. This is not so. Continuous review of existing accounts is necessary to ensure that they do not turn bad.

A valuable method of controlling debtors is the construction of an ageing schedule. This schedule tells the management the proportion of accounts outstanding for particular periods (Table 11).

Table 11

ARDMORE LIMITED
Ageing Schedule of Accounts Receivable
as of 31 December 1986

Period Outstanding	Amount	Percentage of Total
30 days or less	£105,000	25.8%
31—45 days	60,000	14.8%
46—60 days	45,000	11.2%
61—90 days	120,000	29.6%
Over 90 days	75,600	18.6%
	£405,600	100.0%

The terms granted by Ardmore are net 45 days. Only 40.6 per cent of Ardmore customers are abiding by the credit terms. Of more concern is the fact that 18.6 per cent of the debtors are over 90 days. It appears that the Ardmore credit policy is in a shambles. Yet prior to making this decision consider the following:

(a) Sales seasonality may mean that in certain periods more is sold than the average, thus distorting the percentages. In this instance the peaks occur in the spring.

(b) The general trend of credit. In 1986 credit was very tight in Ireland. However, there is evidence that Ardmore Limited has sloppy credit management. The 14 weeks collection period (99 days) is far above the 9.9 weeks, average for Irish engineering firms in the mid 1980s. The customers taking the extended credit need to be examined. It is likely that some bad debts exist in that figure of £75,600. A substantial bad debt could endanger the safety of the business.

One way for Ardmore to reduce the age of accounts receivable is to improve the collection procedures. An increasing number of Irish businesses are finding it necessary to recruit a clerical employee whose sole function is to collect accounts receivable. Among the steps which can be followed to obtain payment are letters, telephone calls, personal visits, use of collection agencies and legal action.

Far too many Irish firms baulk at the use of tough collection policies. As a result there is a general lack of discipline in credit matters. Customers who will not pay should be taken to court. The excuse put forward for not taking legal action is that you will lose the customer. The answer is that you should not want such a customer. It is possible to calculate the value of an increased collection effort. Ardmore Limited, for 1987, is considering hiring a credit control clerk at a salary of £15,000. It is expected that letters, calls and visits to customers by the employee will cost a further £6,000. It is thought that the accounts receivable period would decline to 10 weeks with the addition of this employee. More important perhaps is the likelihood of a reduced level of bad debts.

Expected 1987 Level of Accounts Receivable (90 days' sales)		£393,700
Expected Level with new clerk (70 days)		306,200
Reduction in Investment in Receivables		£87,500
Interest saving at 15 per cent =	£13,125	
Cost of Clerk (wages + expenses) =	21,000	
Saving (cost) to Ardmore	(£7,875)	

This shows that hiring the employee is not worthwhile.

Credit Policy

Management has the power to decide on the level of accounts receivable. Economic conditions do have an effect on payments but by lowering or tightening standards management can either increase or decrease the level of accounts receivable. A lowering of credit standards assists the marketing effort and should increase sales. Offsetting the good effects are greater debt collection costs, increased working capital needs and a greater probability of bad debts.

Credit policy is based on a set of standards. A customer's credit rating is established by means of bank references, credit agency reports and financial information. Two decisions are involved: whether or not to grant credit and, if granted, how much. The latter is known as the *line of credit*. Obtaining information on the creditworthiness of a potential customer has been extremely difficult in Ireland. In practically every other country firms must file copies of their financial statements. In Ireland, up to the passing of the Companies (Amendment) Act, 1986, only public companies, state enterprises and co-operatives filed accounts. The customer can be asked for copies of statements but many will regard this as insulting.

Dun and Bradstreet is the largest provider of business information in Ireland with a database holding information on over 26,000 businesses. Customers may access this service by having a direct computer link from their own desk or by phoning in to the DunsTel Centre in Dublin. The type of information available includes details of business history, operations, bankers, credit rating, directors, payment performance etc. Customers also have direct access to Dun and Bradstreet's databases in Europe, US, Canada, and Australia, and to an international network of offices. Dun and Bradstreet is the world's largest business information company with 265 offices worldwide. Other services include marketing information, commercial collection and Stubbs Gazette.

An additional source of credit information is the Irish Trade Protection Association Limited (ITPA). The ITPA has been in existence since 1882 and is a non-profit seeking company formed to protect the interests of traders. It provides full credit reporting and debt recovery services nationally and internationally including on-line credit information to its members. The ITPA publishes a weekly gazette containing particulars of registered court judgements, bankruptcies, statements of affairs, mortgages, charges, satisfactions and business names.

Further sources of credit information include banks and financial institutions, trade references, competitors, creditors, and the firm's salesmen who have, at least, visited the potential client.

Having obtained information, it must be analysed. Much emphasis in

Ireland is laid on the character of the business and on the reputation of management. In most instances rapid decisions can be made. It is only in cases where information is contradictory and/or where unfavourable indications exist that a detailed analysis needs to be made.

Varying Credit Policy

On many occasions management will be under pressure to relax credit terms. The temptation to do this is particularly strong in those cases where a significant sales increase can result. It is possible to make a quantitative assessment of the effects of changes in sales credit policy.

The marketing department have informed the general manager of Ardmore Limited that they can increase sales by £200,000 during 1987 if they are allowed to offer more liberal credit (Table 12). They have estimated that the effect on Accounts Receivable will be an increase from 12 to 16 weeks' sales. Note that the credit period is on sales of £1,796,700, £1,596,700 plus the incremental £200,000 sales. A marginal increase of £4,000 in administrative costs is expected while bad debts of £10,000 might occur.

Table 12

Incremental Sales	£200,000
Variable Cost of Production (82% of sales) (This comes from the Pro Forma Income Statement: 1,311.6 ÷ 1,596.7)	164,000
Contribution	36,000
Less Bad Debts and Clerical Costs	14,000
Increased Profits	£22,000
Accounts Receivable Under Proposed Terms	553,000
1987 Accounts Receivable on Existing Credit Terms	393,700
Incremental Accounts Receivable	159,300
Increased interest cost at 15 per cent	£23,895
Net effect on profits – reduction (£1,895)	

The first question to be answered is the availability of additional production capacity. Having confirmed that it does exist the next step is to estimate the additional profit which will arise from the proposal. Apart from the profit and loss effect there will be a major increase in cash required to fund the additional sales with the bank overdraft likely to rise to over £150,000 during January—June peak sales period.

The answer is clear. The marketing department proposal will be rejected. Indeed given the existing high level of accounts receivable, management might calculate the effect on the company of tightening up credit standards.

Reservation of Title

A new and powerful force has entered the area of accounts receivable management. Now, by means of a clear statement on an invoice the vendor of products reserves the ownership of these goods until they are paid for. In the event of delayed or non payment the vendor can retrieve the goods in question. Of more value perhaps, is the fact that in the event of bankruptcy goods on which title has been reserved must be returned to the vendor. Where a manager has doubts about the creditworthiness of a particular client he should insist on a title retention clause on each invoice.

Reservation of title also affects lenders and investors. Inventory values may not be what they appear to be. Title retention clauses do not, as of 1988, have to be filed for public inspection; hence there is no way of knowing the effect, if any, on the inventory of a particular firm.

Credit Insurance

The risks insured by a standard policy are insolvency and protracted default. On being asked to provide cover an insurer will first satisfy himself that the credit control arrangements in operation are sensible and are adhered to.

There are a number of different styles of cover available including:
(a) Whole Turnover Basis
(b) Specific Customers Only
(c) Datum Line Policy.

Where at least 50 per cent of annual sales are to a small portion of the total customers, insurers may well be prepared to insure only sales to these specified buyers. This can be an attractive style for both insurer and client in view of the much reduced administration involved and the fact that the client will have concentrated the available resources on being covered against the collapse of substantial customers whose demise would otherwise have been even more painful.

Datum Line Policies apply to all customers with balances above an agreed minimum outstanding. Cover for each customer must be specifically requested. There is no facility for automatic cover in respect of customers already being traded with as there can be with the Whole Turnover Basis.

As for other insurances the insured pays a deposit premium at the beginning of each period of insurance. This deposit premium is based on the anticipated turnover for the year applying the agreed rate. At the end of the period a declaration is completed by the proposer showing the actual insured turnover which has taken place. An adjustment is then calculated with an additional or return premium due to the insured as the case may be.

Amoung the problems in acquiring credit cover at an acceptable price are:

(a) Whilst quite a few insurance companies are licensed to transact this class of business only two or three do so and, finding themselves in a seller's market, they have no pressure to price keenly.

(b) In some sectors suppliers compete so fiercely that credit terms being afforded would not be considered prudent by an impartial underwriter.

Credit insurance is intended to complement good credit management. The basic principle is that the risk be shared thereby giving both insurer and insured a clear interest in good credit management. The insurer will normally pay 90 per cent of a loss up to 90 per cent of the customer's established credit limit.

THE MANAGEMENT OF CASH

Cash management is the maintenance of liquidity in the business. Cash means not only the actual cash held by a business but also the availability of cash from bank accounts and 'near cash' that is, assets which are readily realisable for cash. Near cash assets are known as *marketable securities*.

A business holds cash for two purposes, trading and emergencies. *Trading cash* is money used in the course of day-to-day business activities. This is the money to pay the wages, fuel, light, heat and suppliers. *Emergency cash* is money required to meet unexpected demands for cash. Such demands arise in many ways, for example, a machinery breakdown, strikes, a credit squeeze. No business activity is certain, so variations in the expected outcomes are always likely. To allow for the unexpected businesses keep a 'cash cushion' over and above the sums required for trading. This cushion does not have to be actual cash but usually consists of marketable securities and/or borrowing facilities at a bank. Availability is more important than size.

Defining Cash Needs

How much cash should a business hold? The answer depends on the following:

(1) The expected pattern of cash flows as shown in the cash budget (Table 7 above).

(2) The certainty of cash flows. Some businesses, such as electricity suppliers, can predict revenues with a high level of certainty. At the other extreme are firms operating in competitive markets, selling products with high obsolescence possibilities. The greater the level of uncertainty attaching to cash flows the larger the cash required.

(3) General monetary climate. In periods of tight credit customers can be very slow in paying, therefore, cash inflows can be reduced. As credit gets tighter a firm should continuously monitor cash levels.

(4) Borrowing capacity. A firm with agreed borrowing capacity can afford to maintain very low cash levels.

(5) The efficiency of cash usage. This means the speed with which cash is utilised. Two ratios are used to measure cash usage.

$$(a)\ \text{cash in current assets} = \frac{\text{cash balance}}{\text{current assets}}$$

$$(b)\ \text{cash turnover} = \frac{\text{sales}}{\text{cash balance}}$$

In Ireland the above ratios are rarely used, as most businesses make liberal use of bank overdrafts and so have minimal cash balances. The ratios can be made more meaningful by including bank overdraft in the cash balance figure. Management should aim, over a period of time, to reduce the first ratio and increase the second.

Cash Policy

The correct policy for managing cash is easy to state but difficult to implement. The following is advisable:

(a) Stretch payables as long as possible without damaging the credit rating of the firm. This means delaying payment to suppliers. If very favourable cash discounts are offered then they should be taken.

(b) Reduce levels of inventory to the minimum required to meet sales projections and to enable efficient production.

(c) Have a tight credit control on accounts receivable. Do not, as Ardmore Limited has done, allow control to slip over time.

(d) Improve the collection and deposit of cash receipts.

(e) Invest surplus cash balances.

Stretching accounts payable can ease cash problems, at least in the short term, but may damage the reputation of the firm. Where a supplier is dependent on the firm then there is little danger in slowing up payments. Irish firms have become adept at stretching payables. As a result, suppliers often include interest provisions in their invoices and/or charge higher prices. One method of stretching accounts payable is to offer Bills of Exchange. Instead of paying suppliers on the due date the firm offers to accept a Bill of Exchange for a period of 60, 90, 120 or 180 days. The supplier can usually discount the Bill and receive cash. A previous section has dealt with the concept of inventory management. By using more efficient management controls in purchasing, production and marketing levels then the amount of cash invested in inventory can be reduced. It is possible to release the cash tied up in inventory by borrowing. Specific financial instruments using inventory as collateral are available in Ireland. Together with other sources of finance, they are discussed in later chapters.

Speeding up debt collection has been dealt with at some length. Careful credit control can release large sums of cash. It is also possible to reduce the capital invested in accounts receivable by selling them. This method of raising cash is known as factoring. It is examined in Chapter 10.

A number of techniques exist to speed up the technical process of collecting, depositing and clearing cheques. Many firms lodge receipts irregularly. The cost per day of holding cheques should be noted. At 15 percent interest the cost per day is .041 per cent (15 ÷ 365). Of course the additional administrative cost of daily banking must be offset against interest saved. If a firm has many sales outlets throughout the country then they can make use of *concentration banking*. This is a system whereby accounts are paid into the local branches of a bank. This method reduces the time between cheque mailing and receipt.

Another means of managing cash is the 'float', that is, the money tied up in cheques written but not yet paid. Using the float involves 'cheque kiting', that is, writing a cheque on an account knowing that the funds are not there but intending to lodge the funds before the cheque is presented. Some firms write their cheques on distant banks knowing that it will take much longer to clear this cheque. 'Kiting' is illegal. Care must be taken to preserve the good name of the business.

Investing surplus cash balances, which is the last step in efficient cash management is the subject for the following section.

Investing in Marketable Securities

Marketable securities are short-term near cash investments. Though many firms suffer from cash shortages other firms have excess cash. Some Irish companies such as Merchants' Warehousing and Guinness have substantial cash deposits. The Irish-based Canadian-quoted mining company, Northgate Exploration, had over £100 million in cash or near cash in 1988. It is undesirable to leave cash unused. Excess cash usually means temporary cash surpluses which are available for short-term investment. Firms with cash not needed for trading or emergency purposes should seek long-term investment opportunities in their own business or in diversifications. If no worthwhile investment opportunities can be discovered then consideration should be given to paying out excess funds to the shareholders by means of dividends or by a repayment of capital.

Caution should be exercised when investing in short-term securities. Risk, either to income or to capital value, should be minimised. The main outlets for cash are:

(a) Exchequer Bonds. These are short term, 90-day, securities of the Irish government. The bonds are sold at a discount from their face value. They are readily saleable.

(b) Commercial paper. This is an unsecured promissory note issued by top-quality businesses. Chapter 9 discusses this financial instrument in more detail.

(c) Term deposits with financial institutions. Banks will negotiate a rate of interest for a deposit left with them for a specific period.

(d) Government loans. These are long-term loans to the state. They are quoted on the Irish Stock Exchange. There is, however, a risk that should interest rates rise there will be a loss in the capital value of the investment. Since an active market exists in government loans there is little difficulty in obtaining cash when required.

INFLATION AND WORKING CAPITAL

This chapter has presented a number of techniques for the efficient management of working capital. Despite the best efforts of top class financial managers, many firms have in recent years suffered from severe liquidity problems.

Table 13 Company Failures 1979-86

Year	1979	1980	1981	1982	1983	1984	1985	1986
Receiverships	15	59	33	98	207	111	114	133
Liquidations	121	213	434	626	475	502	460	505
Winding Up Petitions	12	15	36	57	84	122	155	85
Creditors meetings	29	67	188	241	286	342	421	477
Total	177	354	691	1,022	1,052	1,077	1,150	1,200

Source: Irish Trade Protection Association Limited

The data included in Table 13 is incomplete, ignoring closures among sole proprietorships and partnerships as well as receiverships. Inflation can be blamed for much of the financial misery. The world in general and Ireland in particular had high annual rates of inflation during the 1970s and into the early 1980s. In the period of 1970-86 the consumer price index rose by 525 per cent. Firms purchasing raw materials from abroad suffered more as devaluations of the Irish pound increased prices. Firms had to run fast just to stand still. To understand the predicament examine Table 14 which presents statistics from the 1986 Ardmore Limited financial statements.

Table 14 Effect of Inflation

	1986	Effect of 5% Inflation on Investment
Current Assets		
Inventory	£326,400	£16,300
Accounts Receivable	405,600	20,300
		36,600
Current Liabilities		
Accounts Payable	305,300	15,300
Net Increase in Funds Required		£21,300
After Tax Profit — 1986	£81,200	
Proportion of 1987 profits required to maintain the status quo		26%

The important figures are the current assets and accounts payable. In 1987 an inflation rate of 5 per cent was considered likely in contrast with 15 plus per cent annual inflation in the early 1980s. To maintain the liquidity position of Ardmore Limited would take 26 per cent of projected 1987 profits. Otherwise the company would have to borrow from the bank, thereby worsening the various ratios. A little more detailed explanation may help. Assuming that business stays at the exact same level as in 1987, Ardmore would need to invest 5 per cent more in inventory and accounts receivable, because of inflation. This would require an extra £36,600 of funds. However, part of this extra investment would come from Accounts Payable which would also rise with inflation. But the shortfall of £21,300 would have to be made up from profits and/or borrowings. In fact, most of the so called 'profits' of modern business are simply inflation and do not represent a real return on investment. A problem of taxation on inflation rather than on profits was alleviated during the 1980s by an order which exempted inflation on inventory values from taxation. The 10 per cent corporate tax level on manu-facturing profits further reduces the problem. High levels of inflation over long periods of time, unless they are accompanied by extremely high rates of profits, lead to serious liquidity problems and make a nonsense of attempts at efficient working capital management.

CONCLUSION

This chapter on the management of working capital has concentrated on asset management. The techniques of handling short-term liabilities are considered in Chapter 9 which deals with short-term sources of finance. The essence of working capital management is liquidity, the ability to provide cash when it is required. Liquidity can be measured by the time it takes to turn an asset into cash as evidenced by the working capital cycle and by the certainty of the value contained in the asset. The management of liquidity involves decision-making on the types of invest-ment and on the level of commitment to each investment. Business profitability and risk are affected by the decisions made.

Further Reading
Dileep Mehta: *Working Capital Management,* Prentice Hall, Englewood Cliffs, New Jersey, 1984.
L. J. Gilman: *Principles of Managerial Finance,* Harpur, New York 1976.

Chapter 6

Capital Budgeting and Fixed Asset Management

Previous chapters have concentrated on the financial effects of short-term plans. Managing operations in the short term is only one side of the financial management coin. The ultimate profitability of a business depends on the success or failure of the long-term investments selected by that business. The process of selecting these investments is known as capital budgeting, with the primary motive being to increase the value of the firm; this means selecting investments that have a positive net present value and managing them well. The capital budgeting techniques discussed in this chapter can help managers perform this task together with judgement, intuition and a great deal of common sense. Furthermore society has a substantial stake in the firm's capital investment decisions. Capital investments create jobs and promote economic growth, hence increasing the wealth of society. Governments typically pursue policies designed to encourage firms to invest.

Long-term investments are an integral part of the corporate strategy followed by the firm. Corporate strategy can be defined as follows:

'Given the resources available to a firm and the environment facing the business, corporate strategy is that set of policies followed to achieve the objectives of the owners.'

Corporate strategy is decided by the board of directors. To assist decision-making it is common to find that the effects of various policy decisions are all reduced to a common denominator—money. Examples would be of a board of directors considering such projects as an overseas investment, a new domestic factory and/or the introduction of new product lines. To assist deliberation it helps to have the outcomes of these potential investments reduced to annual cash flows and profit and loss statements.

Table 15   Corporate Strategy

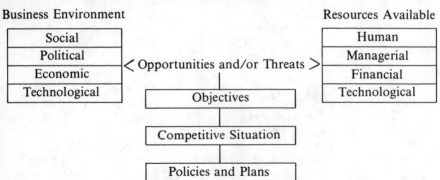

Business Environment   Resources Available

| Social |
| Political |
| Economic |
| Technological |

< Opportunities and/or Threats >

| Human |
| Managerial |
| Financial |
| Technological |

| Objectives |

| Competitive Situation |

| Policies and Plans |

Long-term investments usually involve commitments to fixed assets. Often the commitments are large, indeed large enough to bankrupt the business if the wrong decisions are made.

Generally there are a number of alternative investment opportunities open while resources are limited. Techniques have been developed which assist decision-making in allocating funds to prospective investments. These techniques are known collectively as capital budgeting. Potential investment projects are evaluated to see which of them best meets the objectives of the business. For this reason capital budgeting is known also as project appraisal.

The types of decision which require the application of capital budgeting techniques include the replacement of assets, modernisation, new fixed asset acquisitions and the purchase of other businesses. The size of capital investments ranges from the purchase of inexpensive equipment to outlays which may dwarf the existing assets invested. An example is the Tara Exploration and Development Company Limited whose exploration subsidiary Tara Prospecting Limited had numerous small expenditures on rigs, drill bits, etc., while another subsidiary, Tara Mines Limited, invested over £105,000,000 in the 1970s to bring the Navan zinc/lead mine into production. Generally, the size of capital expenditures decides the level at which they must be approved. In the case of drill bits, the general manager of Tara Prospecting could authorise the purchase. In the case of the Navan mine the full board of the parent company deliberated for a long time before agreeing to proceed.

This chapter examines some of the critical areas involved in capital budgeting. The areas examined are:

(a) Estimating the Total Investment.

(b) Analysing the Timing of Expenditures.

(c) Estimating the Life of the Project.

(d) Forecasting Long Run Cash Inflows.
(e) Forecasting Long Run Costs.
(f) Evaluating the Investment Proposal.
(g) The Effect of Inflation.
(h) The Effect of Uncertainty.

Having examined the theoretical aspects of the process a worked example is presented. This example analyses the long-run return to Ardmore Limited of replacing some existing machinery with new high-speed equipment.

THE TOTAL INVESTMENT REQUIRED

The first task facing management is the estimation of the total investment required. Total investment covers not only the costs of equipment and buildings, but also installation, expenses, taxes, and working capital requirements. For many projects it is very difficult to estimate the total, particularly where lengthy construction periods are involved. Conservative managers usually provide a contingency allowance. Other significant costs which are frequently ignored are architects' and engineering consultants' fees. These costs average 6 per cent of total investment in fixed assets. Interest during the construction period must also be provided for. Rampant inflation in construction costs in the 1970s seriously affected the ability of management to predict costs. Capital intensive schemes, such as the Asahi project at Killala, the Nitrigin Eireann Teo. fertiliser plant at Cork and Tara Mines at Navan, more than doubled in cost from the time they were first planned until they started production. Table 16 provides a framework for estimating the total capital investment in a project.

Table 16	Estimating Capital Investment	
	Item	£
1.	Site, costs and preparation	
2.	Plant and Equipment cost, plus installation	
3.	Ancillary Equipment e.g offices, canteen, hygiene, estimated cost at date of expenditure	_____
	Total Fixed Cost	
4.	Consulting Fees (6%)	
5.	Contingency Fee (15%)	
6.	Pre production Interest	
7.	Working Capital required (Inventory, Accounts receivable)	_____
	Total Cost	
8.	Less Proceeds from Sale of Surplus Assets	_____
	Total Incremental Cost	

In many cases new investments are designed to replace existing assets. This means that the old assets can be sold. The salvage value less the removal costs is deducted from the cost of the new investment. Depending on the price received for the old asset there may be a tax charge. Often assets are fully written off against profits and have no value in the books of the business. If these assets are sold for a price greater than the book value then a 'balancing charge' of corporation tax may arise. If land or buildings are involved there may be a capital gains tax liability.

TIMING OF CAPITAL EXPENDITURE

Often capital projects have expenditure spread over a long period of time, for example, the Alcan project at Aughinish Island took about four years to construct but it was in the planning stage for at least an equal number of years. Having estimated the total investment involved, the timing of expenditures must be calculated. Rarely will the entire cost be payable at one time. For instance, payments for buildings are usually made over a period of months or years—so called 'progress payments'. Working capital will not be required until close to production start-up and then it will build up as output increases.

A chart should be drawn up covering the pre-operational life of the project, that is, from decision time to full output time, showing the outflow of costs. Figure 3 indicates a pattern of expenditure found in many capital projects. This S curve can be explained by the low outflow during the early days of a project. Large payments as equipment arrives are followed by a slowdown as the project goes into operation. The bump at the top of the curve is caused by final payments to a wide variety of interested parties.

THE ESTIMATED LIFE OF THE PROJECT

How long will the project under analysis be economically viable? This simple question is often ignored in project appraisal but the profitability of many projects are determined largely by their revenue earning lives. The economic life of the project is difficult to determine because it is usually quite different from the physical life. A zinc refinery may have an indefinite physical life but a finite economic existence. The major uncertainties are technological obsolescence, currency changes, and inflation. A change in technology could result in a new process which would render existing facilities unprofitable. Technological forecasting is notoriously inexact but management should at least scan the business environment to see if innovations are on the horizon.

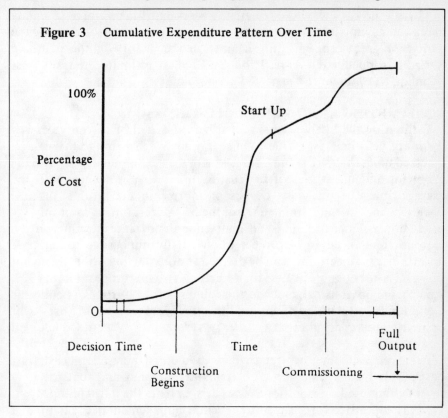

Figure 3   Cumulative Expenditure Pattern Over Time

Inflation attacks the economic lives of projects in an insidious way. At
the time of planning, the process used represents the best available
mixture of capital and labour. Inflation results in increasing labour costs.
Over time labour-saving devices become available but are not used so that
within a period of years existing facilities are relatively high cost because
they are labour-intensive. The effects of currency changes are obvious.
During the 1980s the fall of the US dollar against the Irish pound meant
that in dollars Irish subsidiaries of US firms had at least a 20 per cent rise
in direct operating costs. Apart from technology, inflation and currency,
other variables act to reduce the economic lives of projects. Tastes
change, leading to a decline in demand for certain products, sources of
raw materials dry up, the taxation environment changes or political
attitudes change. An example is the change in political attitudes and in
taxation policy towards mining in Ireland during the 1970s. After the
boom in mining discoveries in the 1960s not one new discovery was
announced in the next decade. Attitudes changed again in the 1980s.

There is no easy way to estimate the economic life of a project. Many companies simply take fifteen years as their planning horizon. During the period of great economic uncertainty in the late 1970s the planning horizon dropped to ten years. Though difficult to estimate, attempts must be made to evaluate the expected economic life.

FORECASTING LONG-RUN CASH INFLOWS

Estimating the likely revenue for a period of ten or fifteen years is a daunting yet vital task. There is no way in which profitability can be assessed unless sales revenue figures are forecast. Chapter 4 dealt with the problems and difficulties of forecasting one year in advance. Now the exercise must be pushed a decade or more into the future. Business operates in an uncertain environment. Uncertainties multiply as prediction is extended. It is difficult enough to place a value on the various risks faced by a project but virtually impossible to estimate uncertainties. Uncertainty can be defined as not knowing what you do not know. It is not possible in 1988 to predict sales of oil storage tanks in 1998. Apart from obvious risks such as the collapse of the European Economic Community, oil shutdowns and the like, other problems could arise—war or pestilence or an alternative energy system which would render oil obsolete.

All revenues from a project are measured on an incremental cash flow basis. This means that non-cash items are ignored and that the only revenues counted are additional ones arising from the particular project.

In attempting to forecast future revenue management needs to predict two variables, price and quantity. It is possible to get estimates of the likely price from market research studies and marketing department estimates. Estimating the likely level of sales is more uncertain. Guidelines may be obtained from the sales levels of substitutes or competing products. If the product in question is replacing existing products then forecasting is easier.

As the forecasts stretch two, five, ten and fifteen years into the future, other assumptions need to be made. Factors such as the growth of the economy and the relationship between the economy and the particular product become important.

An examination of the factors affecting sales will allow management to make estimates of the most likely cash inflows in a particular year. But note that the word used is 'estimates'. It is likely that by changing some assumptions the sales estimates will vary. Therefore a risk is attached to the selection of a best estimate cash flow. To handle the risk and uncertainties attaching to cash flows the following techniques, Sensitivity Analysis and Probability Distributions, have evolved.

Sensitivity Analysis

This provides a simple way of treating risk. Management are asked to provide a range of sales estimates for each year. Generally a series of individuals are asked to provide three estimates, worst, best and most likely. Very little additional work is required to produce these estimates as most individuals tend to operate within a certain range when forecasting.

Figure 4 demonstrates the outcome of a sensitivity analysis.

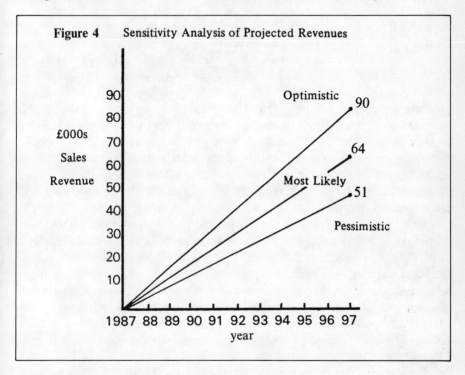

Figure 4   Sensitivity Analysis of Projected Revenues

This illustration shows that management are being reasonably conservative, that is, the most likely estimate is closer to the pessimistic than to the optimistic. Using this data management can now provide three rates of return. This method, which is simple to use, is appropriate in those situations where management are very uncertain about the future.

Probability Distributions

The application of probabilities to outcomes is a refinement of the sensitivity method outlined above. A probability is the percentage chance of a particular outcome occurring. The example below shows the technique applied to the estimates for the third year of a project being considered by Ardmore Limited.

Table 17   Range of Possible Outcomes in Year 3 for Project X
Ardmore Limited

Cash Inflows	Possibility of Occurrence	Expected Value
(1)	(2)	(1 × 2)
£20,000	.05	£1,000
17,000	.15	2,550
15,000	.20	3,000
12,000	.35	4,200
10,000	.15	1,500
8,000	.10	800
	1.00	£13,050

Management, in conjunction with marketing and production staff, have estimated that the net results in year three for Project X could be any of the six outcomes in Table 17, column 1. The top outcome would normally correspond with the 'optimistic' estimate of the previous approach, while the bottom estimate is the equivalent of the 'pessimistic' in Figure 4. The next step is to decide the possibility of each of these estimates being the actual result. Probabilities must add up to one, meaning that the entire range of possibilities is covered. It is decided that there is only a five per cent chance of a net cash inflow of £20,000 but a thirty-five per cent chance of a cash inflow of £12,000. At the other end of the scale, cash inflows are not expected to be much less than £8,000 and in fact it is considered that there is only a ten per cent chance of an £8,000 cash inflow. Multiplying column 1 by 2 gives the expected value of the various estimates. The sum of this column is the expected value of cash inflows for the particular year being examined. The expected value of £13,050 can then be incorporated into the project appraisal. The figure can be put in context by realising that the cash inflow may range from £20,000 to £8,000 but considering the possibilities within this range the expected value or most likely inflow is £13,050.

The above method becomes simple to apply with experience. It should be applied to the cash flows of each projected period, thus giving management some estimate of the risk attaching to the project, and an idea of the likely range of benefits or losses.

Further extension of the analysis of uncertainty by means of probability distributions and their means and standard deviations is useful, but beyond the scope of this text.

In applying sophisticated techniques, remember that the results obtained are only as good as the data. If the original forecasts on which the analysis was based were poor then the final output will also be poor.

Management, using all available data, produce a long-run forecast of cash inflows. In the last year of the project's economic life two non-revenue cash inflows are likely, (a) a salvage value for the plant and equipment and (b) a release of the capital tied up in inventory and debtors. Estimating the salvage value of machinery is difficult, and a low figure is usually taken. The recovery of working capital is often forgotten but since this can be a substantial item care should be taken to include an appropriate figure.

FORECASTING LONG-RUN COSTS

Capital budgeting is only concerned with incremental costs. Incremental costs are those which vary with alternative courses of action. Costs are relevant only if they specifically arise from an investment decision. If a cost will remain the same whether or not a proposed investment is undertaken then it should not be considered in the analysis. The following, though not comprehensive, provides a useful checklist for costs that are likely to be affected by a new proposal.

Direct labour	Material costs	Inspection costs
Indirect labour	Other supplies	Set-up time
Fringe benefits	Insurance	Down time
Maintenance and repairs	Tools	Power and fuel costs
Materials handling	Tool repair	Floor space
Marketing costs	Scrap and rework	Sub-contract costs

Management must attempt to measure the extra or incremental costs attaching to each of the above which would arise if a new investment were made. Costs such as direct labour, materials and power may be easily estimated, but others, such as the costs attached to the salesmen carrying an extra line, fringe benefits, extra maintenance, etc. may be difficult to compute.

It is easier to predict costs than revenues, as management has experience of costs and their trends. Of course costs are a function of sales volume so it is necessary to undertake an exercise to provide a range of costs suitable for the sales estimates generated by the sensitivity analysis or probability distribution analysis. It is important to note that many costs will be fixed across large ranges of output. Three cost items deserve special comment. They are Sunk costs, Capital costs and Closure costs.

Sunk Costs

The concept of sunk costs can be of vital importance in capital expenditure decisions. A sunk cost is one resulting from a past decision which cannot now be reversed. Once an investment is made, it is completely irrelevant to any future decision unless it can be recovered in whole or part. Suppose £40,000 has already been irrevocably invested in the development of a new product, but a further £10,000 is necessary to get it off the ground. Here, all the future benefits must be measured against the incremental outlay of £10,000 and not the original £40,000 or the combined £50,000. This concept applies particularly to situations involving replacement of machinery, buildings, etc. It is not correct to consider either the original cost or depreciated value of existing assets. The only figure of 'cost' to be considered is the market value of the assets.

Capital Costs

The cost of capital is mentioned here because it is most certainly a cost relevant to investment proposals. Estimating the cost of capital is one of the most difficult problems in business finance, and one that may be approached in various ways. For the smaller private firm, an approximation of the cost of capital is the rate paid by the firm on borrowed funds. For larger firms with different sources of long-term funds, the cost can be approximated by the weighted average cost of the various sources used.

The cost of capital as used in capital budgeting is either the required rate of return or cutoff rate. Businessmen examine a project to see if it costs more than it yields, that is, will the cost of the funds raised to finance the proposed investment be greater than the profits from the investment itself. In many instances, the return which a project must offer should equal or better a target rate. This target rate must be higher than the cost of the money if any real profit is to result from the project.

Chapter 14 deals in detail with the cost of capital.

Closure Costs

Modern social legislation places a high cost on people losing jobs. Therefore redundancy payments must be provided for in the final year of operation. Increasingly environmental controls are forcing businesses to clean up projects before leaving an area. This can be costly particularly in the mining industry.

Having estimated the total costs attaching to revenues the net cash position is worked out in a manner identical to that used in the cash budget shown in Table 7. The net difference between cash generated from sales and that paid out to cover costs is the money available to repay the investment made.

EVALUATING INVESTMENTS PROPOSALS

Having gathered together all of the information required on investment, timing, inflows and outflows, management must now combine the data into a framework which produces a measure of investment worth. Four methods are commonly used to evaluate investment. The methods are: Payback, Simple Rate of Return, Internal Rate of Return and Net Present Value.

The first two methods are relatively simple to apply and are used widely. Unfortunately, they each have a major theoretical weakness. The latter two methods of evaluation are more sophisticated, introducing the concept of a time value of money.

Payback

The payback is the period of time required to recover the initial cost of the investment. Two methods are used in calculating the payback.

$$\text{The Average Payback Period} = \frac{\text{Initial Investment}}{\text{Average Annual Net Cash Flow}}$$

The Actual Payback Period = the actual time required for net cash inflow to equal the initial investment.

Generally the payback period is compared with some maximum acceptable standard. If the payback on the project is less than the reference period, the project is accepted; if not, it is rejected. Studies have shown that the payback method is by far the most commonly used project appraisal technique. Most businesses use a reference payback period of five years or less. The popularity of the payback method arises from its simplicity of application. To a limited extent the payback period measures risk, that is, the longer the payback then the greater the risk. It is also a rough measure of liquidity. Payback is commonly used even by large companies in projects where risks and uncertainties are very high.

There are two weaknesses inherent in the payback method. Consider the following two proposals before the board of a company. Each proposal requires a £30,000 investment.

Proposal Outflow		Net Cash Inflows Year						
		1	2	3	4	5	6	7
A —	£30,000	£6,000	£12,000	£12,000	£18,000	£18,000	£18,000	£18,000
B —	£30,000			£30,000				

Project A and B rank equally.

In both cases the payback is three years, but the method ignores all cash flows after that period. It also ignores the magnitude and timing of cash flows within the payback period. In the above example Proposal A provides a cash inflow two years before B, yet both are equally ranked.

Of course no management would simply calculate the payback period and ignore all other data. As a screening device this method of capital budgeting is useful.

Simple Rate of Return

There are many different ways of calculating this measure. It is defined here as follows:

$$\text{Simple Rate of Return} = \frac{\text{Average Profit after Tax and Depreciation}}{\text{Average Investment}}$$

This method is used primarily because the data required is available from the normal accounting statements, and is often known as the Accounting Rate of Return. Average profits are found by adding up the total after-tax profits of the project over its life and then dividing the total by the life of the project. The average investment is simply total investment divided by 2. The logic behind this is that annual depreciation returns part of the capital to the original investors. Therefore over the life of the investment, on average only half of the original investment is committed.

In using this method it must be compared to some standard cutoff rate. Frequently standards for comparison are estimates of the cost of capital invested in the project. If the rate of return on the project under appraisal is greater than the cutoff rate then the project should be accepted. The simple rate of return has numerous shortcomings including the following:

(a) It is based on accounting income rather than on cash flows.
(b) It ignores the time value of money. £1,000 received in year 15 is as valuable as £1,000 received in year one.
(c) It is biased by the method of depreciation used.

It is difficult to find anything good to say about the Simple Rate of Return. It is a dangerous method of evaluating a capital investment. If it is to be used at all it should be as one of a number of methods.

Internal Rate of Return

The two methods outlined above totally ignore the timing of cash receipts. Yet few people, if given the choice, would prefer to accept £1,000 next year instead of £1,000 today. However, change the offer to £1,000 a year from today or £920 today and some people will choose the future receipts. Change the offer to £1,000 next year or £850 today and an even greater number will accept the future cash flow. This simple example points out a fact of life: there is a time value attached to money. An individual with cash today can invest it, spend it, bank it or simply look at it but he/she is better off having the cash now than having to wait for it. The time value of money is the equivalent of the risk free rate of interest. It is that payment which is made for the use of money for a particular period. Numerous experts, among them Keynes and Fisher, have attempted to define the true rate of interest. Inflation and risk mean that no existing interest rates are relevant. The nearest rate would be the rate on government bonds, because it is virtually without risk. From that an allowance for inflation should be deducted. Fisher thought that 5 per cent was a good estimate of the long-run true rate of interest.

The time value which attaches to money plays a very important role in capital budgeting. Most projects have cash inflows spread over a number of years. Frequently annual cash receipts differ substantially in size across years. Table 18 shows cash inflows for three separate projects.

Each of these rather hypothetical projects would have the same pay-back period and a similar Simple Rate of Return; yet quite clearly the Projects are not equally acceptable.

Two methods of project evaluation have been developed which use the time value of money as part of the technique. These methods are known as Discounted Cash Flow or DCF techniques. The methods are the Internal Rate of Return (IRR) which is discussed in this section and the Net Present Value (NPV) which is analysed below.

The Internal Rate of Return is that rate of return which equates the present value of all cash outflows with the present value of all cash inflows. The relationship is as follows:

$$TI = \frac{NCI}{(1+r)^1} + \frac{NCI}{(1+r)^2} + \ldots \frac{NCI}{(1+r)^n}$$

TI = total investment.

NCI = net cash inflows each period.

   r = the time value of money or, as it is more commonly known, the discount rate for the period.

In this instance r is the unknown. A trial-and-error method is used to identify the rate of discount which equates the two sides. A closer examination of the formula will show that it is related to compound interest. Further thought will show that the Internal Rate of Return method is the opposite of Compound Interest. A series of discount tables are readily available to assist the financial analyst. Appendix A (page 299) reproduces a sample discount table.

Table 18

Project Outflow	Net Inflows (£)										Total Inflows
	1	2	3	4	5	6	7	8	9	10	
A (£30,000)	6,000	12,000	12,000	12,000	12,000	12,000	12,000	12,000	12,000	12,000	£114,000
B (£60,000)		12,000	48,000	165,000						9,000	£234,000
C (£30,000)			30,000							84,000	£114,000

To make the Internal Rate of Return meaningful it must be compared with some cutoff rate. The cutoff rate, generally an estimate of the cost of capital, is known as the Acceptance Criterion or Hurdle Rate. If the Internal Rate of Return exceeds the cutoff rate the project is accepted; if not, then it is rejected. The method of trial and error outlined above must seem ponderous to many. Indeed it is, but computer models have done away with much of the drudgery. Where annual cash flows are constant there is a simple and quick method to arrive at the present value of a series of inflows. Tables have been prepared which give the present value of £1 received for a specific number of periods, (see Appendix B).

Consider the following simple example. A young man is in receipt of a trust fund which will provide him with the annual sum of £4,000 net for the next five years. However, he wants to buy a car costing £13,600. A friendly financier has offered him £13,600 in return for all rights to receive the flow of £4,000 at the end of each of the next five years. The young man wants to know the rate of interest which equates the two flows. The sum is as follows:

$$£13,600 = \frac{£4,000}{(1 + r)^1} + \frac{£4,000}{(1 + r)^2} + \frac{£4,000}{(1 + r)^3} + \frac{£4,000}{(1 + r)^4} + \frac{£4,000}{(1 + r)^5}$$

At a 10 per cent rate of discount the figures are

$-£13,600 = 4,000(.909) + £4,000(.826) + £4,000(.751) + £4,000(.683) + £4,000(.621)$

$\quad = \quad £3,636 \quad + \quad £3,304 \quad + \quad £3,004 \quad + \quad £2,732 \quad + \quad £2,484$
$\quad = \quad £15,160$

Check the discount factors in Appendix A (page 299) using a discount rate of 10 per cent.

Obviously the discount rate is higher. At a 15 per cent rate the figures are

$-£13,600 = £4,000(.870) + £4,000(.756) + £4,000(.658) + £4,000(.572) + £4,000(.497)$
$\quad = \quad £3,480 \quad + \quad £3,024 \quad + \quad £2,632 \quad + \quad £2,288 \quad + \quad £1,988$
$\quad = \quad £13,412$

A 10 per cent rate is too low and a 15 per cent rate too high.

Interpolation can be used to approximate the return. Note that the true rate is closer to 15 per cent.

	Discount Rate	Present Value
	10%	£15,160
	15%	£13,412
Difference	5%	£1,748

Since the real rate is only £188 below a 15 per cent rate it can be estimated as

$$\text{Internal Rate of Return} = 15\% - \left(\frac{13,600 - 13,412}{1,748}\right)5\%$$

$$= 15\% - 0.5\%$$

$$= 14.5\%$$

Instead of having to work out individually the present values for each year, it is possible because of the constant cash flows to use the cumulative tables (see Appendix B). Using these tables the present value of £4,000 received each year for five years at 10 and 15 per cent discount rates is as follows:

Discount Rate	Cumulative Rate of 5 Years	Cash Flow Each Year £		Present Value of the Stream
10%	3.791	4,000	=	£15,160
15%	3.353	4,000	=	£13,412

The young man now knows that to accept the £13,600 now will cost him an annual rate of 14.5%. It is up to him to accept or reject the deal.

Net Present Value (NPV)

The Net Present value method of capital budgeting is similar to the internal rate of return except that the discount factor is given. All cash flows are discounted to the present value using the required rate of return. The net difference between the inflows and outflows is examined. If there is a positive present value then the project is accepted, if negative, then the project is rejected. A zero present value means in theory that the full costs of the project are exactly equal to the inflows. Returning to the simple example outlined above, the young man has decided that money is worth 12 per cent per annum to him. He can have £13,600 now or £20,000 spread over five years. The formula required is:

$$\text{Net Present Value} = -£13,600 + \frac{£4,000}{(1.12)^1} + \frac{£4,000}{(1.12)^2} + \frac{£4,000}{(1.12)^3} + \frac{£4,000}{(1.12)^4} + \frac{£4,000}{(1.12)^5}$$

$$= -£13,600 + £3,572 + £3,188 + £2,848 + £2,544 + £2,268$$

$$= + £820$$

The positive present value means that the young man prefers to take the £20,000 spread over five years. If the financier increases his offer to £14,421 then the young man will accept.

The NPV method of discounting is simple to apply and easy to understand but it has one fault. It does not provide a relative measure of profitability. The absolute figure of £820 is the only guide that management has and therefore it is difficult to compare projects.

To enable comparison a Profitability Index can be constructed which enables management to rank projects on the basis of desirability. The Index is defined as follows:

$$\text{Profitability Index} = \frac{\text{Present Value of Inflows}}{\text{Present Value of Outflows}}$$

The higher the index the more desirable the project. Where capital is scarce and management has more investment opportunities than cash then the projects should be ranked by the profitability index as the example in Table 19 demonstrates.

Table 19 Projects Presented to the Board of Directors of Ardmore Limited

Project	Investment	Profitability Index
X	£9,000	1.40
P	£50,000	1.20
R	£15,000	1.12
A	£25,000	1.07
C	£21,000	1.05
M	£15,000	.99
T	£18,000	.75

The capital available for investment is £100,000.

Projects M and T are not profitable and so will be rejected. Projects X, P, R, and A are accepted. Project C, though profitable, is held back due to lack of funds.

DEFLATION/INFLATION AND CAPITAL BUDGETING

It has been said that inflation makes all capital projects profitable. This occurs simply because over time the profits of a project grow in current terms. If the inflated profits are compared with historical costs then the project looks extremely profitable.

The treatment of inflation in capital budgeting techniques is particularly thorny and not fully resolved. Two principal methods are used to handle the problem.

(a) Inflate all costs and revenues up to the time of start-up and afterwards assume constant costs.

(b) Allow for inflation in revenue and costs but at the same time discount inflation by increasing the discount rate.

There would be little difficulty in dealing with the inflation if the rate was low, but double-digit inflation tends, over time, to overshadow all other costs. Remember that in the 16 year period 1970-86 prices rose by 525 per cent and average wages by 400 per cent. These high rates make a mockery of long-term forecasting.

The average project will allow for inflation up to the time of commissioning, thereafter it will ignore it. This approach is both conservative and acceptable. Where management do expect significant differences to arise between the rates of revenue inflation and cost inflation then it may be essential to predict each year separately. In such cases it may be necessary to increase the discount factor by an appropriate inflation rate.

The mid to late 1980s has seen the appearance of deflation. This means that fixed assets decline in price. The best example is industrial property. In the late 1980s good quality factories could be bought for £5—£8 per square foot. The fall in the price of raw materials and energy during the 1980s has led to a fall in the price of many products. Indeed in countries such as Switzerland and Germany the consumer price index has declined.

Deflation can be good for a project in that there may be a lag between falling input prices and the price of the finished products. The result is a fallen gross margin. The rise in agricultural income in Ireland in 1987 was due mainly to failing input prices. Unfortunately deflation can affect the value of inventory particularly in competitive industries. The result is inventory losses as stock is sold at the new lower prices. Careful budgeting analyses tend to ignore deflation as well as inflation, but management need to be aware of a possible impact on their business.

CAPITAL BUDGETING AND UNCERTAINTY

So far this chapter has examined the effects of uncertainty on cash receipts and disbursements. Other techniques have been developed which allow an assessment of the level of uncertainty in the overall project.

Earlier sections have suggested that a series of estimates be obtained for receipts and outflows. At the simplest level three estimates, Optimistic. Most Likely and Pessimistic, were advised. Table 20 shows the number of Net Cash Flows arising from this simple approach to uncertainty.

Nine potential returns are evident ranging from the 'Worst', which would be Pessimistic estimates of costs and revenues, to the 'Best', which would be Optimistic estimates of both. Unfortunately, this simple analysis allows for very little variation. In the cost estimates, variations can occur in labour, power and materials, to name only three important

Table 20 Potential Net Cash Flows to Project X

		Receipts		
		Optimistic	Most Likely	Pessimistic
Costs	Optimistic			
	Most Likely			
	Pessimistic			

elements. To examine changes in these three variables together with three revenue estimates requires 81 sets of calculations ($3 \times 3 \times 3 \times 3$).

If, as is more advisable, a probability distribution of estimates for each variable is produced then manual manipulation becomes virtually impossible. In recent years simple computer programmes have been devised to do all of the work. Now the analyst will be asked to supply a list of variables, a range of probable outcomes and the probabilities attaching to each outcome.

At the push of a button the computer will produce a distribution of expected Internal Rates of Return together with estimates of the most likely outcome and the potential deviations from this outcome. Figure 5 shows the likely outcome. A distribution of Profitability Indices is usually produced.

References at the end of this chapter provide additional information on this area.

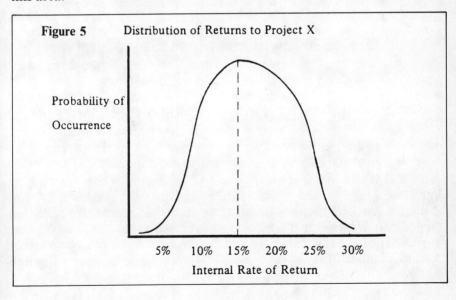

Figure 5 Distribution of Returns to Project X

Probability of Occurrence

5%   10%   15%   20%   25%   30%
Internal Rate of Return

TAXATION AND CAPITAL BUDGETING

The tax policies applying to investment can seriously affect the return on investment. Taxation normally reduces the cash available to a project. In Ireland an extensive system of tax incentives has been developed. When examining the return to the shareholders, after tax cash flows must be used. The incentives available in Ireland are as follows:

(a) Liberal depreciation allowances.
(b) Deductibility of interest.
(c) Offsetting allowances against other income.
(d) Low overall tax rates.

Depreciation Allowances

Ireland has a tradition of liberal depreciation allowances for manufacturing investment whereby the full cost of an investment could be written off against tax in the year in which it occurred. With the passing of the 1986 Finance Act this was amended to read 'net — after grant — investment'.

Interest Deductions

All business interest charges can be offset against business incomes.

Offsetting Allowances or the Tax Shield

A company investing in new machinery can usually offset the depreciation on that machine against the general profits of the business. This provides a 'tax shield' and means that many firms can fully utilise depreciation allowances in the year in which expenditure occurs.

Low Corporation Tax Rate

To encourage manufacturing investment a low rate of 10 per cent is charged on company profits arising from manufacture. It should be noted that the low tax rate reduces the benefit of tax shields.

CAPITAL BUDGETING EXERCISE ON ARDMORE LIMITED

For some time now Ardmore Limited has been pursuing investigations into the possibility of expanding operations into a totally new product area—stainless steel tanks which would be used in the rapidly growing dairy and chemical sectors in Ireland. Eolas (formerly the Institute for Industrial Research and Standards) has assisted with technical information, the Irish Productivity Council has offered a financial appraisal and the Industrial Development Authority has agreed to provide grants for the project. The following data have been presented to the general manager of Ardmore Limited. He wishes to appraise the project before submitting it to the board.

Capital Cost. No new space is required. The expected expenditure is as follows:

Plant & Equipment installed	£80,000
Less IDA Grant	32,000
Net Investment	£48,000
Increased Working Capital	103,000
Total Investment	£151,000

There is little uncertainty here as the machinery prices have been quoted. Note that the IDA grant has been deducted from the cost. The estimate of working capital was arrived at by assuming an inventory to sales turnover of 4.2 and allowing a twelve weeks' credit period. These figures are consistent with forecasted 1987 Ardmore operations.

Investment Timing. The machines can be delivered and installed during January 1988. Full production should be achieved by June 1988.

Economic Life. The physical life of the machines is twenty years or more. The economic life is much more difficult to ascertain. The management of Ardmore Limited have no idea about technological developments but they do know that foreign competition is likely in the future. Based on their assessment of the market they decide on an eight-year life.

Salvage Value. Management find it difficult to estimate salvage value. A figure of £10,000 has been selected. Three-quarters of the working capital will be recovered. A figure of £75,000 is taken as recovered working capital.

Tax Shield. Apart from the free depreciation available management expect to have taxable profits of over £40,000 on other operations (see Pro Forma Income Statement, Chapter 4).

Revenues: The market for stainless steel tanks in Ireland grew from virtually nothing in 1970 to £5 million annually by 1987. Modernisation of dairy farming and a huge increase in chemical/pharmaceutical production has led to the increased demand. The IDA have identified stainless steel tanks as an excellent import substitution product, that is, a product currently imported but suitable for local production. Studies have produced annual growth figures of 20 per cent for the late 1980s.

Ardmore expects to sell to a local readymade market. Within a ten-mile radius of the plant there are a number of agricultural equipment suppliers. The company has also held discussions with a large Dublin-based engineering products distributor who has agreed to carry the new product line.

The sales estimates are as follows:

1988	1989 onward
£230,000	£281,000

By 1988 production capacity will have been reached. No sensitivity analysis was performed.

Costs. A detailed analysis of the costs attaching to the above levels of sales is as follows:

	1988	1989 onward
Raw materials	£88,000	£108,000
Wages	£47,000	£67,000
Factory Overheads	£25,800	£25,800
Marketing & Administration	£41,500	£40,700
	£202,300	£241,500

Depreciation is not included in the above figures. The operating costs in 1988 are disproportionately high due to training costs, extra materials, wastage and general start-up costs. Marketing costs in 1988 reflect expenditure on literature, trade fairs, etc.

Capital Structure. Apart from an IDA Grant of £32,000, Ardmore Limited received a £100,000 seven-year term loan at 15 per cent. The loan had a moratorium on capital payments for one year. The owners of Ardmore will have to put up the balance of the investment, £51,000, as equity.

Cost of Capital. The investment of £51,000 is a strain on the owners of Ardmore Limited. They are very concerned about the investment for two reasons: (a) loss of the money might bankrupt both Ardmore Limited and its owners and (b) the owners have many alternative uses for the money. In addition, since no sensitivity analysis was undertaken on costs or on revenues, they wish to incorporate a risk factor into the analysis. They estimate that their cost of making the investment is

Time Value = 15 per cent per annum
Risk Factor = 10 per cent per annum
_____
Required Rate of Return = 25 per cent per annum

This might on first sight appear very high but considering the fact that the revenue figures are based on selling the full production capacity of the plant then the risk factor is not excessive. Therefore the decision criterion is an Internal Rate of Return equal to or greater than 25 per cent or a positive Net Present Value using a 25 per cent discount rate.

Table 21 shows the cash flow estimates. It is assumed that the loan is repaid in six instalments of £15,000 each plus one of £10,000. All are paid at the end of the year. The taxation position is as follows:

Year 1 The net investment of £48,000 is used in full as allowable depreciation against earnings of £12,700 (£27,700 – £15,000) on the new tank project, and £40,000 profits on other Ardmore projects. This leaves taxable earnings of £4,700 at a rate of 10 per cent rounded to £500.

Years 2-7 Tax is 10 per cent of the after interest cash flows.

Year 8 Tax is chargeable on £38,500 of earnings plus the £10,000 salvage value. Remember that the equipment has a zero value in the books. Tax is charged on £48,500 less interest paid of £1,500. The tax estimate is £4,700.

Financial Appraisal. The data in Table 21 has been analysed as follows:

Payback Period to Equity. The payback period is the length of time taken to recover the owners' investment. The equity investment is £51,000. The inflows to equity are:

Year 1	£15,700
Year 2	6,100
Year 3	8,100
Year 4	10,200
	£40,100

The income of £12,200 in Year 5 would exceed the sum required of £10,900. The payback period is 4 years plus 10,900 ÷ 12,000 of a year, or 4.89 years.

Simple Return on the Project. Note that this examines the rate of return on the entire project not just the equity. The after-tax profits are not available but the Net Cash Flow is a close enough approximation.

$$\text{Simple Rate of Return} = \frac{\text{Average Net Cash Flow less Non Revenue Items}}{\text{Average Investment}}$$

$$= \frac{(£12,200 + 21,100 + 23,100 + 25,200 + 27,200 + 29,200 + 31,200 + 32,300) \div 8}{£75,500}$$

$$= \frac{£25,188}{£75,500}$$

$$= 33.4\%$$

Note: The figure of £32,300 in the above calculation is arrived at by deducting the working capital recovered from the cash flow to equity. The figure of £75,500 is half the total investment of £151,000.

Table 21   Ardmore Limited: Cash Flows Arising From the Stainless Steel Project

	1988	1989	1990	1991	1992	1993	1994	1995
Revenues	£230,000	£280,000	£280,000	£280,000	£280,000	£280,000	£280,000	£280,000
Less Operating Costs	202,300	241,500	241,500	241,500	241,500	241,500	241,500	241,500
Net Cash Flows from Revenues	27,700	38,500	38,500	38,500	38,500	38,500	38,500	38,500
Salvage Value								10,000
Working Capital Recovered								75,000
Net Cash Inflows before Interest and Taxes	27,700	38,500	38,500	38,500	38,500	38,500	38,500	123,500
Interest (figures rounded to nearest 100)	15,000	15,000	12,800	10,500	8,300	6,000	3,800	1,500
Taxes (See Note 1)	500	2,400	2,600	2,800	3,000	3,300	3,500	4,700
Net Cash Flow	12,200	21,100	23,100	25,200	27,200	29,200	31,200	117,300
Capital Repayments	—	15,000	15,000	15,000	15,000	15,000	15,000	10,000
Cash Flow to Equity	12,200	6,100	8,100	10,200	12,200	14,200	16,200	107,300
Tax Saving on £35,300 of taxable Ardmore Profits shielded by using allowances from this project	3,500	—	—	—	—	—	—	—
Increase in After-Tax Cash to the Owners of Ardmore Limited	15,700	6,100	8,100	10,200	12,200	14,200	16,200	107,300
Cumulative Cash Inflow	15,700	21,800	29,900	40,100	52,300	66,500	82,700	190,000

Internal Rate of Return (IRR). To estimate the IRR three rates of discount were tried, 15 per cent, 25 per cent and 30 per cent. The calculations are shown below.

Discount Rates

Year	Cash Flows £	15%	PV £	25%	PV £	30%	PV £
1	15,700	.870 =	13,659	.800 =	12,560	.769 =	12,073
2	6,100	.756 =	4,612	.640 =	3,904	.592 =	3,611
3	8,100	.658 =	5,330	.512 =	4,147	.455 =	3,685
4	10,200	.572 =	5,834	.410 =	4,182	.350 =	3,570
5	12,200	.497 =	6,063	.328 =	4,002	.269 =	3,281
6	14,200	.432 =	6,134	.262 =	3,720	.207 =	2,939
7	16,200	.376 =	6,091	.210 =	3,402	.159 =	2,576
8	107,300	.327 =	35,087	.168 =	18,026	.123 =	13,197
Present Value of Cash Flows			£82,810		£53,943		£44,932

The present values of inflows must be compared with the equity outflow of £51,000. Clearly the IRR is higher than 15 per cent and lower than 30 per cent. Using interpolation the rate has been estimated as

	Discount Rate		Present Value
	25%	=	£53,943
	30%	=	£44,932
Difference	5%	=	£9,011

The rate is £2,943 above the 25 per cent rate so

$$\text{Internal Rate of Return} = 25\% + \frac{2,943}{9,011} \ (5\%)$$

$$= 26\%$$

Net Present Value (NPV). Using the required discount rate of 25 per cent the net present value is as follows:

$$\text{Net Present Value at } 25\% = -£51,000 + £53,943$$

$$= £2,943$$

The Profitability Index on this project is

$$\text{Profitability Index} = \frac{£53,943}{£51,000}$$

$$= 1.06$$

Recommendation Relying on the information provided and on the results of the analysis the project should be accepted.

Note 1: Allowable depreciation against tax is the net cost of plant and equipment which is £48,000. The following tax calculations apply:

		1988	1989
Taxable Profits			
(a)	From Stainless Steel Project	£12,700	£23,500
(b)	Depreciation	12,700	23,500
	Allowance available for offset against other profits	35,300	—
	Other taxable profits (approx.)	40,000	40,000
	Allowance remaining for following year	—	—

Please note that the tax shield of not paying tax on other profits is £3,500 in year 1 and none in year 2 because the net investment of £48,000 has been fully allowed in year 1. Thereafter tax is 10 per cent.

CONCLUSION

This chapter has examined capital budgeting decisions in the context of overall corporate strategies. The examination of total cost, economic life and particularly projected cash flows require all the skill and experience at the command of management. A mistake in capital budgeting can ruin a firm. The methods of appraisal presented are designed to lower the possibility of this occurring. No one method provides all the answers. Though four methods of analysis were presented, two were stressed. These are the so-called discounted cash flow methods of capital budgeting.

These techniques are being increasingly applied, particularly to large projects. Despite their apparent complexity they become easy to apply with practice. It must be remembered that they are only techniques and do not of themselves provide correct information for decision-making. If the information regarding cash flow projections, economic life, etc. is not correct then the techniques will not provide the correct answers. The methods themselves are not perfect and are criticised on the basis of re-investment rate assumptions and on the fact that they ignore the need of management to provide a constant or increasing stream of earnings per share.

The use of capital budgeting techniques depends very much on the human, financial and time resources available to the individual firm. Some firms will not have skilled personnel to gather the information and analyse it fully. Others may consider that the expenditure of time and money may not be worth the results. If possible, it is recommended that all four methods be used. The extra work necessary to apply discounting methods may well be worth the effort. For the smaller firm, the use of the firm's auditors as financial analysts may be both advisable and fruitful.

Further Reading
H. Bierman & S. Smidt: *The Capital Budgeting Decision,* (5th Ed.), Macmillan, New York 1984.
J. P. Dickinson (Ed.); *Risk and Uncertainty in Accounting & Finance,* D. C. Heath, Lexington, Mass. 1975.
H. L. Beenhakker: *Handbook for the Analysis of Capital Investments,* Greenwood Press, Westport, Conn. 1977.
J. C. Van Horne: *Financial Management & Policy,* (7th Ed.), Prentice Hall International, London 1986.

Chapter 7

Irish Financial Institutions

An earlier chapter pointed out that financial management involved not only the management and control of investments, but also the efficient raising of the funds required to undertake the investments. Money is raised from a variety of sources. It is the purpose of this and the following chapter to examine the various institutions which provide finance to Irish business. Chapters 9 to 13 analyse the types of finance provided by the institutions. To understand the role played by financial institutions it is useful to be familiar with the market for capital. The availability of funds which can be invested depends on the level of savings. Individuals and corporations save for a multiplicity of purposes, a holiday, a house, to protect against the 'rainy day' or to provide security. There are many ways of saving. Table 22 shows some of the more popular methods of saving together with the sums saved at the end of 1986. Note that the savings are liquid insofar as they can be easily realised. The huge sum of almost £15,000 million provides the funds for the capital market.

Table 22   Savings in Ireland

Method of Saving	Totals Saved as End 1986 (£m)
Building Societies	2,901.2
Post Office and Trustee Savings Banks	1,045.4
Deposits in the Banking System	7,919.5
Deposits in State Sponsored Financial Institutions	403.2
Government Savings Schemes	1,001.6
Currency	1,130.0
Inter-Institutional Adjustment	368.6
	£14,769.5 million

Source: Central Bank of Ireland Annual Report 1987. Table 14.4

The various financial institutions in which the funds are lodged know from experience what their inflows and outflows are likely to be. Funds not likely to be withdrawn by savers can be loaned to areas which need money for investment purposes. The length of time for which savings are likely to be held range from hours to decades; so too, does the payoff on the various investment opportunities which exist. The financial institutions which hold the savings have developed special financial products which best market their funds. These products are known as financial instruments.

Business is a major, but by no means the only, participant in the demand for capital. Apart from providing capital to business, money is also provided for private mortgages, personal credit and for state borrowing. Indeed, one of the major problems in Ireland in the early 1980s was that the demand for capital far outweighed the supply. The state in particular was a major borrower, often at the expense of the private business sector. Late in the decade demands for funds declined dramatically.

The methods of saving outlined in Table 22 above are by no means the only methods. Insurance policies, pensions, stocks, shares, and fixed asset purchases are other methods of saving.

HISTORICAL BACKGROUND

Financial institutions have a long and chequered history. Saving is a method of reducing future uncertainty, so historically people have saved. The concept of saving money on which interest could be paid is one which taxed many brains during the Middle Ages. In the Christian world usury, that is, a payment for the use of money, was frowned upon, but it did exist. Paying interest is still illegal in most Moslem countries. Institutions in which money in the form of metals could be deposited, have existed for millennia, but it was not until the growth of trade in the seventeenth and eighteenth centuries that modern financial institutions appeared.

Ireland lagged behind the United Kingdom in the development of banking. Though the Bank of Ireland was chartered in 1783 it was not until after the passing of the 1821 Banking Act that modern banking developed. The 1821 Act permitted branch banking. It was passed in the aftermath of the financial crash of 1820 which saw many Irish financial institutions go bankrupt. Between 1825 and 1836 the ancestors of Allied Irish Banks, the National Irish Bank and Ulster Bank were formed.

Remember that at this time Ireland was part of the United Kingdom and the UK financial system obtained in Ireland. This had one unusual effect — the institutions which developed in Ireland did so as part of an advanced United Kingdom economy.

Independence saw the country with over 950 bank branches, a well-developed Post Office Savings Bank network, insurance offices and building societies. Though it was a poor country, there were some savings. These were generally channelled from Ireland to the United Kingdom. This was not a political decision: the demand in Ireland was low and the period between the two world wars was a time of financial confusion in Ireland. In 1927 the Currency Act provided for an indigenous currency and in 1942 the Central Bank Act established the Central Bank. Yet, until 1979, the Irish financial system was tied closely to that of the United Kingdom due to the link with sterling. Since the establishment of the state the Irish punt had been on a parity with sterling. This, in effect, provided for a free capital market in the British Isles and it meant that Irish financial policy was dominated by events on the London capital markets. In March 1979, when Ireland joined the European Monetary System, the link with sterling was broken. Chapter 16 returns to this topic.

Irish financial institutions developed slowly during the first half of the 19th century. As economic growth rates improved in Ireland, the demands on the financial institutions grew. Older institutions adapted and new ones appeared. Merchant banks, industrial banks, North

Table 23   Irish Financial Institutions

Category	Number
Central Bank	1
Associated Banks	4
Non-Associated Banks	
Merchant and Commercial	
Irish	7
Other EEC	11
Other International	7
Industrial Banks	14
State-Sponsored Financial Institutions	2
Post Office Saving Bank and Trustee	
Savings Bank	5
Building Societies	16
Hire Purchase Finance Companies	34
Insurance Companies	49
Stock Exchange	1

Source: Central Bank of Ireland Annual Report 1987.

American banks and European banks opened offices in Ireland. Many of these institutions introduced new financial instruments into the country. Ireland, for her level of economic development, has a highly sophisticated set of financial institutions. Table 23 sets out the major types of such institutions in Ireland.

Each of the categories in Table 23, with the exception of the Stock Exchange, is dealt with below. Chapter 8 deals with the Stock Exchange.

THE CENTRAL BANK

The function of a Central Bank is to safeguard the integrity of the currency of the country. The primary function is subdivided into six major tasks.

(1) Controlling the level of credit available is one way of controlling the growth of an economy. By forcing banks to either increase interest rates and/or reduce the amount of credit outstanding, the Central Bank reduces inflationary pressures. If economic growth is sluggish then credit can be relaxed and investment encouraged. By selling government loans the Central Bank drives up interest rates and reduces the amount of cash available. This dampens down the growth in credit. By purchasing bonds, interest rates decline and credit is relaxed. These latter two methods of controlling credit are known as 'Open Market Operations'.

(2) Acting as state banker. A modern state has very many complex cash flows, such as tax, loans, salaries, social welfare. The Central Bank acts as banker to the state, monitoring and co-ordinating the finances. As an example, consider the work involved in controlling the many state loans. In 1987 there were over 100 loans totalling almost £8,500 million.

(3) Issuing currency. Imagine the situation whereby a state finances expenditure simply by printing more money. The currency becomes debased and worthless. It is the function of the Central Bank to issue and control currency. As of 1987 there was £1,130 million in outstanding currency.

(4) Acting as lender of last resort. Financial institutions should maintain adequate liquidity. Should they get into difficulties they can borrow from the Central Bank. In practice, this function is used to control credit.

(5) Acting as banker to banks. This function is similar to (4) above. The Central Bank may require the commercial banks to deposit certain sums in the Central Bank on special terms.

(6) Holding the external reserves of the country. Many countries, including Ireland, have very strict controls on the movement of funds across borders. This is largely due to the weak level of external reserves. As of January 1988 the external reserves of Ireland amounted to slightly

above £21,700 million. By controlling all reserves, the Central Bank is in a better position to defend the currency against undesired devaluations. It also plays a very active role in deciding Irish economic policy.

As the 1990s approach Irish financial institutions are facing a major upheaval as regulations on competition are relaxed.

REGULATORY CONTROL OF THE IRISH FINANCIAL SYSTEM

The Irish regulatory environment is most uncertain. This is due in part to the lack of a single regulator responsible for all deposit-taking institutions. Despite the small size of the Irish financial system, there are multiple Government agencies involved. In addition to the Central Bank, there are other regulatory agencies; the Department of Finance is responsible for the control of the state banks and the TSBs; the Department of the Environment is responsible for the building societies; the Department of Industry and Commerce is responsible for the insurance companies as well as those lending under exemptions from the Moneylenders Acts. As a consequence of this fragmented regulatory environment, a co-ordinated approach to deregulation appears less likely.

It would appear that, with the exception of the building society regulators, the trend in regulation in Ireland is largely to copy trends in the UK. This should be a matter of major concern to the Irish Financial institutions. The UK expects to benefit from regulatory change because it has helped to establish London as the major European financial centre.

Irrespective of how far Ireland deregulates, it will not be feasible to turn Ireland into a major European financial centre. The proximity of the London market, with its existing infrastructure and position, precludes this. Deregulating, in the same fashion as in the UK, will not help Irish industry. It is already clear, from the actions of the directly foreign controlled financial institutions, that they have minimal interest in all but the premium credit customer in Ireland.

Historically, the Irish regulatory environment has discriminated against the associated banks in favour of the non-associated banks and against the Irish based banks as opposed to the non-Irish based banks. Asset constraints were imposed at a higher level on the associated than on the non-associated banks. Equally, the high level of primary reserve requirements imposes a substantial cost on Irish based institutions. The net effect of these impositions is to direct business towards the least cost supplier of funds, that is, those lending from outside the Irish market. The high level of secondary liquidity imposed on the associated banks is currently not a binding constraint. Largely because of the lack of loan demand, neither group of banks is currently restricted by this constraint.

However, in the event of loan demand increasing in the 1990s the associated banks may once again be restricted by the secondary reserve requirement.

Similar and additional problems exist for the building societies. A substantial portion of their growth has been due to tax advantages and their dominant position in the mortgage market. Historically, they have been less subject to competition. If foreign competitors in their native markets are given greater freedom of action at an earlier stage than the Irish building societies, then the Irish societies will not have the opportunity to develop the skills necessary to compete when the Irish market is opened to foreign competition under EEC directives.

The initial thrust of regulatory change for the building societies was not aimed at allowing them more freedom to compete. Its objective was to remove tiered interest rates and other practices which are deemed to be non-competitive. However, to the extent that these items increase the profitability of the building societies, the consequence of the legislation, if it is effective, will be to reduce their profit levels. Building societies, because they are mutual societies, do not have ready access to capital. In addition, because of the small size of the domestic Irish market, the Irish societies have a much lower capital base than their potential foreign competitors. Proposed legislation, not yet enacted, may go a long way towards establishing this principle and in so doing create a 'fairer' environment for all interested parties.

There is a major need to co-ordinate Irish regulatory policy. This could best be done by establishing the Central Bank as the sole regulatory authority for all deposit taking institutions.

Deregulation should be a gradual process. Institutions, particularly those who have been historically shielded from competition, should be given an environment which would encourage them to compete and a period of time in which to build up the necessary skills. They should not be expected to compete overnight with foreign institutions whose native environment has promoted their competitive development. Full competition should be encouraged but on a phased basis.

If one is intent on imposing burdens or restrictions on institutions while at the same time hoping to maximise competition, then every effort should be made to ensure that identical restrictions are imposed on all players. If this is not the case, then competition is not maximised, it is simply distorted.

A co-ordinated Irish regulator could do a substantial amount to encourage the development of the Irish financial markets. The range of financial instruments available in Ireland on a formalised basis is narrower than elsewhere. The development of a clearing house for all corporate treasury product markets would be a major benefit. It is in everyone's interest to develop the liquidity and range of instruments in the market.

THE ASSOCIATED BANKS

The term 'associated banks' comes from the Central Bank Act 1942 which defined a special relationship between the four associated banks and the Central Bank. These four banks, two Irish-owned, one UK-owned and one Australian-owned, dominate Irish finance with total assets of almost £10,000 million or 57 per cent of total bank assets.

The four associated banks, together with Guinness and Mahon, an Irish merchant bank, provide a clearing house for cheques. The four associated banks are Bank of Ireland, Allied Irish Banks, Ulster Bank — which is owned by National Westminster Bank (UK) — and National Irish Bank — a subsidiary of an Australian group. Bank of Ireland and Allied Irish Banks control the bulk of business in the Irish Republic.

Until the 1960s there was little demand for loans in Ireland. Excess funds were invested in the London money market. Industrialisation in the 1960s and agricultural growth in the 1970s placed severe financial and organisational strains on the banks. Growing demands for credit were met by improved lending procedures. The difficulties of understanding the needs of new industries and technologies were handled by hiring experts. In the 1970s and 1980s the two Irish-owned associated banks began to expand overseas to better serve both domestic and international clients.

In the mid 1960s, at the time the two major banking groups were formed, the associated banks controlled about 70 per cent of the domestic resources with deposit taking institutions. By the end of 1987, this high level of concentration had fallen to about 45 per cent. Table 24 compares the pattern of lending by the associated banks and that of the non-associated banks. During this period there was increasing fragmentation of the savings and lending market, spurred by uneven tax policies and the entry and growth of new competitors into the market.

To minimise the diversion of resources away from them and in response to the needs of a growing Irish economy, the associated banks transformed themselves with each setting-up merchant and other banking subsidiaries. They began to participate, if indirectly, in the life insurance market through the management and/or marketing of investments with a tax efficient life insurance dimension. They also began to expand overseas to better serve both domestic and international clients.

Table 24 Pattern of Lending by Irish Banks, 1987

Categories of Borrowers	Associated		Non-Associated		Total	
	£ million	%	£ million	%	£ million	%
Agriculture	979.0	20.5	117.7	2.8	1096.7	12.2
Energy	51.8	1.1	387.2	9.2	439.0	4.9
Manufacturing	744.0	15.6	848.5	20.2	1592.5	17.8
Building & Construction	142.5	3.0	106.5	2.6	249.0	2.8
Distribution, Garages, Hotels & Catering	693.7	14.6	468.6	11.2	1162.3	13.0
Transport	209.6	4.4	299.6	7.1	509.2	5.7
Postage Services & Telecommunications	17.3	0.4	483.3	11.5	500.6	5.6
Financial	189.1	4.0	658.2	15.7	847.3	9.4
Business & Other Services	473.0	9.9	391.1	9.3	864.1	9.6
Personal	1263.5	26.5	434.9	10.4	1698.4	19.0
Total	£4763.5	100%	£4195.6	100%	£8959.1	100%

Source: Central Bank of Ireland

THE NON-ASSOCIATED BANKS

There are basically two categories of non-associated banks, merchant/commercial and industrial banks. Merchant and commercial can be further analysed under the headings of Irish, other EEC and other international. Table 25 gives a profile of the number and size of the different categories of banks, and for comparative information the associated banks in summary form.

Table 25 Non-Associated Banks, 1987

Category	No. Banks	Total Assets £ million	Non-Government Lending £ million
Merchant and Commercial:			
Irish	7	£2,903.8	£1,490.2
Other EEC	11	£1,644.4	£1,033.4
Other International	7	£946.5	£576.1
Total Merchant and Commercial	25	£5,494.7 (32%)	£3,099.7 (35%)
Total Industrial	14	£1,900.8 (11%)	£1,095.9 (12%)
Total Non-Associated Banks	39	£7,395.5 (43%)	£4,195.6 (47%)
Total Associated Banks	4	£9,963.9 (57%)	£4,763.5 (53%)
Total Irish Banks	43	£17,359.4	£8,959.1

MERCHANT AND COMMERCIAL BANKS

Today merchant banks specialise in financing business. They can be termed wholesale banks in that they deal in very large sums. As of 1987 the twenty-five merchant/commercial banks had total assets of £5,500 million or 32 per cent of total bank assets. Their non-government lending, manufacturing being the largest category of borrower, amounted to over £3,000 million or 35 per cent of total non-government lending.

The dramatic increase in the number of merchant/commercial banks operating in Ireland is due to the entry of non-Irish owned banks. This began with the entry of North American banks in response to US and Canadian firms investing in Ireland, initially in the mining industry and later in the chemical and electronic industries. This development was followed by the entry of a number of powerful European banks in the 1970s following on Ireland's accession to the EEC in 1972. The major strength of these institutions is their ready access to international expertise and extensive networks throughout the world. In addition, through their parents, they have close links with most of the multi-national corporate clients. Within Ireland, they have a small geographic base and a small, but premier quality, corporate customer base. Because these banks have instantaneous access to international expertise, they tend to be product innovators within the Irish market. They have a less rigid regulatory environment and are not subject to Irish capital adequacy requirements. They are given the flexibility to get into new activities for which the associated banks would require permission from the Central Bank. The non-Irish banks are subject to a lower tax burden than their Irish competitors and to less restriction on their assets. The branches operating in Ireland are subject to minimal Irish control, as they are presumed to be adequately controlled by the authorities in the country where the parent is located. Whilst historically they have had a competitive disadvantage relative to the associated banks in that they couldn't write Section 84 or lease type financing, recent legislative changes have greatly reduced the value and use of these forms of finance and consequently eroded the competitive strength of the associated banks. With the equalising of lending facilities and the expertise in these merchant banks, one might have expected them to continue to increase their share of the corporate market. Surprisingly the US banks have found it difficult to make profits in Ireland. A number have closed (Chase Manhattan, Bank of America and First National Bank of Chicago), while others have moved into different financial sectors. Citicorp bought into J.&E. Davy (stockbrokers) and Gandon (money managers), while the Bank of Nova Scotia bought First Southern Bank (a hire purchase and leasing company).

Four of the merchant banks are owned by the associated banks, one

Guinness and Mahon is an old Irish bank, and the remainder are subsidiaries of non-Irish owned banks. Table 28 lists all the financial institutions operating in Ireland in 1987, and Table 29 ranks the top fifty in terms of gross assets.

INDUSTRIAL BANKS

This group of fourteen banks provides instalment credit in the form of hire purchase and leasing. The smaller banks provide loans to consumers on durables while the larger banks offer services such as block discounting, bridging loans and export finance. A number of the larger industrial banks have branches but not on a large scale. Total assets amounted to £1,900 million in 1987. Their non-government lending amounts to over £1,000 million or 12 per cent of total non-government lending. Property, construction, car and household durables comprise much of their lending.

The largest industrial banks are United Dominions Trust, Credit Finance, Allied Irish Finance and Bank of Ireland Finance.

HIRE PURCHASE FINANCE COMPANIES

Hire purchase finance companies are not licensed banks but in common with the industrial banks their principal business is the extension of instalment credit. The industrial banks engage in a considerable amount of other lending as well, whereas the hire purchase finance companies do not. These companies derive their main resources from loans made to them by their own banking affiliates or from the non-associated banks, and are prohibited from accepting deposits from the public. There are thirty-four such companies and in 1987 total domestic credit extended by them amounted to over £100 million.

The bulk of the business done by hire purchase companies is in financing private and commercial motor vehicles.

The principal business users of hire purchase are small companies. The principal companies are Allied Finance, Bowmaker, Lombard, Mercantile Credit and Wallbrooke Limited.

POST OFFICE SAVINGS BANKS (TRUSTEE SAVINGS BANK AND AN POST)

Over 100 years ago the state established a mechanism to encourage small individual savings by utilising the extensive network of post offices. No sum was too small. Many diligent savers learned thrift by purchasing savings stamps at a couple of pence each. These stamps could be redeemed at any post office.

Around the same time Savings banks were established in Dublin, Cork,

Waterford and Limerick. Their function was similar to that of the Post Office Savings Bank. Generally the Savings banks paid a higher rate of interest on deposits than did the associated banks.

In the 1970s the Savings banks began to provide other services, such as current accounts and loans. Their expansion was assisted by long drawn-out strikes in the associated banks.

Trustee Savings Banks (TSB)

Following the merger of the Cork and Limerick Savings Banks, the three remaining TSB's (Dublin, Waterford and Cork/Limerick) are involved in discussions with a view to an eventual merger of all operations under a single management structure.

In 1986, the TSBs were affected by the impact of Deposit Interest Retention Tax. Deposits in the Dublin bank fell by about 5 per cent to £263 million resulting in a decrease in the annual surplus from £1.15 million to just over £1 million. Loans to customers increased marginally to £49.9 million while cash on deposit with the Government declined by over 13 per cent to £186 million.

Post Office Savings Bank (An Post)

The freedom from Deposit Interest Retention Tax liability strongly benefitted the savings schemes administered by An Post in 1986. During the year, there was a net inflow of £383 million to Savings Certificates, Bonds and Instalment Savings resulting in a growth of over 47 per cent in the combined amount held under the three schemes. Savings Certificates funds grew by £174 million to £549 million. In contrast, the popularity of conventional Post Office Savings Bank accounts continued to decline with funds falling by £26 million to £382 million. The total amount invested in Post Office savings schemes stood at £1,249 million at the end of 1986.

Table 26

	Amount on Deposit at 31 Dec. 1986	Net Inflow during 1986
	(£m)	(£m)
Savings Certificates	549	174
Savings Bonds	220	99
Instalment Savings	98	10
Post Office Savings Bank	382	−26
	1,249	257

This group of banks which, in 1986, had deposits of over £1,200 million, deals almost exclusively with personal deposits and loans. Being state-owned, they are not required to hold banking licences from the Central Bank.

BUILDING SOCIETIES

The building societies are an important part of the financial sector. They are the largest single providers of mortgage finance for housing in Ireland, accounting for approximately 70 per cent of such finance. Although the building societies have primarily long-term assets they solicit and incur short-term liabilities in the form of shares and deposits. Of the sixteen building societies only five are relatively large. These larger societies have branches in most of the bigger urban areas. The increased competition in the savings market in 1987 resulted in a marked slowdown in the rate of growth in building society assets. The slower growth in lending reflected both the generally sluggish demand for home loans and increased competition from the major banks. In 1987 their lending for housing purposes amounted to over £2,400 million while their shares and deposits were £3,000 million.

The principal building societies are the Educational Building Society, the Irish Civil Service Building Society, the Irish Permanent Building Society, the Irish Nationwide Building Society, the First National Building Society, the Irish Mutual Building Society, the Midland and Western Building Society and the Irish Life Building Society.

In the coming years, building societies are likely to experience continued pressure to offer a growing range of services to customers which will make it difficult to contain the growth in management expenses. Net interest margins will remain low and net income in the societies is not expected to improve. On the lending side, the market share of the major banks is likely to grow at the expense of the societies and increased flexibility in society lending terms will be necessary.

At the end of 1986, the Government passed new legislation in relation to the building societies which permitted unsecured lending for specific purposes and increased the power of the Minister for the Environment to regulate the activities of the societies. Unsecured lending, allowed for bridging finance and home improvement purposes only, is limited to 4 per cent of the total assets of the society and can only be engaged in by societies that have a minimum reserves to total assets ratio of 4 per cent.

In 1987, the Minister introduced additional regulations governing certain society activities. The new regulations outlawed the charging of tiered mortgage rates and redemption fees, provided for choice of insurance company and for access to valuation reports by borrowers, obliged societies to pay their own legal fees and provided for changes in the way society directors are elected. These changes met with strong resistance from the societies, some of which have been slow to comply fully with them. In response to this resistance and to contribute towards the development of the building societies in general, the Minister established a working party comprising representatives of the societies, the Department of the Environment, the Department of Finance and the Central Bank. The working party's brief included reviewing difficulties resulting from the recent legislation and the construction of a framework for comprehensive legislative changes in relation to the societies. It is expected that the draft legislation, expanding the permissible range of activities, will be tabled in 1988.

The ongoing changes in the UK are likely to have a strong influence on future revisions to legislation and regulations in Ireland. In particular, the UK Building Society Act (1986), which expanded the range of services that societies can offer and allowed up to 20 per cent of society funds to be raised on the wholesale money markets, is a pointer to possible developments here. Given the structural differences between the sectors and markets in the two countries, however, legislative change here will not be a carbon-copy of what has occurred in the UK and may come about more slowly. Innovations such as mortgage-backed securities may also be slow in reaching Ireland.

In addition to developments in the UK, the EEC Mortgage Credit Directive is expected to come into effect in 1988 and will impinge in a major way on the Irish building societies. The directive envisages barrier-free trade for credit institutions offering mortgage credit within the EEC and is likely to result in serious competitive pressures on the Irish societies. The increasing sophistication of available technology will encourage cross-border developments and make it easier for foreign institutions to transact lending business with a minimal physical presence in Ireland.

Given the strong impetus for change from the market, the Government and the societies themselves, the nature of the building society movement is likely to evolve rapidly over the coming years. It is inevitable that the present level of competition between the societies and the banks will intensify as the range of services offered by the societies is extended. Any new activities undertaken by societies are likely to encroach on the traditional realms of the banks. The growing overlap between the two groups will eventually create a conflict between the mutual nature of the societies and the need to maximise profits in an increasingly competitive market. As a result, the degree of mutuality of these organisations is likely to be reduced gradually and societies of the future will closely resemble their banking counterparts. The need for change is highlighted by the declining profitability of building societies over the past year, mainly due to a heightened level of competition in the savings market. If building societies are to survive further increases in competition, they will need to be given greater flixibility in access to funds and in adapting to changes in the marketplace.

INSURANCE COMPANIES

Insurance companies provide essential protection for both the individual and the business sector. They also play a major role in providing long-term savings and investment facilities. The insurance industry in Ireland is a key sector of the economy. Collectively, insurance companies in Ireland employ over 8,000 people and many thousands more jobs are created in spin-off areas such as insurance broking and loss adjusting. The combined turnover of Life and General insurance companies in Ireland in 1987 was in excess of £2,000 million. The total funds managed by them was in excess of £6,000 million, of which approximately 90 per cent is invested directly in Ireland to the benefit of the Irish economy.

The Irish Insurance Federation (IIF), which represents most Life and General insurance companies, was established in March 1986 with the primary objective of creating a strong, unified and authoritative voice for the Irish insurance industry. It has forty members who account for over 95 per cent of the total insurance business underwritten in Ireland. Membership is open to all authorised insurers operating as Irish-registered companies, or as branch offices of overseas firms.

There are forty-nine insurance companies in Ireland, of which five are Irish-owned. Many of the foreign-owned firms are British and have been in Ireland since the nineteenth century. With the EEC making rapid progress towards the completion of the internal market in 1992, the recent establishment of American and European multi-national insurers will have a profound effect on the structure and competitive operation of the Irish insurance market.

Among the leading companies are Irish Life, Insurance Corporation of Ireland, New Ireland Assurance, Hibernian Insurance, PMPA, General Accident, Guardian Royal Exchange and Sun Alliance and London. The largest company by far is the state-owned Irish Life. This company has a pre-eminent position in the life insurance market and is the dominant investment force on the Irish Stock Exchange. As a state-owned company Irish Life is prohibited from holding majority control of a life assurance company in a number of US states and this seems to have increased the likelihood of some degree of privatisation in the near future.

LEASING COMPANIES

The most spectacular growth among financial institutions has been the leasing companies. These companies, currently not subject to stringent control and not having banking licences, have grown at exponential rates during the 1980s.

Such companies use their own equity and bank borrowings to lease assets to users. Most leases are simply financial leases, in that at the end of the lease period, for a small payment, the user will take over ownership of the asset. Leasing companies use the taxation allowances available in the State and the tax haven status of the Shannon Free Zone and Dublin Custom House Docks Zone to offer cheaper capital to domestic and international customers.

During the 1980s Guinness Peat Aviation (GPA), based in Shannon, developed into the world's largest aircraft leasing company with turnover of hundreds of millions of pounds and profits greater than those of the Bank of Ireland. Originally Irish-owned, Japanese, US and Canadian companies bought into GPA.

Domestically, Woodchester Investments grew in the 1980s into the dominant force in leasing. A publicly quoted company, Woodchester was in 1988 capitalised at over £200 million. In late 1987 a computer leasing company Reflex made their debut on the Irish Stock Exchange.

Other substantial leasing companies are Cambridge Finance, Capital Leasing and Irish Air Services at Shannon.

OTHER FINANCIAL INSTITUTIONS

Credit Unions play an active part in promoting small savings. This modern movement prospered in Canada and the USA from where it eventually spread to Ireland in 1958. Dramatic expansion took place and has been maintained over the last three decades, so that today, the credit union is recognised in Ireland as a unique and practical expression of self-help through co-operative endeavour. The essential element of any credit union is that all members and potential members should have something in common with each other. The law provides for a number of different common bonds. Two types generally exist: community bond and occupational or associational bonds.

There are about 500 credit unions in Ireland; 100 in Northern Ireland and 400 in the Republic. These credit unions are directed by over 8,000 volunteers and employ over 500 full-time staff. Total credit union membership is over 800,000.

Each credit union is separate, autonomous and completely in control of its own affairs. Credit unions are regulated by Acts of Parliament and the Government official responsible is the Registrar of Friendly Societies.

By law a credit union may charge not more than 1 per cent per month on the unpaid balance of a loan. This represents an interest cost of about 6.5 per cent on a loan of £100 repaid in twelve equal monthly instalments.

The state operates a number of financial institutions. The Agricultural Credit Corporation was established to finance agricultural development; the Industrial Credit Corporation acts as a development bank; and the Industrial Development Authority provides a wide range of financial incentives to business. These institutions are examined in more detail in Chapter 13.

THE DUBLIN MONEY MARKET

A money market deals in short-term funds, and until the 1970s there was no such market in Ireland. It acts like any other market: buyers and sellers attempt to match each other's needs. Prices, in this case interest rates, are a function of supply and demand.

By 1988 a small but thriving money market existed in Dublin. It is made up of two main segments — the market for Exchequer bills and Central Bank deposits and the interbank market.

The Central Bank controls credit to some extent by imposing certain liquidity requirements on the licensed banks. The banks can meet the requirements by holding non-interest bearing cash or by depositing funds with the Central Bank for agreed periods at agreed rates. Banks unable to meet the liquidity requirements can borrow from the Bank at high rates.

The Central Bank also curbs credit by controlling the issue of Exchequer Bills, which are ninety-day loans. By purchasing such bills money is released into the economy; by selling such bills funds are tightened. Exchequer bills are negotiable and an active market exists in these bills. Banks selling cash can sell or rediscount Exchequer Bills at the Central Bank.

The interbank market is based in Dublin. It developed during the 1970s primarily in response to the needs of the non-associated banks. While the associated banks deal in this market, the main participants are the non-associated banks. Compared with the associated banks, these banks, particularly the merchant and North American banks, do not enjoy the same degree of continuity in the flow of domestic savings to them or in their domestic lending. Some banks draw temporarily on the interbank market to mobilise the necessary funds for lending to customers, while others find that their liquidity becomes excessive at times and they lend to other banks in Dublin or place deposits with the Cental Bank. Deposits in the interbank market are repayable at call, two and seven days' notice, and are also placed for fixed periods ranging from seven days to twelve months. Most activity is centred in the call to one month range. The growth in the market has been rapid and the establishment of three money-brokers in Dublin in recent years has stimulated activity in the interbank market. Because it is competing with other investment outlets, the rates offered in this market reflect conditions in London and in other money markets abroad.

Since the break with sterling access to the London money market is much restricted, so activity has increased in Dublin. The industrial banks tend to be net borrowers while the merchant banks are net lenders.

A series of new instruments have evolved:

(1) Financial Futures Contracts;
(2) Interest Rate Hedges;
(3) Interest Rate Swaps;
(4) Interest Rate Options.

A *financial futures* contract is a binding agreement to buy or sell through an established exchange, at a definite date and at a specified price, a standard amount of financial paper of predetermined quality under fixed conditions of delivery. Actual or anticipated risks in money and bond markets (cash markets) can be minimised by taking an equal and opposite position in a futures market. Any cash market loss resulting from adverse interest rate movements should be offset by profits on futures contracts.

Future rate agreements are similar to financial futures contracts in that they also allow a customer to hedge against a future interest rate risk. However, unlike a financial futures contract which is provided by a bank which then lays off the risk in a traded futures market, the risk in a future rate agreement is taken on by the bank itself.

An *interest rate swap* consists of a set of forward exchanges of interest payments between two companies. Interest rate swaps allow a corporate treasurer to change the nature of the interest rate payments on the company's debt. The swap does not involve any exchange of principal amounts. It consists only of an agreement to exchange interest flows. The only payment that is made is the difference between the fixed and floating interest rate calculations on an amount stated in the agreement.

An *interest rate option* allows corporate treasurers to insure against adverse interest rate movements on anticipated drawdowns of new debt or on rollovers of existing floating rate funds.

Banks offering an interest rate option essentially sell their customer the right, but not the obligation, to borrow a specified amount at any time during the option period at a fixed rate for the stated period of the option. The option gives the corporate treasurer a combination of a pre-set fixed borrowing rate and the flexibility of choosing the drawdown date or choosing not to drawdown at all. For that right the treasurer pays a premium. The premium cost will depend on the degree of interest rate volatility, the intrinsic value (the difference between the current borrowing rate and the exercise rate) and the time value (the longer the option period, the more the option costs). Interest rate options can also be tied to a futures instrument to lock in a fixed rate for some point in the future, that is, an option on a future rate agreement.

The most common use of interest rate options by corporate treasurers is to provide an 'interest rate cap' on floating rate debt through an option on a future rate agreement.

THE CAPITAL MARKET

Apart from a short term money market a capital market exists in Dublin. The stock exchange is the location of the capital market but a narrower definition provides only for government loans. Trends in the rate of interest on government loans reflect accurately changes in interest rates in the economy. The capital market is dominated by the Central Bank which by either buying or selling government issues controls interest rates. As of 1987 there were over fifty Irish government loans totalling over £13,000 million. Trading in government loans dominates activity on the Irish stock exchange. The next chapter deals with the stock exchange.

THE FOREIGN EXCHANGE MARKET

Ireland has an open economy. That means that a large part of the Gross National Product is accounted for by foreign trade. Foreign trade must be financed; exporters must receive foreign currencies and bills of exchange which they need to convert into punts. Importers seek foreign currencies to pay their suppliers.

Up to 1970 most foreign exchange business was done in London. In 1970 the Central Bank commenced dealings in the major foreign currencies. Buying and selling rates for foreign currencies are quoted throughout the day by the Central Bank. Until March 1979 the task was simple. Parity with sterling meant that Irish and British exchange rates against other currencies were identical; otherwise arbitrage took place. Breaking of the link with sterling resulted in a major expansion of the Dublin foreign exchange market. Now the Irish punt has a quotation against every major currency. But since more than 34 per cent of all foreign trade is with the United Kingdom, the punt/sterling rate is the critical foreign exchange rate.

To protect the punt the Central Bank has instituted a series of restrictions on overseas investments. This enables it to exercise limited control over movements in the punt. The foreign exchange market is maintained by telephone and telex links and is confined almost exclusively to banks.

Financial innovation in international banking has been stimulated by a wide range of factors, such as:

(1) The changing regulatory environment which reduced structural rigidities worldwide and increased financial competition. The increased competition reduced the profitability of traditional banking services and forced the development of new specialised products to compensate.

(2) Due to the international problems with some major loans, regulatory pressure in the form of a demand for a strong capital basc in financial institutions emerged. This led to the development of 'off balance' sheet hedging and liquidity management techniques such as futures, swaps, options and note issuing facilities (NIFs).

(3) Technology improvements which reduced the costs of tele-communications and information processing, while also encouraging greater competition in traditional standardised services.

(4) The sharp rise in inflation and the increased volatility of interest rates and exchange rates. This higher volatility has increased the risk in financial institutions which do not exactly match the term structure of their assets and liabilities. Consequently, there has been an incentive to develop effective hedging devices to deal with these increased risks. The new financial instruments have largely focussed on this risk shifting and hedging.

(5) Fundamental shifts in the allocation of international funds
   (a) Sharp fall in OPEC investible surpluses.
   (b) Reduced access to credit by major LDC countries.
   (c) Switch in the role of the US from large net provider of funds to large net taker.
   (d) Growth in current account surpluses in Europe and Japan.

The key changes which have resulted from these forces for innovation have been:

(1) The emergence of new financial instruments — mainly focussing on off balance sheet commitments, for example, futures, options.

(2) Securitisation of the capital markets. Large international loans have shifted to the direct credit market rather than using the banks as intermediaries. This shift has been helped by some of the new instruments, such as NIFS (Note Issuing Facilities).

(3) Financial markets have become far more closely integrated worldwide — partially because of communications.

(4) The volume of transactions has increased.

(5) The mobility of capital has increased.

Financial innovations have offered a broad range of products for borrowing, deposits, and for managing interest rate and exchange rate exposures.

FINANCIAL SECTOR AND THE ECONOMY

While the macro environment in 1986 was ostensibly stable, there were very large differences between sectors. The financial sector in particular experienced major changes stemming from tax changes and exchange rate uncertainty, although the basic flow of savings remained relatively steady.

The changes in the financial sector can be seen by looking at the distribution of financial flows between Banks, Building Societies, Post Office, Government savings schemes and State-sponsored financial institutions (ICC, ACC). These data exclude flows into pension funds and life assurance companies (Table 27).

Table 27

Financial Flows (£ millions)	1985	1986
Currency	46.70	54.30
Licensed Banks:		
Current Accounts	–16.20	50.60
Deposit Accounts	420.40	–192.80
POSB and TSB	135.40	17.60
ICC and ACC	63.50	–77.10
Building Societies	332.60	206.90
Govt. Savings Schemes	198.40	243.30
Less		
Inter-institutional Deposits	102.20	–28.90
Money & Other Liquid Assets	1,078.60	331.70

The coming decade will see major changes in Irish financial institutions. Deregulation will lead to a scramble to lend. Traditional policies and patterns will become blurred. New lenders and new lending instruments will appear.

The challenge facing the Associated Banks is severe. They are large traditional labour intensive institutions used to operating in a cartel, which ensured that interest rates charged were high enough to cover all costs and leave a profit.

New aggressive lending institutions such as leasing companies have little or no overheads and tailor loans to the needs of the client. Building Societies can become major lenders to private customers.

Bank opening hours will have to adapt to the needs of the customer. The merchant and industrial banks will struggle to find a profitable role in the new environment. Some US banks have already decided that they are not equal to the task and are withdrawing. The Associated Banks are merging many of the activities of their merchant bank subsidiaries into their main banking activities.

It is likely that the number of banking licences will decline through merger and acquisition. The 1990s will see the rapid development of Irish financial institutions.

CONCLUSION

As a business grows and develops it will find that contacts with financial institutions also develop. The credit union, local bank or the building society which provided the second mortgage to get the business started will become less relevant with growth. Greater financial needs result in contacts with industrial banks and merchant banks. Overseas deals may require the permission of the Central Bank and the assistance of the North American or European banks. Larger ventures may result in loans from insurance companies or a quotation on the stock exchange.

Ireland has a range of well-developed financial institutions which have a selection of financial products, one or more of which can suit practically every financial need. Table 28 shows the financial institutions listed per the Central Bank Annual Report. Table 29 shows the top fifty in terms of gross assets.

Table 28   Financial Institutions with Banking Licences

Associated Banks
Allied Irish Banks plc
The Governor and Company of the Bank of Ireland
National Irish Bank Limited
Ulster Bank Limited

Non-Associated Banks
Merchant and Commercial Banks: Irish
   Allied Irish Investment Bank plc
   Anglo Irish Bank Limited
   Ansbacher and Company Limited

The Investment Bank of Ireland Limited
Northern Bank Finance Corporation Limited
Smurfit Paribas Bank Limited
Ulster Investment Bank Limited

Merchant and Commerical Banks: Other EEC
Algemene Bank Nederland (Ireland) Limited
Banque Nationale de Paris (Ireland) Limited
Barclays Bank Ireland Limited
Barclays Bank plc
Guinness and Mahon Limited
Hill Samuel and Company (Ireland) Limited
Irish Bank of Commerce Limited
Irish Intercontinental Bank Limited
Standard Chartered Bank Ireland Limited
Trinity Bank Limited

Merchant and Commercial Banks: Other International
Bank of America National Trust and Savings Association
The Bank of Nova Scotia
Chase Bank (Ireland) plc
Citibank NA
The First National Bank of Chicago
The Hongkong and Shanghai Banking Corporation

Industrial Banks:
Allied Irish Finance Company Limited
Anglo Irish Bank Corporation plc
Bank of Ireland Finance Limited
Bowmaker Bank Limited
Credit Finance Bank plc
Equity Bank Limited
First Southern Bank Limited
Lombard and Ulster Banking Limited
Mercantile Credit Company of Ireland Limited
The Thrift Company Limited
UDT Bank Limited
Waterford Penny Bank Limited

State-Sponsored Financial Institutions
Agricultural Credit Corporation plc
Industrial Credit Corporation plc

Post Office Savings Banks and Trustee Savings Banks
Post Office Savings Bank
Trustee Savings Bank Cork and Limerick
Trustee Savings Bank Dublin
Trustee Savings Bank Waterford

Source: Central Bank Annual Report.

Table 29   **Banks and Building Societies**

Rank			Gross Assets	Profit (Loss)		
1987	1986	Company	£m	£m	Year End	Main Activity
1	1	Allied Irish Banks	8516.0	102.10	31/03/87	Financial services
2	2	Bank of Ireland	8017.0	81.50	31/03/87	Banking
3	4	Central Bank of Ireland	2661.6	1178.0	31/12/86	Central bank
4	3	Ulster Bank	2660.0	34.9	31/12/86	Banking
5	—	Post Office Savings Bank	1250.0	N/A	31/12/86	National savings
6	7	Irish Permanent Building Society	1223.0	9.69	31/12/86	Building society
7	10	First National Building Society	798.4	3.65	31/12/86	Building society
8	11	Educational Building Society	661.1	6.53	31/12/86	Building society
9	9	Agricultural Credit Corporation	614.3	0.24	31/12/86	Banking
10	13	Industrial Credit Corporation	513.2	3.36	31/10/87	Development banking
11	8	GPA Group	486.0	47.8	31/03/87	Aircraft leasing/ financing
12	12	National Irish Bank	483.6	N/A	31/12/86	Banking
13	17	Banque National de Paris (I)	430.5	N/A	31/12/86	Banking
14	15	Banque Nationale de Paris (I)	415.2	N/A	31/12/86	Banking
15	21	Irish Intercontinenal Bank	405.0	N/A	31/12/86	Merchant banking
16	22	Cork & Limerick Savings Bank	383.0	1.25	30/11/87	Personal banking
17	24	Trustee Savings Bank — Dublin	290.0	1.00	20/11/87	Banking
18	16	Citibank N.A.	285.0	N/A	31/12/86	Banking
19	23	Bank of Nova Scotia	259.2	N/A	31/10/87	Banking
20	27	Irish Nationwide Building Soc.	234.0	9.09	31/12/86	Building society
21	25	Hill Samuel & Co. (I)	228.1	N/A	31/03/87	Merchant banking
22	29	Barclays Bank	192.2	N/A	31/12/86	Bank
23	35	ICS Building Society	183.9	0.98	31/12/86	Building society
24	28	Chase Bank (I)	183.0	N/A	31/12/86	International banking
25	36	Bank of America NT & SA	169.9	N/A	31/12/86	International banking
26	32	Smurfit Paribas	163.0	N/A	31/12/86	Corporate banking
27	30	Standard Chartered Bank Ire	163.0	N/A	31/12/86	International bankers
28	43	Woodchester Investments	157.0	7.40	31/12/87	Leasing/financial banking
29	34	UDT Bank	150.0	N/A	31/10/86	Banking
30	—	Anglo Irish Bank Corporation	140.0	1.45	30/09/87	Bank
31	38	Irish Bank of Commerce	120.6	N/A	31/12/86	Merchant bank
32	39	Mercantile Credit Co.	112.0	N/A	31/12/86	Industrial bankers
33	40	First National Bank of Chicago	100.0	N/A	31/12/86	Corporate banking
34	—	Ansbacher & Co. Ltd.	85.5	N/A	31/12/86	Merchant banking
35	42	Irish Life Building Society	81.0	N/A	31/12/87	Building society
36	44	HongKong/Shanghai Bank. Corp	79.0	N/A	31/12/86	Banking
37	47	Trustee Savings Bank-Waterford	63.5	0.04	20/11/87	Personal banking
38	—	Irish Mutual Building Society	58.0	0.69	31/12/86	Building society
39	46	First Southern Bank	57.0	N/A	30/09/87	Bankers

Insurance Companies

Rank 1987	1986	Company	Premium Income £m	Profit (Loss) £m	Year End	Main Activity
1	5	Irish Life Assurance plc	449.7	N/A	31/12/86	Life assurance
2	—	Voluntary Health Insur. Board	112.0	2.8	28/02/87	Healthcare insurance
3	26	Hibernian Group	105.6	7.7	31/12/86	General insurance
4	41	PMPA Insurance plc	86.1	9.8	31/12/86	General non-life insurance
5	48	Shield Life Insurance Co. Limited	83.3	N/A	31/12/86	Insurance
6	19	Insurance Corporation of Ireland	77.5	6.1	31/12/86	Insurance
7	33	Prudential Life of Ireland Limited	56.6	N/A	31/12/86	Life assur./pension/ invest.
8	14	Canada Life Assurance	55.7	N/A	31/12/86	Life assurance pension, PHI
9	49	FBD Insurance plc	41.6	1.4	31/12/87	General insurance
10	—	Abbey Life Assurance	37.7	N/A	31/12/86	Insurance
11	20	New Ireland Assurance Co. plc	36.5	1.6	31/12/86	Life assurance

Source: *Irish Business*, January 1988

Chapter 8

The Stock Exchange

Investors owning shares or debentures in businesses of various types often need to liquidate their investment. Companies, on the other hand, may wish to raise new capital from the public at large. The solution to both problems lies in the Stock Exchange—a market where shares and debentures may be bought and sold. Over 8 million people in Britain and Ireland invest in more than 9,000 different shares and bonds on the Stock Exchange.

The buying and selling of shares has gone on for hundreds or even thousands of years. In the eighteenth century business became widespread with a consequent growth in the amount of shares and debentures traded. Specialists, who bought and sold, developed in business centres such as Amsterdam, Stockholm and London. These specialists would meet daily to do business. At first, they had no formal meeting place so they used coffee houses or restaurants. Amsterdam was the first city to have a formal location. By 1772, the London Stock Exchange occupied premises in Sweeting Alley in the City of London. Business at that time was confined mainly to shares and debentures in trading companies, mining companies, canal building companies and government loans.

Wealthy people living in Ireland also wished to participate in the buying and selling of shares and debentures. A number of stockbrokers opened up for business. In 1793, twelve Dublin stockbrokers thought that they were doing sufficient business to organise a Dublin-based market. The market consisted largely of shares in canal companies, mining companies and government stocks. An Act of Parliament in Dublin in 1799 firmly established the Dublin Stock Exchange. The rules of the Dublin exchange were similar to those of its London counterpart. The Cork Stock Exchange opened for business on the South Mall in 1886.

At the same time as the Irish exchanges were developing, regional exchanges were growing throughout England. By 1960 it was realised that this multitude of local exchanges was not offering the best service to the investing public. Developments in communications meant that anyone in the British Isles using a telephone could be in instantaneous contact with a central exchange. A series of mergers took place in the United Kingdom, and also in Ireland, which culminated in the Irish exchange merging with the London exchange in 1973. The Irish exchange now operates in Anglesea Street in Dublin as a unit of the London Stock Exchange.

FUNCTIONS OF A STOCK EXCHANGE

The Stock Exchange performs many functions in a modern economy. Its primary functions are:

(1) To channel savings into investment. In 1987 alone, over £500 million was invested in new issues on the Irish unit of the stock exchange and eleven new companies were launched onto the exchange.

(2) To provide a market for existing shares and debentures. For example, in one ten-day account in March 1987, total purchases and sales amounted to £1,737 million, as shown in Table 30.

Table 30 Transactions on the Irish Stock Exchange in the Account Ended 20 March 1987[1]

Security	Number of Deals	Turnover £million
Irish Government Loans	2,630	1,532.1
Ordinary Shares of Irish Companies	7,796	192.6
Debentures of Irish Companies	112	0.24
British Government Loans	53	0.62
Ordinary Shares of British Companies	1,395	11.95
	11,986	1,737.51

1 Turnover for all of 1987 was in excess of £38,000 million.

(3) To act as an indicator of the economic health of the country. Trends in the prices of shares and debentures reflect the business confidence in the country. Governments keep a close eye on the Stock Exchange as trends there are reflected later in the economy.

(4) To provide safeguards for investors. The Stock Exchange carefully examines and regulates the activities of those businesses which are quoted on the exchange. In addition, its members, the stockbrokers and jobbers, have to abide by stringent rules which are designed to protect the investing public. Not many businesses would pass the examination of the Quotations Committee—the group that decides which shares may be quoted on the exchange. A special Stock Exchange Compensation Fund exists to pay in full investors who lose money because of actions by stockbrokers.

(5) To advise investors. The stock exchange, through the stockbroking members, provides a pool of competent advisors to assist the public.

ORGANISATION OF THE STOCK EXCHANGE (LONDON/DUBLIN)

Only Stock Exchange members may deal on the exchange. The general public buy and sell shares and other securities through agents, known as stockbrokers, who are members of the Stock Exchange. Membership is very tightly controlled and at present numbers 3,300. Prior to September 1986 and deregulation the members were split into two distinct groups: stockbrokers and jobbers.

Stockbroker

A stockbroker is an agent who buys and/or sells on behalf of clients. Apart from acting on behalf of clients, brokers often act as financial advisors. For their services stockbrokers receive a commission equal to $1\frac{1}{2}$ per cent of the value of the business carried out. They occasionally specialise in certain groups of shares or securities.

Stock Jobber

A jobber is a principal in that he buys or sells for his own account. Jobbers deal only with stockbrokers. A jobber may be called a wholesale buyer and seller of shares. A jobber operates by quoting two prices when approached by a broker or another jobber. The party approaching the jobber simply names the share of interest without stating whether they are buying or selling. Thus a jobber would quote two prices, say, 100—105. The higher quote, 105, represented the price at which the jobber would sell the share, and the lower quote, 100, represented the price at which he was prepared to purchase the share. The difference between the two quotes, 5, was known as the jobber's turn. Because a number of jobbers were active in any given type of share the prices quoted tended to be competitive and, as scope existed for shopping around a number of jobbers, quotes usually gave an accurate reflection of the worth of a share. Jobbers tended to specialise in certain categories of shares, for example, mining, oil, banks, stores, rubber. Jobbers disappeared in 1986.

Other parties may be involved in transactions on the exchange. An authorised clerk is usually a senior member of a jobbing or stockbroking firm who has the authority to trade on behalf of his employer. An unauthorised clerk is one who can enter the Stock Exchange building on behalf of his employers. To enter the building, the clerks used to wear buttons, the colour of which represented the work which the clerk could perform. Blue button men were senior clerks who carried orders between the stockbroker's office and the broker trading in the exchange. Red button men were junior clerks whose job it was to check the transactions made by the principals of their firm. This system of dealing which had survived for over 200 years came to an end in 1986.

Deregulation

'Big Bang' is often referred to as the deregulation of the financial markets. It could more correctly be referred to as re-regulation as what happened in September 1986 was the exchange of one set of rules for another. In the London context, the major changes were:

(1) The amalgamation of the role of stockbroker and the jobber. Since the Big Bang brokers and jobbers do the same work.

(2) Deregulation of commissions. Companies were allowed to compete when they were offering commissions on deals. Until the Big Bang the commissions were strictly set. Theoretically, since the changes investors are able to shop around not only for the best price for a share from position takers in the market but they can also look for the best commission from a market maker.

(3) Other changes include allowing outside companies to buy into existing Stock Exchange member companies and the buying of brokerages by banks.

(4) New types of gilt-edged dealers.

(5) New screen-based dealing systems.

(6) New investor protection legislation.

In Dublin the changes have been slower to take place and may not be as drastic. There are no jobbers in Dublin but brokers act as agents for investors executing their orders. It is still not clear whether Irish brokers will end up making a market in shares as the market is being deemed to be too small for that. It is likely that commissions will fall though, probably in line with London.

Under deregulation stockbrokers 'make markets' in certain shares. That is, they offer buy and sell prices for agreed lot sizes. Market makers are large prestigious well-financed companies.

All of the companies quoted on the Exchange are listed into four groups: Alpha, Beta, Gamma and Delta. The Alpha group comprises the largest and most secure companies such as Shell, ICI, Hanson, General Electric. There are numerous market makers in the shares of these companies. Quotations are competitive and lot sizes large—100,000 shares and up. Beta, Gamma and Delta companies have fewer market makers. In the case of Delta companies there may be no active market. As a consequence the share prices have a wider spread between bid and offer (buy and sell) and lot sizes are much smaller.

Irish companies trading in London are Beta or Gamma in most cases. Active shares such as Cement Roadstone Holdings and Smurfits may have up to four market makers.

The Big Bang has meant very little change in Dublin. Shares are still traded between brokers though most deals are now done by telephone. In

London the changes are greater. The new types of Gilt-Edged dealers created were primary dealers and inter dealer brokers. The primary dealers, being the market makers in government stock, play a vital role in the smooth operation of the market. They provide the market with its liquidity by being willing to quote two way prices in government stocks. To do so they need access to large amounts of capital. The Bank of England recognises the service they provide and assists them in several ways, by dealing only through them and also by allowing them both stock and cash borrowing facilities. In addition, they have certain tax advantages and access to the inter dealer brokers. These inter dealer brokers act as agents for transactions between the primary dealers and thereby facilitate the market by enabling transactions to be carried out by market makers without disclosing their positions.

The introduction of an electronic screen based dealing and pricing system—SEAQ—for the equity market was an overdue necessity for a market which was expanding rapidly. The millions of new investors created by the privatisation issues and the additional dealing created by the market makers in equities necessitated a 'real time' dealing and pricing system which could keep the market fully informed.

The final area of change was in relation to the introduction of legislation designed to regulate the activities of the participants and to protect investors. The legislation tries to combine the US method of pure statutory regulation with the British tradition of self-regulation. Whether the foreign firms in London, who are used to coping with statutory rules or no rules, will cope with the 'gentlemens' agreement' aspects of the new British system remains to be seen.

GETTING A STOCK EXCHANGE QUOTATION OR 'GOING PUBLIC'

There are only sixty-two Irish companies quoted on the Stock Exchange—Irish. The number was much higher but mergers, takeovers, and closures have reduced the total. For many years, the gaining of a stock exchange quotation was regarded as the pinnacle of success for a business. Recently, many companies have questioned the value of being quoted. Irish private companies such as Clerys, Dunnes Stores, Denis Coakley and Bell Ferries are larger than most of the quoted companies but for many reasons they have decided to remain unquoted.

The advantages of a Stock Exchange quotation are as follows:

(1) Access to a wider source of funds. A quotation on the exchange enables a company to raise larger sums from the public and, more importantly, from the large financial institutions These institutions,

insurance companies, unit trusts, investment trusts and pension funds, are generally unwilling to invest in private companies.

(2) The creation of an efficient market in the company's shares. This provides an opportunity for the original owners of the company to realise some or all of their reward for building up the company.

(3) Because the shares are marketable and have a value, it is possible to use them as means of paying for the takeover of another company. The share quotations reflect the fact that the company is a true entity distinct from its owners and that it has continuity apart from the original founders.

(4) The prestige attaching to having a Stock Exchange quotation. Greater publicity is possible, which results in benefits such as better credit ratings, consumer and government confidence, employees' morale, better management. Scope exists for using share option schemes as a carrot to attract top managers and workers.

The Stock Exchange insists on four main prerequisities for a company seeking a public quotation:

(a) A minimum market capitalisation of £15,000,000, that is, share price times number of shares. This is for a full listing.
(b) A minimum percentage of the shares to be held in the hands of public shareholders.
(c) At least 300 shareholders.
(d) A proven trading record which indicates that it is a company of a reputable nature achieving good profits.

The quotation being sought, Full-Listing, Unlisted Securities Market or Third Market decides the particular criteria to be used. Before the public can be approached to buy shares, the Stock Exchange itself must be satisfied that the company can be given a quotation. This initial procedure, prior to quotation, can be quite rigorous. The company usually appoints financial advisors to prepare the documentation and reports required to satisfy the Stock Exchange. The exchange, however, will only deal officially with one of its own members, so a stockbroker must be appointed to represent the company in negotiations. The advisors and the sponsoring broker will carry out a considerable amount of investigation into the business prospects and financial position of the company before a formal approach is made to the Stock Exchange. The detailed procedure for applying for a quotation is given in the 'Yellow Book' published by the exchange.

Once a company has been accepted by the exchange a decision must be made on the method whereby the public will be asked to buy shares. A company can 'go public', using one of the following five methods.

(1) Issue by Prospectus. A company offers shares to the public at a

given price. The advisors to the company prepare a prospectus which gives details of the firm's assets, earnings and management. It also gives details of the number of shares offered and their unit price. Strict regulations on drafting a prospectus are enforced by the Stock Exchange. A broker or merchant bank agrees to underwrite the issue, that is, they agree to buy any shares not applied for at the price stated in the prospectus. This method of issuing shares is rare in Ireland. It is also very expensive, costing up to 5 per cent of the proceeds.

(2) Offer for Sale. Often a merchant bank will buy a large block of shares in a private company. Over time, they will prepare the company to go public. When ready, the bank will offer their block of shares for sale to the public. This method is the most common form of going public in Ireland.

(3) Stock Exchange Placing. Raising new equity money is very expensive. A cheap way to 'go public' is to get a stockbroking firm to sell blocks of shares to various clients. The shares are 'placed' before the price is quoted on the exchange. The exchange expects at least 35 per cent of the shares to be sold to other stockbrokers. Money is saved by not having to issue a prospectus and by not having the operation underwritten.

(4) A Stock Exchange Introduction. The Stock Exchange will allow an 'introduction' only when the security in question is already quoted on another stock exchange or when it is widely distributed among the investing public. Usually an introduction is suitable only when the company is fairly well known. A sufficient number of shares must be made available to make a quotation meaningful. Normally this method is not a means of raising new finance for a company.

(5) An Offer by Tender. An unusual method of raising money is to issue a prospectus but no price. Bids are accepted at or above a stated price. Individuals can then decide how much a share in the company is worth and submit a tender. On a certain day the issue is closed, the tender bids are examined and a price accepted. All tenders above this price are accepted. People who tender at very high prices pay only the accepted price.

In 1987 eleven new companies went public in Dublin raising £24 million in new funds and valuing themselves at a total of £97 million. Almost all the new listings were Smaller Companies Market or Third Market. Only one, Power Securities, received a full listing. Two exploration companies, Burmin and Ovoca were introductions raising no new capital.

Often companies wish to raise new capital but do not want to affect the ownership or control of the company. They raise capital by means of a 'Rights Issue'. This means that existing shareholders are given the right to subscribe for new shares. The shares are priced attractively. Owners not wishing to take up their right to subscribe can sell the rights to other investors.

It was pointed out above that companies often do not pay out all the profits earned. Over time the returned profits can grow large and one effect may be a high share price. The psychology of the market is such that investors prefer a low price per share so that their investment purchases a large block of shares. Companies reduce their share prices by Bonus Issues of shares, that is, they capitalise earnings by turning the reserves into issued capital. Bonus issues are 'free' shares but they should not affect the total value of the company.

LISTING CATEGORIES AND DESCRIPTIONS

There are four levels of Stock Exchange listing:
(1) Full list.
(2) Unlisted Securities Market (USM).
(3) Third Market.
(4) Smaller Companies Market (SCM).

Full List

This has the most stringent set of listing requirements. Companies must have:
(a) A clean audited record for at least five years.
(b) A market capitalisation of £15 million when quoted.
(c) Profits of £750,000 per annum.
(d) At least 25 per cent of shares in the hands of the public.
A full listing is important for prestige, and because certain institutions have restrictions on their investment rules which confine them to shares of fully-listed companies.

Few Irish companies have the credentials for a full-listing. The listing of Power Securities in 1987 was only the second full-listing in fourteen years.

To accommodate the needs of companies wishing to have their shares quoted and to maintain the integrity of the Stock Exchange new categories of listings evolved in the 1980s.

Unlisted Securities Market (USM)

The USM was launched in November 1980 with a two-fold purpose. Principally, it was to provide a formal, regulated market designed to meet the needs of smaller less mature companies unlikely or unable to apply for a full official listing. Secondly, the USM brought under formal regulatory control of the Stock Exchange those unlisted companies whose securities were being freely traded under the provisions of Rule 163 (2) of the Stock Exchange. That rule permitted occasional bargains, subject to the permission of the Council, in the shares of unlisted public and private companies and whilst it will still be available in the future, it will be only on a more restricted basis. The USM was therefore designed as a separate, distinct market within the Stock Exchange, standing between official listing, on the one hand, and the restricted dealing facility of Rule 163 (2) on the other.

A further factor in the introduction of the USM was the low number of new entrants to the Stock Exchange during the 1970s.

The easiest and least costly way to get a quotation on the USM is by way of introduction. A broker/bank must be prepared to sponsor the company, and provided the company has a three-year profit record and minimum capital in public hands (10 per cent) then the only remaining hurdle is size. A USM company must have a capitalisation of at least £7 million.

Certain documents must be lodged with the Stock Exchange but there is nothing of an unduly onerous nature. If an introduction is taking place there is no need for a prospectus or an accountant's report though a report to shareholders may be sought.

A placing is the most common route used where there is a marketing operation by either the existing shareholders disposing of shares, or by the company in raising new money. The Stock Exchange has limited the sum to be raised on the USM by this method to IR£5 million. Where there is a placing, 25 per cent of the shares must be offered to the market.

In Ireland there is little evidence that the ratings given to USM companies are lower than they would achieve if they had a full listing. There appears to be no disadvantage in regard to share price between USM and full listing. However, there is a significant advantage in being on the USM compared to a full listing insofar as continuing obligations are concerned.

The requirements for circulating shareholders with information are not as stringent on the USM as the official market. Under a full listing a company is obliged to send a circular to its shareholders in the event that it makes an acquisition or disposal, where the profits or assets acquired or disposed of are greater than 15 per cent of its own profits or assets.

Where such profits or assets are greater than 25 per cent, the company must obtain its shareholders' approval for the transaction. In the case of USM companies the level at which a circular must be sent to shareholders is 25 per cent and not 15 per cent, and there is no specific obligation to obtain shareholders' approval if a transaction is above a certain size.

A USM company, however, must notify the Stock Exchange where the above tests shows a figure of 100 per cent or more and it is felt that in these circumstances, the Stock Exchange would generally require the transaction to be conditional on shareholders' approval.

The USM is a most versatile market in that it can accommodate quite small companies and ones with a large market capitalisation, such as FII plc valued in excess of £100 million in mid-February 1988.

Unfortunately, the USM market in Ireland has not taken off as was originally anticipated with only five companies quoted on the market at the moment. Once again costs and procedures were cited as the reason for the lack of interest, and the Stock Exchange response was to form the Third Market.

The Third Market

This over-the-counter (OTC) market is designed to make it easier for companies to raise equity finance than would be the case if they had to meet the requirements of a USM quote. It is a follow up to the initiative taken by the London Stock Exchange in providing an accessible market place with a suitable standard of investor protection for many of the shares, which are at present being traded outside the Stock Exchange on the OTC market. This new market is characterised by simplified, unexacting admission procedures and disclosure requirements which, while formal, are not onerous.

Companies must have a minimum capitalisation of £200,000 with no non-voting equity. Audited accounts and projections must be submitted to the Stock Exchange in time to permit adequate examination. Dealing will only be carried out in the open market. In other words, no after hours dealings. In addition, the Stock Exchange will make it clear that the companies quoted on the OTC are not officially listed on the Exchange and are not subject to scrutiny by the quotations department of the Stock Exchange.

The Irish Stock Exchange has adopted the Third Market for Irish mineral exploration companies, which means these companies will be subject to the same set of requirements in both Dublin and London. It would appear in Ireland that the Third Market will only apply to these mineral exploration companies, with other smaller companies being accommodated on the Smaller Companies Market.

Eglinton Oil and Gas plc is one of the four companies in Ireland to date to have joined the Third Market.

For a company to be considered for admission to the Third Market, a Member Firm of the Stock Exchange, that is, a stockbroker must have accepted the company's formal invitation to act as a sponsor. The guidance of candidate companies through the approval procedures will rest very much in the hands of the sponsoring stockbrokers and they will not be allowed to relinquish their responsibilities without informing the relevant Stock Exchange Committee.

Investors in companies traded on the Third Market should be appraised of the nature and extent of the risk which they are accepting in making such investments. Broker-dealers will, however, be required, under the new financial services regime, to demonstrate that any investment in a Third Market Stock is a suitable investment for the individual client for whom it is purchased and to be able to show a customer agreement letter in which Third Market stocks are explicitly mentioned before they may recommend or, if they have discretion, buy such stocks for a client. The Stock Exchange for its part has specified the wording of a 'risk warning' for inclusion in advertisements, circulars, and contract notes.

All investors in the Third Market initially will enjoy the full protection of the Stock Exchange Compensation Fund. This is designed to meet costs suffered by investors as a consequence of the failure of a Member Firm of the Stock Exchange.

Smaller Companies Market (SCM)

In March 1986, the Irish Stock Exchange, in response to the Government's concern with the limited flow of Irish private funds into small Irish companies set up a new market called the Smaller Companies Market. It was specifically designed to attract:

(a) Existing small Irish companies whose shareholders require a market quotation for their shares and the facility of disposing of all or part of their holdings.

(b) Small growth oriented companies wishing to finance their expansion through additional equity capital and reduce their reliance on borrowings.

(c) Companies approved for grant aid by the Industrial Development Authority.

(d) Companies approved under the Business Expansion Scheme.

Entry requirements are less onerous than for the Unlisted Securities Market (USM) and on the other hand there is less regulation by the ISE. There is a greater reliance on the professional advisers to the company to ensure compliance with legal requirements.

Provided a company has a sufficient spread of shareholders so as to enable a market to operate, has a trading record of at least one year and has the support of a sponsor (stockbroker/bank) then application can be made for quotation on the SCM. Costs are kept to a minimum by this way of entry. If there is a marketing operation—that is, if an SCM entrant wants to raise capital through the issue of securities to the public—it must produce a prospectus which will need an accountant's report in compliance with the Companies Acts 1963 to 1986.

The principal ongoing disclosure requirement for a company on the SCM is to disclose to the ISE any information necessary to enable shareholders to appraise the trading and financial position of the company and to avoid the establishment of a false market in the securities of the company.

After a slow start the response to the SCM has been enthusiastic. In 1987 eight companies went public on the SCM. These were: Sportsfield Equipment, Castletown Press, Oglesby and Butler, Superwood Holdings, Sunday Tribune, Classic Thoroughbred, Printech International and Reflex Investments. It is expected that a continuous stream of companies will come to this market.

A significant advantage of the SCM is the range of taxation reliefs which can apply to companies quoted on that market. Companies benefitting from the reliefs given to investment in certain corporate trades, commonly known as Business Expansion Scheme companies, and in research and development, retain those advantages on the SCM.

In addition, ownership of shares quoted on the SCM gives the shareholders a considerable advantage in terms of any capital gains tax payable on the sale of the shares. There is some doubt as to whether institutional investors would be interested in acquiring shares in companies listed on the SCM, due to the lack of regulation compared to the USM or official list, the likely size of the companies involved, lack of liquidity and investment rules in relation to certain investors.

DEALING ON THE EXCHANGE

The Stock Exchange operates in a series of accounts. A year is divided into twenty-three accounts, each of two weeks' duration, and two three-week accounts. The account begins on a Monday morning and ends the following Friday week. During the long history of the exchange a number of unusual and indeed rare practices have grown up, many of which derive from the slow communications of earlier times. One result is that payment for deals done is not due or made until nine days after the account ends. This gives adequate time for buyers to send in their money and for sellers to send in their share certificates.

The traditional procedure for dealing on the London Stock Exchange was as follows:

(1) An investor, having read an article on North Sea Oil, decides to buy some shares in British Petroleum. He telephones his stockbroker on a Tuesday morning, discusses the potential of BP and finally decides to buy

500 shares. The price of BP at the close of business on the previous day was £2.40 per share. The investor is willing to pay up the £2.50 for each share.

(2) A stockbroker telephones the order to his partner who is working in the Stock Exchange, that is, he is 'trading on the floor'.

(3) The partner goes to the section of the exchange where the oil jobbers are. He approaches a jobber and states 'BP'. The jobber will answer '240—260'. Since the price at which the jobber will sell is outside the investor's limits the stockbroker must do one of three things: go to another jobber seeking other quotations; challenge the jobber by offering £2.50 for shares in BP; ask the jobber to reconsider his quotes.

(4) The stockbroker moves onto another jobber who quotes '240—250'. The stockbroker strikes a 'bargain' for 500 BP shares at £2.50 each. He then transmits this information to his home office.

(5) Within forty-eight hours the investor will receive a contract note which informs him of the purchase, gives the total sum due and the date of settlement, that is, the day on which the jobber must be paid. Additional information on the note relates to stamp duty, commission, the date of the bargain and the type of share bought. An example of a contract note is shown in Table 31.

(6) Should the investor decide to sell BP shares before the end of the account he can do so without paying any additional commission and without having to pay the stamp duty. Assume for example, that the price of BP went to £3.10 in the week following the original purchase. The investor might decide to sell at £3.10, thus realising £1,550. Since his purchase price was £1,250 for the shares plus £20.63 commission for a total of £1,270.63, the profit for the venture would be £279.37.

(7) In this instance the investor decides to hold on to the shares. From the time of purchase until the Wednesday following the end of the account nothing happens.

(8) Ticket day is the Wednesday following the end of the account. It is on Ticket day that the process of linking the original seller and the final buyer begins. The buying broker, using a red button, issues a name ticket to the jobber from whom he bought the shares. The name ticket gives the full name and address of the buyer, the name of the share bought and the number of shares bought. From the jobber, it is sent to the seller's broker. If the shares have been dealt in more than once during the account, it will pass through several hands before reaching the seller's broker. From the name ticket, the selling broker prepares a transfer form, giving the name and address of his client and the buyer, and the details of the shares sold.

(9) On the Monday week following the end of the account, settlement

Table 31

Contract Note

GOODBODY JAMES CAPEL
Members of the Stock Exchange

Incorporated in the Republic of Ireland No. 54223
A COMPANY WITH UNLIMITED LIABILITY.

5 COLLEGE GREEN, DUBLIN 2.
TELEPHONE: 793888.
TELEFAX: 793868
TELEX: 93719

By order of:

JOHN TEELING ESQ.,

Bargain Date and Tax Point	Security	Account	Contract Ref.	Settlement Date
14 Sep. 87	+0664901	S(19)		05 Oct 87

WE THANK YOU FOR YOUR INSTRUCTIONS AND HAVE BOUGHT ON YOUR BEHALF AS AGENTS
OVOCA GOLD EXPLORATION I£0.02

Time	Quantity	Price	Consideration
09:37	3000	0.50	I£ 1,500.00
	3000		I£ 1,500.00

TRANSFER STAMP (N)   15.00

COMMISSION   7.50

	TOTAL
	I£ 1,522.50

Members of the Stock Exchange

Please retain this document for Capital Gains Tax and VAT purposes.

CONTRACT NOTE AND TAX INVOICE

/15

JOHN TEELING ESQ.,
BELGROVE ROAD,
CLONTARF,
DUBLIN 3.

Notes for your attention:-

EFFECTED IN ACCORDANCE WITH THE RULES &
REGULATIONS GOVERNING THE THIRD MARKET. THIS
INVESTMENT MAY CARRY A HIGH DEGREE OF RISK.

Subject to the Rules and Regulations of the
Stock Exchange including any temporary
requisitions made by, or under its authority at
the Council of the Stock Exchange.

E. & O.E.

day is reached. On settlement day, cash changes hands, as do share certificates and share transfer forms. The share certificate is then sent to the Registration Department of BP. The company registrar will issue a new certificate in the buyer's name.

It is important to note that the investor is not involved in the complicated dealing pattern outlined above. He simply gives the order to the stockbroker and pays cash on or before the settlement day. Table 32 gives a visual description of the workings of the stock exchange account.

Two unusual items appear in Table 32, Contango Day and New Time Dealings. Contango Day is the day on which buyers can persuade sellers to postpone seeking payment for a further account period. If the seller agrees, then the buyer receives a further twenty-two days credit, that is, until the next settlement day. Contango is the fee charged by the seller to the buyer. It is a rate of interest usually higher than that charged on overdrafts. In certain circumstances, the seller cannot deliver the shares to the buyer and asks for a postponement. If this is granted, the buyer is paid a fee known as backwardation.

New time dealings are transactions completed for the new account during the last two days of the old account. Buyers using new time dealings effectively get an extra fourteen days' credit. They pay a charge, often one penny extra per share, for this privilege.

'Big Bang' caused a change in the way shares were bought and sold. Now a broker watches a video screen. An order can be immediately filled by accepting the offers or bids as the case may be which market makers have placed on their screens. The floor of the exchange is now empty, jobbers are extinct. Every bargain is now made electronically.

Dealing on the Stock Exchange—Irish Unit

The main difference between the two parts of the exchange is that there is little market making in Dublin. There would be insufficient business to support market makers since there are less than 200 quoted securities in Dublin compared to 9,000 plus in London.

The seventeen stockbroking partnerships in Ireland make up a broker-to-broker market. Once an Irish stockbroker receives an order to buy an Irish share he will attempt to find a seller. Stockbrokers in Ireland operate in two ways.

(1) They meet twice daily to fix prices. At these meetings each security is called out by name. If there are buyers and sellers, attempts are made to match, buy and sell orders. If a deal is struck the price is marked on a large board which contains the names of all of the securities with Irish quotations. It is expected that this ancient method of marking deals will disappear in coming years.

Table 32   The Account of the Stock Exchange

Monday	Day 1	Account begins
	2	
	3	Bargain made. Bought 500 BP
	4	
	5	
	6	} Closed
	7	
	8	
	9	
	10	
	11	New Time Dealings
Friday	12	Account ends Contango Day
	13	} Closed
	14	
Monday	15	New Account begins
	16	
	17	Ticket Day
	18	
	19	
	20	} Closed
	21	
Monday	22	Settlement Day

(2) Outside the exchange, stockbrokers are in constant contact,· attempting to match, buy and sell orders. If a deal is done outside the exchange it is marked in the exchange at the next meeting of brokers.

Apart from broker-to-broker dealings, the Irish unit of the Stock Exchange operates in an identical fashion to the London exchange. If an Irish investor wishes to purchase shares quoted in London he can do so through Irish stockbrokers who will approach a market maker on the floor of the London exchange.

TYPES OF SHARES AND DEBENTURES QUOTED ON THE STOCK EXCHANGE—IRISH

The range of securities quoted in Ireland has been declining in recent years, so that in early 1988 a total of only 187 issues existed. These are divided as follows:

Government Lands and Land Bonds	61
Transport Company Stocks (CIE)	3
Corporation and Semi-State Loans	23
Commercial Fixed Interest Loans and Preference Shares	33
Ordinary Shares of Financial Institutions	5
Ordinary Shares of Industrial Companies	62

Government Bonds

These are divided between Government Funds and Land Bonds. They are securities issued by the government and represent their borrowings from the public to meet capital expenditure on such items as roads, hospitals and defence. They are gilt-edged securities with no risks attached. They bear a fixed rate of interest guaranteed by the government, and in most cases are repayable at their face value on some future date.

Corporation, Semi-State and Transport Bonds

These are identical to government bonds except that they are indirectly guaranteed by the state. These are gilt-edged securities and are generally used to finance major capital investment projects. The major borrowers include the Dublin and Cork Corporations, Coras Iompair Eireann and the Electricity Supply Board.

Debentures and Preference Share Issues

These include all preference shares, debentures and loan stocks issued by commercial concerns. Debentures and loan stocks represent borrowings by companies at a fixed rate of interest. Usually such issues carry a promise of repayment at a future date. The security to the investor in each case therefore is as good as the company's credit. Often these loan stocks are secured on certain assets of the company which, in the event of it getting into financial difficulties, means that loan stockholders must be paid off in full before any payment is made to shareholders.

Preference Shares are shares entitled to a fixed rate of dividend and this dividend must be met from profits prior to any payment of dividends to the ordinary shareholders.

Ordinary Shares

The holders of these shares are the owners of the company. All remaining profits, after loan interest and preference dividends are paid, belong to these ordinary shareholders. However, it is both customary and prudent to provide for the replacement of existing assets and future expansion (purchase of new assets) and so companies tend to retain some of the profits that in theory the ordinary shareholders can claim in full. Those profits not retained are then distributed to the ordinary shareholders in the form of dividends. Dividends on ordinary shares generally fluctuate in line with profits; often dividends are not paid in bad times. Ordinary shares, while carrying the greatest risks, also hold the best prospects of future growth, particularly in capital appreciation, that is, an increase in the market price of the share. The marked price of ordinary shares is determined not so much by past results as by expected future results.

First-class shares are known as 'blue chip'. This denotes low risk and stable earnings.

There are two markets in Dublin, one in the government stocks and the other in the ordinary shares. The gilt market is by far the more important, accounting for around 80 per cent of the total market value. The person who makes the market in government stock is the Government Broker (the GB). He works for the Department of Finance and the Central Bank, buying and selling gilts. As of 1988 the GB is Ken Beaton of Butler and Briscoe. He is appointed for a set term.

In theory the market happens in this way. In the morning the gilt dealers, who work for the stockbroking firms, take a market overview. They look at money market interest rates, international rates, foreign exchange rates and other factors such as political ones which could affect a market. Having done this they take a position on the market and then ring their customers who are mainly the pension funds and advise them on a course of action. When the funds work out what they should do they give a sell or buy order to the gilt dealers who in turn go to the GB and offer to buy or sell stock. Depending on the amounts of stock to be dealt the GB can make a rapid or a very slow decision on what he plans to do. The decision can take up to two hours to come to. These decisions have to be made twice a day and the system is called 'call over'.

As can be seen it is a slow and inefficient system and one with which many if not all of the main players are dissatisfied. Fund managers are often left not knowing what direction the market is going and this can last for several days, as has happened recently. It is also very uneasing for those interested in interest rate directions since the yields on the various government stocks determine, to an extent, the money market rates or at least mirror them. Money market rates can move around if the GB effectively does not want to deal, while for days on end the yield on the gilts does not move at all.

It is estimated the gilt market in Ireland is worth roughly £8 billion. This pales when compared with the size of the British gilt market, which is worth £100 billion. The number of players in the market is also very small, with only ten main institutions making up the bulk of the market and three of those, Irish Life, AIB and the Bank of Ireland, accounting for over 40 per cent of the market.

There are really only four leading stockbroking firms in the gilt market. Figures are never released but it is estimated that there would not be a huge difference between Davys, Riada and National and City Brokers/Dillon and Waldron while Goodbody Dudgeon would be in the fourth place. Davy's has sold a third of the company to Citicorp, Riada is owned by a Dutch bank, NCB/Dillon and Waldron are believed to want to remain independent while Goodbody Dudgeon has sold 40 per cent to James Capel.

Activity on the Irish Stock Exchange was at a very low ebb in the 1970s and early 1980s. The five-year 'bull' market which came to an end in October 1987 saw a major increase in activity. Table 33 shows the equity funds raised in Dublin in the five years 1981–1985.

It must be acknowledged that the size of the Irish market is not independent of the industrial structure and tax regime. Agribusiness is

Table 33   *Funds raised on the Irish Stock Market 1981-85*
(Expressed as £'000,000)

	Industry	Financial	Oils	Other	Total
1985	16.5	0.3	27.9	16.7	61.4
1984	34.4	46.4	20.5	2.0	103.3
1983	13.9	1.9	28.8	6.3	50.9
1982	14.2	2.8	2.0	2.5	21.5
1981	25.5	33.6	23.3	3.8	86.2
Total 1981-5	104.5	85.0	102.5	31.3	323.3

mainly undertaken by co-operatives, which to date, with the exception of some co-ops, have relied on a narrow equity base and heavy borrowings. Industry has been dominated by wholly-owned subsidiaries of multi-national or transnational corporations whose funding comprises IDA grants, bank borrowings and parent company loans and equities.

The capital gains tax rates of as high as 60 per cent have also had a negative impact on the domestic equity market leading to a potentially volatile market where holders of stock are unwilling to sell as prices rise, thus creating an artificial shortage; as prices fall, a substantial supply of stock is forthcoming adding to the downward pressure on prices.

Balanced against the foregoing is the high cost of bank finance relative to inflation and the modest cost of raising funds in the various markets now available. The cost of a fund-raising exercise in Dublin is far lower than in the US with normal underwriting commission in Dublin of 2 per cent to 2.5 per cent versus New York of around 7 per cent. Fund-raising on the new SCM is likely to be even lower with the fixed cost element of covering professional fees under £0.1 million.

SPECULATION

Ever since time began people have speculated. They have been prepared to invest capital in the hope that their reading of the situation is better than that of the market as a whole.

The Stock Exchange is an ideal medium of speculation. The delays between arranging the bargains and making the settlement provides outstanding opportunities for speculation. Speculators on the Stock Exchange are referred to by different names, depending on the nature of their speculative activities. The major types of speculators are bulls, bears, stags, and pigs. 'Lame ducks' also exist.

Bulls

A bull is a speculator who buys now, expecting an immediate rise in price. Bulls buy shares in the hope that they will quickly rise in price so that they can be sold at a profit before settlement day. Should this occur then no actual financial outlay is required on the part of the bull. If, however, the expected rise in price fails to materialise within the account period, the bull has a choice: he can sell the shares and suffer a loss or he can postpone settlement until the next account, hoping the price will have risen by then. In the event of postponement, he may either pay a fee to the broker from whom he bought the shares (contango) or sell the shares for cost at a fixed price to a dealer and then buy them back again at the same price for the next account. He pays a commission of $1\frac{1}{2}$ per cent to do this.

Bears

A bear is a speculator who sells shares he does not own, anticipating that he can buy them back at a lower price before the end of the account. If such a fall does not materialise the bear either buys at a higher price and suffers a loss, or postpones settlement by paying backwardation to a broker who lends him shares to complete the deal he has made with the original buyer.

Stags

A stag is a speculator who applies for a large quantity of a new issue expecting that the initial price of the share when quoted on the stock exchange will be higher than the issue price. He can then sell his shares at a profit.

Prior to the 1970s the stag's operation was easier, as new issues often required only part payment on application and allotment. Now, however, almost all new issues require payment in full on application. Irish issues of recent times have tended to be over-subscribed, causing the initial stock exchange price quotation to be in excess of the issue price. The stag's problem, then, is to be allotted enough shares. Stagging declined in the mid 1970s but recently it has become more prevalent in the United Kingdom. In general, new share issues are priced to cause a premium when quotation begins so the stag is usually successful.

Pigs

A legendary United States speculator was once asked to account for his great success. 'I always bought and sold at the wrong time,' he declared. The pig is a speculator who does not know when to take a profit. He is determined to make every last penny, forgetting that speculative changes in share prices are volatile and can easily reverse themselves. Stock exchange lore has a saying, 'pigs never make profit'.

Lame Ducks

A 'lame duck' is one who cannot meet his commitments. One early account of the London Stock Exchange recalls how in 1787 at one account day 'twenty-five lame ducks waddled out of the Alley', that is, the location of the exchange. A lame duck is a very rare bird on the modern exchange though rampant speculation in oil stocks in 1984 produced a small number.

OPTIONS

A sophisticated form of speculation is by means of options. These are rights to buy, sell or buy/sell at previously agreed prices.

An option is a contract between a buyer known as a 'holder' and a seller, known as a 'writer'. Options may be of three types: call options, put options or put and call options.

A call option entitles the buyer to purchase shares from the writer at a fixed price called the 'striking' price. The buyer of a call option expects the price to rise. The price paid for this right is known as an 'option premium'. It is usually a price per share.

A put option is a right to sell a certain share at an agreed price. The purchaser of a put option expects the price of the share to fall.

Sometimes, an individual expects a swing in the price of a share though he is unsure of the direction. For example, an investor expects that the price of Aran Energy will be subject to a heavy movement up or down depending on the results of exploration drilling. In such a situation one buys the right to either buy or sell the shares at an agreed striking price. This is the put and call option.

Options are normally for periods of three months. At any time during the ninety-day period the option can be exercised. Options are expensive. In early 1980 a call option in Northgate, then selling at $7.50 per share was $1.50 or 20 per cent. In Silvermines it was possible to purchase a put option to sell the shares at £1.40 each at a cost of 20 pence per share. To all intents and purposes options do not exist on the Irish Stock Exchange.

An option is a way of gearing up or levering one's investment while at the same time hedging one's risk. An example will illustrate.

An investor with £3,000 is interested in purchasing shares in Blue Sky plc. He can purchase 3,000 shares at £1 each or he can:

(a) Purchase an option to buy 3,000 shares at £1 each at an option price of 12 pence each or £360.

(b) Buy £3,000 worth of options giving him the right to buy 25,000 Blue Sky shares

$$\text{that is } \frac{£3,000}{12 \text{ pence}} = 25,000 \text{ shares}$$

Assume that the share stands at £1.20 at the end of the option period. Our investor now has one of the following outcomes.

Investment	Cost	Value	Profit
3,000 shares at £1 each	£3,000	£3,600	£600
Options on 3,000 shares	360	600	240
Options on 25,000 shares	3,000	5,000	2,000

However, if the price rises to only £1.12 the option agreements provide no profit while the straight investment does.

The London Stock Exchange introduced the concept of traded options in 1980. This system currently applies to a small number of top-quality British shares. Under it call options may be negotiated for a three-, six-, or nine-month period. The call options are for lots of 1,000 shares. These options can be traded in the market thereby reducing the risk exposure of the investor. It is expected that the number of shares on which traded options may be written will expand.

THE FINANCIAL PAGES OF THE NEWSPAPERS

Movements on the Stock Exchange have long held a fascination for the ordinary man in the street.Newspapers and periodicals report trends in share prices in great detail. In Ireland the morning newspapers carry at least one full page of financial news, most of which is devoted to activity on the Stock Exchange. Each Monday morning the national dailies carry a review of each quoted bond or share. In addition to giving the current market price the papers also provide information which will assist investors in deciding whether or not a share is a worthwhile investment.

Among the measures used by the media are:
(a) Earnings per share.
(b) Earnings yield.
(c) Price earnings or P/E ratio.
(d) Dividend yield.
(e) Cover.
(f) Ex and cum dividend.
(g) Redemption yield.
(h) 'Blue chips' or 'first line' shares.
(i) 'The Index'.

Earnings per share (EPS)

This is the annual profit (earnings) of the business divided by the number of shares outstanding. It is that portion of the annual profit attributable to one share. Note that the profit figure used is that reported by the company.

Earnings Yield

This is the earnings per share divided by the current market price. For example in early 1986 Abbey Ltd had earnings per share of 15.85 pence and a then price per share in the market of 185 pence. The earnings yield is as follows:

$$\text{Earning yield} = \frac{15.85}{185} = 9\%$$

This percentage figure is a rough measure of the return on the investment, that is, every 185 pence investment earned profits of 15.85 pence. This yield is an historical yield in that it divides the present market price into the reported profits of the company. Remember that profits are reported months after the end of the financial year, so it is possible that major changes in earnings will have taken place.

Price/Earnings Ratio

This widely used measure of investment worth is defined as follows:

$$\text{P/E Ratio} = \frac{\text{Market Price of the Share}}{\text{Earnings Per Share}}$$

This represents the period of time required to recover the purchase price assuming that earnings per share remain constant. It is the inverse of the earnings yield.

In this case of Abbey the ratio was:

$$\frac{\text{Market Price}}{\text{Earnings Per Share}} = \frac{185}{15.85} = 11.7$$

The P/E ratio for all shares quoted in Dublin are published each Monday morning. An investor can cast his eye along the list, picking out anomalies. In early 1988 the average P/E ratio was between 11 and 12, so Abbey appeared average.

Dividend Yield

Typically a company pays out a proportion of its profits to the shareholders. The cash payout is known as a dividend. The dividend yield is defined as follows:

$$\frac{\text{Dividend Per Share}}{\text{Market Price Per Share}}$$

In 1987, Abbey paid a dividend of 5 pence on each share. Therefore, in 1987, after the market price adjustment of October 1987 the dividend yield for Abbey was:

$$\frac{5}{185} = 2.7\%$$

Confusion often arises in this area because dividends are declared as a percentage yield on the nominal value of the share. Every share when first issued has a nominal value of, say, £1.00, 25 pence or 10 pence. The issue price is very often above the nominal price, thus creating a share premium. The nominal price is a hangover from olden times and has little relevance apart from the fact that dividends are declared on it. Abbey shares are in 25 pence units. In 1987 a dividend of 20 per cent was declared on the nominal price. This produced a yield of 2.7 per cent on the market price.

Cover

Total profits are rarely paid out as dividends because the directors usually decide to retain some to assist investment. The 'cover' is the relationship of earnings to dividends. It is defined as:

$$\frac{\text{Earnings Per Share}}{\text{Dividends Per Share}} = \frac{15.85}{5.00} = 3.17$$

A high cover means that the dividend can continue to be paid even if earnings drop. It may also mean that there are many investment opportunities open to the business so there is the possibility of rapid growth in future earnings. A cover of less than 1 means that the business is paying dividends out of reserves.

Ex and Cum Dividend

Shares which are sold with the right to collect an imminent dividend are sold 'Cum Div'. If the seller retains the right to the dividend the shares are sold 'Ex Div'. In theory the share price should reflect the value of the dividend.

Redemption Yield

This measure applies to loan stocks. Loan stocks are repaid or redeemed at some future date. Usually the market price differs from the repayment or redemption price. Therefore an investor obtains not only the right to the interest payments but also the right to the premium or discount on redemption. Loans are rarely priced above the redemption price but they are frequently at a major discount. For example, in early 1988 an ESB loan paying $7\frac{1}{4}$ per cent annual interest and repaying £100 per unit of stock, sometime between 1988 and 1993, could be purchased at

£84.00. The redemption yield is the annual earnings yield plus the capital profit. This equals:

$$\frac{7.25\% \times 100}{84} + \frac{16}{5}\ \%$$

$$= 8.6\% + 3.2\ \%$$

$$= 11.8\%$$

where

7.25	=	annual interest.
100	=	issue and redemption price.
84.00	=	market price January 1988.
16.00	=	discount between market and redemption price.
5	=	length of time in years until redemption.

This overestimates the redemption yield because £100 in 5 years time will have less value than £100 now. The exact formula for redemption yield is

$$\text{Redemption Yield} = \text{Flat Yield} + \left(\frac{[RP - MP]\ \frac{r}{100}}{\left[1 + \frac{r}{100}\right]^n - 1} \right)\%$$

where

RP	=	redemption price
MP	=	market price
r	=	annual interest rate
n	=	number of years to redemption.
Flat Yield	=	$\dfrac{\text{annual interest rate}}{\text{current market price}} = 8.6\%$

Luckily stockbrokers issue daily lists of the redemption yields on loan stocks so it is rarely necessary to work out the above formula. Applying the formula to the ESB stock gives a redemption yield of 11.54 per cent.

Blue Chips

Blue chips are the strongest and most reputable shares on the market. These are shares with a history of top-class financial performance. In Dublin, shares such as AIB, Bank of Ireland, Cement Roadstone Holdings and Smurfits rank as 'blue chip'. Such shares are also known as first-line shares in that they are the first to rise at the outset of a bull market.

Second-line shares are regarded as being of a lower quality in that they may have less stable earnings patterns, be in a poorer quality industry, have suspect management or simply be relatively unknown or closely held, thus providing a poor market in the shares. At the opposite end of the spectrum from blue chip are blue-sky shares. These are highly speculative issues where there is no pattern of earnings or management. Small speculative exploration stocks epitomise this term.

The Index

There are a number of stock exchange indices in use. In the United States the Dow Jones index is the most important while in the United Kingdom movements in the *Financial Times* index are carefully monitored. In Ireland the *Irish Times* and *Irish Independent* each produce an index.

The Dow Jones index is composed of thirty blue chip shares. Every company in the index is valued at the number of shares times the market price per share. The index is the arithmetic average of the sum of the market value of all of the shares in the index. A change in a share price will change the total value and thus change the index. The *Financial Times* index is also based on thirty shares.

The two Irish indices were developed in the mid 1970s. Each is an aggregate index which means that it is the sum of the market value of all quoted shares. In theory the movements of an index reflect general investor sentiment. An upward movement suggest more buyers than sellers while a downward trend suggests an excess of sellers.

A glossary of stock exchange terms is presented in the final section of this chapter.

PORTFOLIO SELECTION

Ultimately an investor must decide what shares and loan stocks to purchase. The combination of shares purchased is known as a 'portfolio'. An investor selects a portfolio of shares whose risk, expected income and expected capital gains best meet his needs. This apparently simple statement is fraught with complexity. Every investor dreams of shares such as Eglinton which rose from 20 pence to £12 in one year. Attaching to the Eglintons of this world is a huge risk. Many investors, while seeking the return, will not take the risk. In fact, investors in Eglinton saw the share price crash back to virtually nothing. Investors have different preferences and needs, some want little risk of loss, others want income, while others wish to speculate in the hope of significant capital gain. Determining the mix of shares which an investor should purchase is known as portfolio composition or selection. A simple approach to the problem involves two steps: (a) decide on investment objectives; (b) select shares to meet the objectives.

Investment Objectives

Investors objectives can be broken into four categories: (a) income; (b) income and capital gain; (c) capital gain and income; (d) capital gain. The length of time for which an investor is willing to invest funds is also part of the objective. Examples of investors at either end of the investment spectrum would be a retired couple with school-going children and a capital sum to invest. Compare this to a wealthy individual paying the top rate of income tax seeking to speculate a sum which he/she can easily afford to lose. The main determinant is the degree of risk which the investor is willing to take.

Selecting Shares to Meet Objectives

Once the objectives are known, a portfolio of shares must be selected and a decision made on how much to invest in each. The retired investor seeking secure income might look no further than government loans. The wealthy speculator might split his investment between oil exploration shares such as Aran Energy and Kenmare Resources, recovering companies such as Seafield and maybe a takeover prospect such as Heitons.

Not surprisingly, a great deal of research has gone into portfolio selection. A body of principles called portfolio theory now exists. Much of the seminal work was done by Harry Markowitz who developed a model of investor behaviour. Markowitz assumed that investors sought the highest return at the lowest possible risk. His model became known as the Mean-Variance Portfolio Composition Model. Readers interested in pursuing the topic are referred to the readings at the end of this chapter.

At a more basic level a number of steps can assist an investor in selecting a portfolio which meets his objectives. Such an investor should:
   (a) Identify objectives.
   (b) Decide on industries and/or business sectors with risk profiles suited to the objectives.
   (c) Gather information on the industries, trends over time, relationship to the economy, structure, competitive advantages, future threats or opportunities.
   (d) Examine the companies in each sector to identify those likely to perform in a way most suited to the objective of the portfolio.
   (e) Analyse the past performance of the company using the measures presented above and those in Chapter 3.
   (f) Identify the availability and marketability of shares in selected companies.
   (g) Discuss potential purchases with a stockbroker.
   (h) Purchase shares in round figure lots.
   (i) Monitor the performance of the portfolio on a regular basis.

The following is a simple summary of portfolio selection.

Object	*Portfolio Strategy*
Major requirement, income with no risk.	Invest in government bonds.
Income a requirement but want some opportunity for capital appreciation.	Mixture of gilt-edged bonds and blue chip shares.
Want investment to keep up with inflation.	Blue-chip shares assuming a medium-term investment period.
Capital appreciation more important than income, willing to take some risk.	Mixture of first and second-time securities.
Want high returns, willing to take high risk.	Look for speculative shares.

REGULATIONS ON THE STOCK EXCHANGE

The Stock Exchange is very careful to avoid, where possible, any suspicion that share prices are manipulated or that the small investor is getting less than a fair deal.

Each company quoted on the exchange abides by a listing agreement which controls information on such things as notification of profits, changes in the directors, issuance of accounts and share transfers. One aspect of Stock Exchange activity which is now strictly regulated is that of takeovers. It is an investor's dream to have inside knowledge of a proposed takeover. To protect investors a Panel on Takeovers and Mergers was established. This panel issued a series of rules for takeovers. These rules are known as the 'City Code on Takeovers and Mergers' and are contained in the 'Blue Book'. The principal rules refer to (a) the need for secrecy, (b) the behaviour of the bidders and (c) the behaviour of the directors on both sides. In effect a company which buys 30 per cent or more of the voting shares of a quoted company must bid for all of the shares.

STOCK EXCHANGE CYCLES

The period 1955-79 was not good to the Stock Exchange. Investors gradually became disenchanted with low returns and moved their funds to other areas such as property, art and stamps. Gradually the large institutional investors such as pension funds, insurance companies and unit trusts came to dominate the market. Such investors had income with the prospect of some capital gain as their objective and so they concentrated on low-risk 'blue chip' shares and government loans. Rampant inflation proved disastrous for investors. For generations it was believed that share prices were a hedge against inflation. The '60s and '70s proved otherwise. Towards the end of the 1970s life began to re-appear in stock exchanges. Many shares were simply cheap. They had good earnings or alternatively high assets. Inflation during the '70s made many companies asset-rich. Shrewd investors found it cheaper to buy rather than build, that is, it was cheaper to take over existing business than to build new ones from scratch. New terminology evolved to define unacceptable bidders as 'grey knights', rapid takeovers as 'Saturday night specials' and acceptable purchasers as 'white knights'.

The Irish Stock Exchange experienced a pattern of evolution similar to that experienced in the United Kingdom and United States.

The 'Great Bull Market' began in 1982 and lasted for over five years — a record length of time for a bull market. Substantial rises in share prices took place in each of the years 1982-6. The US Dow Jones Index rose by 350 per cent, in this period the Financial Times Index did even better rising over four times (see Figure 6). The good times also visited Ireland.

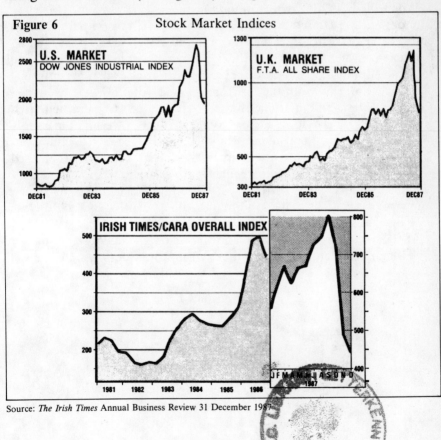

Figure 6   Stock Market Indices

Source: *The Irish Times* Annual Business Review 31 December 1987

The few shares available, exchange restrictions and rising institutional cash inflows combined to produce a strongly rising market: this despite a weak and declining economic performance in the country.

As happens in most bull markets, prosperity led to growing confidence. Confidence fed on itself to produce euphoria. In 1987 worldwide stock markets boomed at a rapid rate. Despite the huge rises of the previous five years the markets grew by a further 40 per cent between January and October 1987.

Fundamental values and negative economic signals were ignored. Markets operated on the 'Greater Fool Theory', that is that there would always be a buyer available at even higher prices.

Certain companies' share prices were selling at values which anticipated almost impossible outcomes. Gold mining shares were selling at up to 100 years' earnings though the companies had gold reserves for only twenty years. The expectation was of a rapidly rising gold price.

Blue chip companies such as Smurfit were selling on Dividend Yields of 1 per cent thus anticipating high rises in capital values.

When the fall came it was unique in the level of severity. 'Meltdown Monday' in the United States, 19 October 1987, saw 25 per cent of the entire value of Wall Street wiped out in one day. This compares with 12 per cent on the worst day of the 1929 crash. Around the world panic replaced euphoria. Almost without exception stock exchanges crashed by 40 per cent and more in the last three months of 1987.

The greatest bull market of the twentieth century crashed in the greatest fall in the long history of exchanges. Overnight pessimism replaced confidence and fears of a substantial recession in the United States economy became a reality in 1988. World stock markets entered a bear market phase where weak rallies in share prices were snuffed out by precipitous falls. After 'Meltdown Monday' subsequent peaks were below previous highs while lows plumbed new depths. By 1988 a classic bear market seemed to be in progress.

At the beginning of the nineteenth century a French observer of stock exchange movements categorised activity into the following cycle.

Period	Relevance to Recent Stock Exchange Activity
Quiescence	— 1975-9
Confidence	— 1980-81
Prosperity	— 1982-6
Euphoria	— 1987
Convulsion	— 19 October 1987
Panic	— October 1987-early 1988
Quiescence	— Early 1988-?

Every share price represents hope—a price is the present value of the sum of all future expectations. In good times hopes are high, in bad times expectations are low, hence the large swings in share prices between 'bull' and 'bear' phases.

The 1988 bear market will cease when panic and forced selling is over and when investors refuse to sell because they believe the prices to be too cheap.

GLOSSARY OF STOCK EXCHANGE TERMS

Account Day
This is the day on which payment is made, or received, for business done in the previous account. It is normally the Monday of the week following the end of the account.

Allotment Letter
A person who applies for a new issue of shares is informed by allotment letter of the number of shares which he has been allotted.

Anomaly
This is a share price which, for one reason or another, is out of line with market prices.

Application Form
This is a special form on which application for share issues must be made. The forms are printed in the daily press and are available from stockbrokers and banks.

Backwardation
A bear who cannot deliver shares which he has sold can postpone delivery by borrowing shares to deliver. The fee paid to borrow the shares is known as backwardation.

Bargain
Any transaction on the stock exchange.

Bear
A person who has sold shares which he does not own, in the hope of buying the shares back at a lower price before he has to deliver the shares.

Bearer Shares
Shares which have no central register. Whoever holds the share certificate owns the shares.

Big Bang

September 1986, when deregulation was introduced to the stock exchange. The principal effect was the replacement of jobbers by market makers.

Blue Chips

Top-quality shares, usually in large stable industrial or financial firms. Irish blue chips include Bank of Ireland, Cement Roadstone Holdings, Allied Irish Banks and Smurfits.

Bull

A person who has bought shares, hoping to sell them at a profit before he has to pay for them.

Call

Certain shares are only partly paid up. Demands by the company for some or all of the unpaid amount is a 'call'. There are no partly paid shares on the Irish stock exchange.

Call Option

The right to buy a share at an agreed price for an agreed period.

Capitalisation Issue

Where a company has reserves of undistributed profit they may capitalise part or all of the reserves by issuing additional shares to existing shareholders. This is also known as a Scrip Issue or Bonus Issue.

Commission

The fee charged by a stockbroker. Usually $1\frac{1}{2}$ per cent. It is also known as 'brokerage'.

Consideration

The price paid for a purchase exclusive of commission and stamp duty.

Contango

This is the price paid by a bull to postpone paying for shares which he has bought. The contango is a rate of interest charged to 'carry over' the deal for one account.

Contango Day

The last day of the account. The bull now decides that he cannot clear his position so he arranges a two-week postponement.

Cover

This is the ratio of the earnings to the dividend paid. The higher the cover the more conservative the dividend policy.

Cum Dividend

A share is cum dividend when the price paid includes the dividend which is due. Shares may also be 'cum capitalisation' or 'cum rights'.

Debenture

Loan stock issued to the public.

Discount

Occasionally shares, when they are first quoted on the exchange, are priced lower than the issue price. The difference between the issue price and the market price is the discount.

Dividend

The amount of profit paid to shareholders. Usually dividends are declared as a percentage of the par value of the share.

Ex Dividend

A share may be bought without the right to receive a dividend which is due to be paid. In such cases the seller receives the dividends.

Ex Rights

New shares may be issued to existing shareholders at a preferential price. When the new shares are issued the old shares become 'ex rights' which means that the price adjusts downwards to take account of the new shares.

Interim Dividend

Most companies pay two dividends each year: an 'interim' and a 'final'. The final dividend must be approved by the shareholders.

Issue of Shares

This term covers the mechanism of moving new shares from the company to the new owners.

Jobber

Jobbers made a market in certain shares. They were called share wholesalers in that they never dealt with the final customers of the exchange.

Letter of Indemnity

Often share certificates get lost. Before issuing new certificates the company must be idemnified by the shareholder against any legal claims. Banks and/or insurance companies may have to sign the indemnity.

Letter of Regret

Applicants who are not allotted shares in an issue are sent a 'letter of regret'.

Limit

This is the price above which a stockbroker cannot buy for a client or below which he cannot sell.

Mark

This is the price at which a bargain was completed. This is the price quoted in the papers for shares dealt in on the stock exchange — Irish.

Market Guide Prices

A set of 'bid' and 'offer' prices for shares quoted on the stock exchange—Irish. Some prices may be out of date.

Market Makers

Stockbroking firms who offer to buy or sell certain shares at published prices.

Middle Price

London share prices quoted in British newspapers are usually the mid price between the bid and offer price of two market makers.

Nominal Value

The par value of a share.

Offer

This is the price at which a market maker offers to sell shares. In Ireland it is the price at which a stockbroker is willing to sell.

Option

A right to do business with a broker at an agreed price for an agreed period in an agreed share.

Passed

If a company decides to miss a dividend payment they are said to have 'passed the dividend'.

Pig
Someone who holds on to make the last few pence profit on a share. Often the market turns and the pig loses.

Pink Slips
In new issues certain individuals are offered preference in buying the shares. The application form issued to preferential buyers is coloured pink.

Premium
New issues whose first quoted price is above the issue price are quoted at a premium. Issues are priced to open at a 'premium'.

Price/Earnings Ratio (P/E)
This is the ratio of the current market price to existing earnings per share (EPS).

Put Option
A right to sell a share at an agreed price for an agreed period.

Put and Call
An option to buy or sell at an agreed price for an agreed period. This is also known as a 'double option'.

Put Through
A stockbroker may be able to match buy and sell orders among his own clients. He puts the deal through a jobber for a small fee.

Redemption
The repayment of a loan.

Redemption Yield
Government bonds which are redeemed at par often sell at a discount. The redemption yield is the rate of interest received on purchasing the bond plus the additional payment received by holding on until the bond is redeemed divided by the number of years to redemption.

Rights
Existing shareholders may be offered the right to subscribe for new shares. Rights issues rarely affect the control of the company. Shareholders not wishing to subscribe for new shares can sell the rights.

Securities
An American name for bonds and shares quoted on a stock exchange.

Squeeze
Sometimes investors realise that bears will have to buy stock to meet their commitments. In such cases prices rise and the bears are 'squeezed' as they have to pay the price to acquire the necessary shares.

Stag
New issues are a source of speculation to individuals who apply for shares hoping to sell them to individuals wanting the shares but who were unlucky in the allotment.

Stale Bull
A person who has bought shares expecting a price rise which has not occurred.

Stamp Duty
Payable at the rate of $1\frac{1}{2}$ per cent on the transfer of shares.

Stock
Historically money was raised by issuing stocks in lots of £100. Stock could be sold in fractions. Now all issues are of shares. 'Stock' is now interchangeable with 'shares'.

Stock Exchange Official List
This is a daily listing of every share on the exchange. It includes details of dividends, the ex-dividend date and the date of dividend payment.

Turn
The difference between the bid and offer price. The larger the turn the greater the uncertainty about the market for the share.

Underwriter
A bank which agrees to buy any shares not purchased by the public. There is a fee for this service.

Warrant
Cheques sent to shareholders in payment of dividends are known as 'dividend warrants'.

XD
An abbreviated form of 'ex dividend'.

Yield

This may be the earnings per share divided by the market price of the share which is the Earnings Yield or the dividend per share divided by market price which is the Dividend Yield.

Further Reading
E. V. Morgan & W. A. Thames: *The Stock Exchange,* Elek, London 1962.
C. R. Sprecher: *Introduction to Investment Management,* Houghton Mifflin, Boston 1976.
H. D. Berman: *The Stock Exchange,* Pitman, London 1987.
The Stock Exchange: *Admission of Securities to Listing,* Stock Exchange, London 1987.
Investors Chronicle, weekly journal.
Business Week, weekly journal.
The Economist, weekly journal.

Chapter 9

Short-Term Sources of Finance

The introduction to this text defined one function of the financial manager as that of treasurer. The job of the treasurer is to have the right type of money in the right place at the right time. This is easier said than done. Money can be raised in many different ways from overnight funds which must be repaid within twelve hours to permanent finance. Each type or source of finance affects a business in three distinct ways — risk, income and control.

Each source of finance has a risk attaching to it. The risk is that the business will not be capable of meeting the financial commitments relating to the source, that is, principal and/or interest. A business generally uses a multiplicity of sources. The total risk of the mix of capital sources is known as the 'financial' risk of the business. The financial risk is very different from the commercial or business risk of the enterprise. The business risk relates to the possibility that the products produced by the venture will produce losses. The financial risk is the risk arising from a mis-match, often deliberate, between the sources of funds and the uses to which such funds are put. Chapter 14 examines this area in more detail.

The income effect of financial sources relates to the cost of funds. Each source of finance has a cost attaching to it. Reducing the cost of funds should increase the income of the owners. Examples of the income effect include accounts payable, which may have no cost to the individual company, government grants, which are costless, and raising new equity by an issue of shares on which dividends may have to be paid during the lifetime of the business.

The control effect of financial sources refers to the possibility of new sources of finance affecting management or ownership control. New shares usually have voting rights, thus diluting the control of each existing share. Term loans often have covenants which restrict the activities of management in areas such as dividends and directors' salaries. Bank overdrafts usually have collateral which restrict the freedom of management to sell the assets.

It is the job of the financial manager to provide the required finance at minimum risk and loss of control while at the same time maximising the income to the owners. The task is exceptionally difficult if for no other reason than the wide range of financial sources available. Table 34 provides a listing of the major sources of finance available to Irish business. It should be noted that all sources are not available to every business. As a rule of thumb the larger the business the greater the number of sources which tend to be available. This, and the following chapters, discuss the sources in detail. This chapter covers the many short-term sources of capital available to Irish business. Smaller businesses tend to make extensive, and often excessive, use of short-term funds. Chapter 10 examines medium-term sources of finance. Two medium-term sources, leasing and term loans, are highly developed in Ireland. Chapter 11 extends the analysis of funds into long-term sources.

Table 34 Source of Finance

	Short Term	*Medium Term*	*Long Term*
Period	Up to one year	1–7 years	Longer than 7 years
Sources	1. Trade Credit	13. Leasing	16. Debentures
	2. Accrued Expenses	14. Hire Purchase	17. Sale and Leaseback
	3. Taxation	15. Term Loans	18. Section 84 Loans
	4. Bills of Exchange		19. Indexed Bonds
	5. Commercial Paper		20. Project Financing
	6. Acceptance Credits		21. Capital Grants
	7. Bank Overdraft		22. Preference Share Capital
	8. Inventory Financing		23. Equity Share Capital
	9. Trust Receipts		
	10. Factoring		
	11. Accounts Receivable & Invoice Discounting		
	12. Insurance Premium Loans		
Uses	Seasonal fluctuations in trade	Plant and Equipment	Fixed Assets such as Buildings

As Irish business grows and develops greater use is being made of sophisticated forms of long-term financing. The thorny problem of ownership funds is tackled in Chapter 12. Giving away control to obtain money is always difficult, no more so than in small firms. In recent years in Ireland a number of 'seed' capital and 'venture' capital sources have appeared. The role of the state in providing financial assistance is highlighted in Chapter 13. The Industrial Development Authority and the Industrial Credit Corporation are the best known state-owned financial institutions; other state organisations also offer financial help to Irish business.

SPONTANEOUS SOURCES OF FINANCE
Spontaneous sources of finance refer to those sources of finance which arise through the normal course of business. They are also known as 'non negotiated' in that the receiver usually has to do nothing to obtain the use of the funds. These sources are unsecured and are usually 'free' insofar as no interest is charged for their use.

The three principal spontaneous sources of finance are (a) trade credit, (b) accrued expenses and (c) taxation.

Trade Credit
Trade credit normally arises when a business orders raw materials. The seller usually extends a period of credit to the purchaser. The importance of trade credit can be seen from an examination of the Accounts Payable figure on a balance sheet. A United Kingdom study found that trade credit accounted for as much as 15 per cent of all sources of finance. The figure in Ireland could be higher. Smaller businesses tend to make extensive use of this form of finance. Note that the accounts of Ardmore (Chapter 2) show a heavy reliance on this source of finance.

The terms of credit are normally stated on the invoice delivered with the goods purchased. Chapter 5 examined trade credit from the viewpoint of the issuer. The cost of giving cash discounts was examined. The analysis applies equally well to not taking cash discounts offered on purchases. The trade terms 2/10 net 30 mean in theory that a company is foregoing a 2 per cent discount for 20 days' use of the money. This is an annual interest rate of 36.5 per cent. However, few people observe the normal credit terms. If a company instead of paying after 30 days waits until 90 days have elapsed, the cost of foregoing the discount is,

$$2\dot{\%} \times \frac{365}{80} = 9.125\%$$

This is an attractive rate of interest. Trade credit has another important characteristic. In times of crisis it can be stretched. Very often suppliers will continue to supply goods though the payment record of the purchaser is disimproving. There are many reasons for this; it takes time for the payment record to filter through the suppliers' organisation and suppliers usually want to hold customers and so are lenient. Trade credit can act as a 'buffer' in bad times. The practice of stretching accounts payable is known as 'leaning on the trade'. It is generally believed that the cost of trade credit is zero. Even where discounts do not exist trade credit may not be free. A slow-paying customer may be paying more for his goods than will a cash-or fast-paying client. Apart from paying more it is possible that slow payers will be refused supplies or else made to pay cash. This latter requirement can have a traumatic effect on a business.

The amount of trade credit available to a firm depends on (a) the proportion of raw materials in the product, (b) the terms of credit offered by the supplier and (c) the payment policies of the purchaser.

The objective of trade credit management should be to stretch the payment period as far as it can go without affecting the credit rating of the business.

Accrued Expenses

The average business obtains services and inputs from a wide variety of sources. The expenses of these sources are usually paid in arrears. Wages are weekly in arrears, salaries monthly, electricity and telephones bi-monthly. These sources are spontaneous and costless if bills are paid when due. Though the sources are costless to the individual firms it is likely that the price of the service is higher because money is not received immediately. Consider the case of the Electricity Supply Board (ESB), providing power as and when required but not receiving payment for a number of months. While awaiting payment the ESB must pay their bills for oil, wages and other expenses. They must finance the period of credit by borrowing or by issuing new equity. Borrowing increases costs which in turn are passed on to the customer in the form of higher power prices.

Accrued expenses are usually a small but useful source of finance.

Taxation

Taxation can be a very large spontaneous source of finance. Under current legislation businesses act as tax collectors for the state. The two important taxes collected by business are Value Added Tax and Income Tax.

Value Added Tax (VAT) is charged on all invoices but is only returned to the state every two months. In fact, the tax due is payable within nineteen days of the end of the two-month tax period. VAT can be a very important cash item, amounting to 25 per cent of an invoice. Should the business not remit the tax in the permitted time then they may be guilty of an offence and liable to interest on sums due. The lax credit policies of Irish business can cause havoc with VAT. VAT is payable on all invoices sent out on a two-month period — that includes invoices sent out on the last day of the period. Therefore, assuming that invoices are sent out on a regular basis over the period, the average period before VAT is due is one month plus nineteen days. The average period of credit taken in Ireland is longer than fifty days so it is possible that in many cases VAT is a *use* of finance rather than a source.

Income tax and Pay Related Social Insurance are other major cost items in business. The Pay As You Earn (PAYE) system of income tax requires a business to deduct tax from wages and salaries. This is then remitted to the Revenue Commissioners. Since 1979 Social Welfare contributions are been handled in a similar manner. Many businesses, particularly small firms, are slow in remitting payments to the state. This practice is illegal and unethical.

Corporation tax is yet another spontaneous source of finance. The profits of a business are liable for tax with the normal payment date being 6 months from the end of the accounting period. During the period between the generation of profits and the payment of tax a business enjoys an interest-free loan. It should be noted that as a spontaneous source of finance corporation tax is very sensitive to any changes in the fortunes of a business.

Consider the example of a service business which grew rapidly during the 1970s but suffered a setback in the late 1980s due to the increasing burden of personal taxation and stiff competition.

Table 35   Taxation as a Source of Finance

Year	1984	1985	1986	1987	1988
Taxable Profits	£20,000	£30,000	£40,000	£20,000	0
Taxation 50%		£10,000	£15,000	£20,000	£10,000
(Payable 6 months in arrears)					

Note that in 1987 the tax payable is equal to the profits earned while there is a real cash outflow in 1988. Thus the business finds itself facing difficult trading times with the added complication of tax liability. Arrears of taxation incur interest at a rate of $1\frac{1}{2}$ per cent per month. This interest is not tax deductible.

NEGOTIATED SOURCES OF FINANCE
Bills of Exchange

A bill of exchange is an unconditional order in writing addressed by one person to another, signed by the person giving it requiring the person to whom it is addressed to pay on demand or at an agreed future time, a certain sum of money to, or to the order of, a specified person or to bearer. It is in effect a financial contract which enables the buyer with the agreement of the seller to delay payment, usually for a period of 30, 60, 90 or 180 days. The buyer 'accepts' a bill of exchange by writing 'accepted' across it and by signing it. The seller can either hold the bill to maturity or else he can discount it at a bank and get immediate cash. The bank will pay the face value of the bill less a rate of discount.

Bills of exchange are common in foreign trade but have virtually died out in domestic commerce. In the 1980s they made a re-appearance mainly as 'trade bills', that is, an agreement between seller and buyer. An alternative form is a 'bank bill' where a bank issues a letter of credit to a buyer. This is discussed below under 'Acceptance Credits'.

The growth in trade bills in Ireland was partly a reflection of tight credit. By offering sellers bills of exchange buyers were extending the period of credit which they would normally obtain from the seller. Often the seller was happy to obtain a bill in that he had a fixed payment date and it was possible to discount the bill with a bank.

Commercial paper

Large businesses often wish to borrow substantial sums for periods up to six months. Such companies have a variety of short-term sources open to them including commercial paper. Commercial paper means the IOUs or promissory notes of large firms. These notes are sold in the money market. Sometimes other substantial businesses with excess liquid funds are the purchasers of these notes. The commercial paper market in Ireland evolved some years after an explosive growth in the United States' market. There, many finance companies found it cheaper and easier to borrow direct from the money market rather than the banks. The industrial banks are large users of the Irish commercial paper market. The advantages of commercial paper are: (a) an interest cost below overdraft rate; (b) a simple and cheap negotiating procedure; (c) the status and prestige connected with the ability to borrow by this method.

The main disadvantage of using commercial paper stems from the impersonal nature of the paper market. If a firm encounters financial difficulties and cannot redeem its paper, it will find it hard to get extensions of time from the investors who hold the firm's paper. Banks are more inclined to help the firm work things out in times of distress. The introduction of Deposit Interest Retention Tax (DIRT) caused a movement out of the interbank market into commercial paper.

The two most common types of commercial paper are Government-Guaranteed Notes issued by Semi-State bodies and Bank-Guaranteed Notes issued by major Irish companies. What are the main attractions of such notes for the parties involved? Top quality issuers of notes can normally issue such paper at the Dublin Interbank Offered Rate (DIBOR) + 0.15% whereas a term loan for a similar period could be as high as DIBOR + 0.375%, a significant difference. Issuers can borrow cheaply in this way as a result of the growth in demand for commercial paper from depositors seeking to invest in a negotiable instrument and/or to avoid DIRT. Depositors are willing to accept lower returns to avoid

DIRT which causes cash flow problems for many companies as the tax is deducted at source. In cases where tax would otherwise not be payable, DIRT can reduce the overall return by 35 per cent if it is not recoverable.

While Government-Guaranteed paper has proved most popular with investors, many are now willing to accept the paper of other issuers, provided in most cases that the placing bank adds its name to the note by way of endorsement. Such bank guarantees are off-balance sheet contingent liabilities and therefore require a lower capital allocation than the more traditional form of bank lending. This allows the bank to offer cheaper funding to the corporate borrower and a better return for the depositor while reducing pressure on the bank's scarce capital resources. The bank can still achieve the same return on equity as a deposit/term loan structure although halving its margin, with the benefit being passed on to the borrower and lender.

This market comprises Note Issuance Facilities (NIFs) and Promissory Notes (PNs) and is currently estimated to be of the order of IR£500 million/IR£750 million. PNs comprise by far the bigger portion of the market.

The move towards commercial paper or 'securitisation of assets' as bankers convert illiquid loans into marketable securities has been a worldwide phenomenon. The advantage for the bankers was that it helped free up balance sheets and eased capital adequacy demands while it offered cheaper credit to borrowers by avoiding reserve asset costs (RAC). However, the banker continues to fulfil the role of the risk underwriter. While NIFs have been in the market for a number of years the PNs really burst into life with the introduction of DIRT. At its simplest PNs are DIRT-free instruments. A borrower arranges with his bank to issue a PN with a duration of up to six months. The banker then finds an investor who discounts the paper and through the bank remits the net proceeds to the issuer. On maturity the issuer pays the face value through the bank to the investor. Under current taxation legislation discount does not equate with interest and hence the PN is DIRT-free.

The attraction of PNs to issuer, banker and investor are that all get a slice of the action. The issuer raises cheaper finance, mainly through avoiding RAC. The bank gets a spread between the issuer and investor, and the investor, if he is a corporation, avoids paying DIRT up front which would be the case if he had made a conventional deposit. For the pension fund an investment in a DIRT-free instrument is exceptionally attractive as it cannot reclaim any DIRT which it incurs on a conventional deposit.

In the case of corporate investors in PNs the DIRT is merely delayed for a period between the time of the interest payment and agreement of accounts with the Revenue Commissioners. For the pension funds the attraction of PNs are enormous and they are the first port of call for any bank with PNs to sell. Given the difficult state of the nation's finances, it is hard to imagine that the Department of Finance will allow such a substantial pool of revenue pass them by in a year when revenue generation will be extremely difficult (1988).

The major issuers of PNs are the state-sponsored bodies and the major Irish and multi-national companies.

The growth in PNs, which are off-balance sheet for the banks, has caused headaches for the regulatory authorities worldwide. The Bank of England has issued a consultative paper on the subject indicating the authority's concern at the growth of this phenomenon. In assessing banks capital adequacy, the Central Bank of Ireland gives a weighting of 50 per cent to PNs which of course adds to their attraction from the banks point of view (that is, a margin of 0.25 per cent on a PN is the equivalent of 0.5 per cent on a conventional loan from a capital adequacy point of view, while no asset is created on the balance sheet).

Acceptance Credits

Acceptance credits are a form of 'Bank Bill of Exchange'. A bank issues a letter of credit to a business. The management of the business can draw bills of exchange on the bank for specific amounts and specific periods. These bills can be discounted by another bank. The market for acceptance credits was, until recently, restricted to large Irish firms and to the subsidiaries of overseas firms. Restrictions on other forms of bank credit led to a rapid expansion in acceptance credits.

Acceptance credits are an excellent supplement to other short-term sources of finance.

Bank Overdraft

Bank overdraft facilities are widely used by business. Though not as large a source of finance as trade credit, it is more important in that many firms use bank overdraft as their cash cushion, that is, if for some reason or other the firm is caught short of cash it relies on bank overdraft to cover the situation. Bank overdraft facilities are intended to meet specific short-term capital needs. Ideally, banks prefer a STISL—a short-term inherently self-liquidating loan. A retailer using bank overdraft to finance stocks of Christmas toys should be in a position to repay the loan within a short period.

Bank overdraft is a negotiated source of finance in that consultation with bank officials is necessary to gain sanction to use the facilities. Generally a credit line is set, that is, overdraft up to a fixed amount. Once the credit line is agreed the firm may borrow and repay money within that limit. This flexibility is one of the advantages of bank overdraft. A further advantage is that it tends to be one of the cheapest sources of finance available. Interest charges are generally tied to current interest rates; interest is charged only on the outstanding daily balance; furthermore, bank interest is an allowable charge against profits for tax purposes. A disadvantage of bank overdraft facilities is that they can be called in at any time.

In granting an overdraft, banks often require security for the loan in the form of a mortgage or lien. This can be restrictive on business particularly if the mortgage 'floats' over all of the assets, that is, every asset is part of the mortgage. The difficulty here is that management may not pledge any of their assets for further finance without first clearing the bank overdraft or re-negotiating the security provisions. In many instances banks do not require the security of a mortgage but instead accept either formal or informal guarantees from management. Such practices undermine the concept of limited liability. This aspect of bank lending highlights the benefits of a sound relationship with local bank officials. If the bank knows the management of the firm, the history of the firm and has had previous dealings with the principals, it is inclined to look more favourably on requests for overdraft facilities. A sound relationship with a bank can be built in the following manner:

(1) By keeping all the firm's accounts with the one bank. In this way the bank can profitably use any of the firm's deposits and can build a case history of its 'financial record'.

(2) By supplying the bank with all pertinent information. This includes not only annual accounts but also quarterly or other accounts, cash flow forecasts, marketing plans and staffing plans. By doing this a firm will provide the bank with the necessary information on which to base decisions. A bank will look favourably on a client who provides information showing that he has a logical objective in business and is planning and organising to attain this objective. It is advisable to present adverse reports along with optimistic reports as there is little advantage in attempting to hide what a good analyst will undoubtedly find.

(3) By preparing and presenting well thought out proposals showing the reasons for the loans, collateral and repayment schedules.

Historically Irish firms have regarded bank overdraft as a source of permanent capital. As long as the banks had surplus deposits requiring profitable outlets, they were content to have them invested profitably. Theoretically, bank overdraft was, and is, recallable at short notice, but this feature has rarely been employed by banks. In recent years, as the Irish economy has expanded, demands on all sources of finance have increased. Banks have found their deposits insufficient to meet the total demands. The ability of banks to create credit became subject to government policy. In times of credit restrictions, where banks were expected to curb lending, they discovered that it was difficult if not impossible to call in bank overdrafts. This was due to the fact that the borrowers had invested short-term bank money in medium- and long-term assets. Had the banks insisted on being repaid, many firms would have been unable to comply with the demand.

In order to bring discipline into bank lending and to relate investment opportunities both to the risk involved and to the money supply available, banks have replaced many overdrafts by term loans. This approach requires firms to present to the banks a reasonable application for the provision of a loan. Among the requirements is a timetable of repayments. Bank loans are tailored to individual requirements in terms of interest rates applied and repayment terms allowed. Where the term of borrowing exceeds seven years or cannot be determined a custom-made loan account may be established.

The purpose of the revised approach is to avoid short-term bank deposits being invested in long-term business assets, with the result that the bank can only recover by foreclosing on the firm — something that no lender wishes to do. The replacement of the present form of bank overdraft should enable the banks to use their own scarce resources more efficiently while at the same time it should force the businessman to plan his financial requirements. From this point of view, the change in bank policy appears beneficial to both sides.

Negotiating a Bank Overdraft

Remember that a bank overdraft is meant to be a short-term loan. In practice banks require the borrower's account to be in credit for a period of thirty days in a year. In presenting a request for bank facilities borrowers should have a cash budget drawn up along lines similar to that developed for Ardmore in Chapter 4 above. A cash budget shows the peak needs of the firm and it is this maximum figure which the company should seek to borrow.

The rate of interest charged on a bank overdraft depends on the risk category of the borrowers. In early 1988 the following were the categories used and the appropriate overdraft rates charged by the associated banks.

Category	Type of Borrower	Overdraft Rate
AAA	The state, local authorities, publicly quoted companies, schools, churches and hospitals	8.75%
AA	Large private firms	10.5%
A	Small firms and personal borrowers	13.0%

The amount of the overdraft facility may be called a 'line of credit'. The borrower may borrow up to this amount. Occasionally a bank allows a customer to overdraw the limit. This usually means an interest penalty which may be as high as 6 per cent per annum.

The interest rate outlines above are those charged by the associated banks. Other banks base their charges on the cost of money plus a premium.

Inventory Financing

Earlier chapters highlighted the importance of the investment in inventory. Irish firms often have high levels of raw materials, work in progress and finished goods. In theory, inventory is a liquid asset and as such it is suitable as collateral for short-term loans. Inventory financing or 'stock loans' have recently become popular in Ireland. The lender examines the inventory and decides to provide loans up to a certain percentage of the market value of the inventory. The more marketable the inventory the higher the percentage. An example in Ireland is the grain trade. Farmers sell their grain to merchants in September. These merchants dry and store the grain until the spring, when it is sold. Grain, with a fixed Common Market price, is a liquid asset and so certain Irish financial institutions will advance up to 80 per cent of the purchase price to the merchant.

On the other hand there are items which are so specialised that there is little or no market for them. These items would not qualify for an inventory loan. The size of the loan as a percentage of the market value of inventory is decided by the bank on the basis of marketability and perishability.

A lender obtains security by means of a 'floating lien' or by means of a chattel mortgage. Under a floating lien all of the inventory is part of the security. Usually a floating lien covers other current and fixed assets. It often encompasses any additional inventory which arises during the life of the lien.

Under a chattel mortgage the borrower provides the bank with an itemised list of inventory. This acts as security for the loan. The inventory can be sold only with the permission of the lender. This method is suited only to large slow-moving inventory items.

Inventory financing, particularly using a chattel mortgage, is growing in popularity, mainly because it releases much of the funds tied up in current assets.

Trust Receipts

This form of financing is also known as 'warehousing finance'. It is a sophisticated form of inventory financing whereby the borrower holds the inventory in trust for the lender. As goods are sold the funds are remitted to the lender. Inventory can be stored in the borrower's facilities or else warehoused in a public store. Terminal warehousing is where goods are stored in a public warehouse. The warehouse management informs a lender who provides funds to the borrower. When goods are sold the lender orders their release from the warehouse. 'Field warehousing' is where the goods are stored in a designated area on the borrower's premises. A company which specialises in monitoring and controlling warehoused inventory controls the flow of goods into and out of the field warehouse on behalf of the borrower.

Because of the costs of warehousing and clerical activity trust receipt financing is more expensive than bank overdraft financing.

Factoring

The origins of modern factoring are rooted in the old colonial practice of using mercantile agents. Because of the risks, great distances and slow communications involved when dealing in colonial markets from the sixteenth century onwards, European producers would appoint such agents or factors to receive, sell, distribute and collect payment for their goods.

This method of doing business ensured that producers could sell their goods abroad without fear of non-payment. It developed strongly on the east coast of Northern America especially in the textile, clothing and related industries. Factors gradually began not only to hold stocks and sell goods on behalf of principals, but to guarantee payment as *del credere* agents.

In time, it was this role of guaranteeing payment for goods which began to supersede the factor's selling functions. In tandem with this change, the burgeoning domestic cotton and textile trade of the United States was increasingly using factors to ensure payment for goods.

By the middle of this century factoring had matured to its modern state and in the 1960s it was imported to Ireland via textile associated business.

Factoring is another method for reducing the investment of long-term funds in current assets. It generally involves a combination of provision of finance, insurance against bad debts, sales accounting service and a cash advance.

Factors offer four main services:
(a) They take over the debt collecting function of the client.
(b) They may offer insurance against bad debts.
(c) They pay the client agreed percentages of invoices on agreed dates.
(d) They may pay cash to the client in advance of invoice payment.
The factor begins dealing with a client by examining the client's

accounts receivable. A list of approved customers is prepared. The factor agrees to provide complete protection against bad debts on all subsequent sales to these customers provided certain limits are maintained. Naturally, the customers selected by the factor tend to be those on which there would be, in any event, no credit risk. If the client company wants to introduce new accounts or to increase the limits on approved accounts the factor must first be consulted.

Having established the service the factor agrees to pay the invoice on an agreed maturity date. For example, a medium-sized textile company began factoring debtors. The factor examined the accounts receivable ledger and discovered that the average credit granted by the firm was fifty-five days. The factor agreed to pay the firm fifty-five days after receipt of invoice. The advantage to the firm was that instead of a varying, somewhat uncertain, cash flow from customers they now had guaranteed receipts.

A prepayment facility exists in most factoring agreements. An agreed percentage of the debtor balance, usually 70 per cent, is advanced to the client on the day the invoice is issued. Factoring may be 'with recourse' which means that in the event of bad debts the factor must be reimbursed by the client. More commonly the service is 'without recourse' in which there is insurance against bad debts.

The firm's customers are informed by a notation on the original invoice that the debt is due to, and should be paid, to, the factor. To avoid public knowledge of the use of factoring, the factor may establish a wholly-owned subsidiary with a name similar to that of the client firm, for example, Ardmore (Sales) Limited. Invoices can then be made payable to this company.

The cost of factoring depends on the amount of work involved and the firm's industry, product and customers. The total cost is made up of three segments: (a) interest charges which are about 4 per cent above AA overdraft rates; (b) a charge for insuring bad debts; (c) a service charge to cover debt collection, accounting records etc. Normally the insurance and service charges together will not exceed 2 per cent of the net sum factored.

Factoring is only considered worthwhile, both from the firm's and factor's point of view, if total credit sales are in excess of £100,000 per annum and the average invoice value in excess of £100.

The Benefits of the Financial Facility from the Factor

Companies using a factor, therefore, have immediate access to cash that they would not normally receive for up to two, three or more months. The facility can stabilise the timing of cash flows and make accurate cashflow planning a reality.

The factor's financial facility enables businesses to:

(1) Pay suppliers more promptly giving enhanced credit reputation.
(2) Obtain cash and quantity discounts on supplies thus improving profit margins.
(3) Cope with seasonal and other peak demands for cash.
(4) Make future purchasing and other plans knowing the working capital that will be available.
(5) Finance a higher level of sales.
(6) Obtain off balance sheet finance.
(7) Improve the return on their capital without giving up equity or control.
(8) Savings in the cost of maintaining own sales administration.
(9) Savings on management time previously spent supervising sales accounts or chasing slow paying customers.
(10) Swifter payment by customers, giving cash flow improvement and interest savings.
(11) Sales relationships with customers are not damaged by sales staff and management repeatedly requesting payment.
(12) More time for sales and business development.

Offsetting the advantages are the costs and a disturbing image problem. In many countries, but particularly in Ireland, factoring accounts receivable is seen as a sign of financial weakness. This misconception of the role of factoring is prevalent among Irish financial institutions. The logic behind the setting up of a like named firm now should be clear. A customer paying invoices to Ardmore (Sales) Limited may not realise that Ardmore has factored its debtors. An example of invoice discounting is shown below. It is important to note that less than 40 per cent of UK companies using factoring are manufacturers, some 35 per cent are distributors, often engineering and metal distributors, while printing and publishing, catering and other business services make up 25 per cent. The average business using factoring has an annual turnover of between £250,000 and £500,000.

As of 1987 debts of about £175 million are being factored annually in Ireland from a base of about £35 million in 1980. The client base has more than doubled in that period to over 800. Textiles, clothing and engineering product manufacturers are the principal users of this source of finance.

A recent innovation has been export factoring. Using a worldwide network of offices and contacts, International Factors can advise Irish exporters on the creditworthiness of foreign customers. Where overseas customers are accepted by the factor cash collection is improved due to the local contacts with the customer. Export financing also guarantees the Irish exporter an agreed price in punts; the factor assumes the currency exchange risk. Removal of both the credit and currency risks makes exporting more attractive to Irish businessmen.

Accounts Receivable Financing and Invoice Discounting

Occasionally a bank will loan money against the collateral of accounts receivable. Because it is very difficult to assess the worth of accounts receivable the loan is rarely for more than half their total book value. Where a borrower submits a list of debtors and the lender accepts only the best quality accounts then the loan may go as high as 80 per cent of the face value of the accounts. Lenders are usually interested in only a few large accounts. The monitoring cost on a collection of small accounts would be too high for the lender.

A development of accounts receivable financing is where a potential borrower submits individual invoices to a lender. If the customer is an acceptable risk then the lender will advance to the borrower up to 80 per cent of the face value of invoices. This is known as invoice discounting.

Invoice discounting has been designed to release funds tied up in debtors without running the risk of losing creditworthiness by having accounts paid directly to a factor. Using this facility involves an examination of the debtors ledger similar to that for a straightforward factoring operation. Once credit levels are agreed on selected accounts, all further sales invoices are assigned to the factor. An agreed proportion of the gross invoices is paid to the client firm. When the invoices are paid the client passes the proceeds to the factor.

Example: Invoice Discounting

Summary of financial position before and after discounting

Nature of business; Supply of Technical Staff to Industry.
Turnover: Forecast £7.5m (Year 4).
Customers: Large national companies.

This company provides technical staff to industry (that is, labour hire). The nature of this business requires a sizeable workforce which is paid on a weekly or monthly basis, dependent on individual contracts, and which therefore calls heavily on the cash flow of the business.

Nevertheless, during years 1 and 2 the company showed considerable growth despite a competitive marketplace. A significant element in this achievement was the investment in a computer system to streamline the company's administrative functions. In a competitive market this had a positive effect on margins by reducing the cost of administration thereby allowing the handling of a greater volume of work which ultimately meant a higher level of service whilst maintaining competitive prices.

The company's principal method of funding at this stage was a bank overdraft facility secured by a fixed and floating charge on the company's assets and the personal guarantees of the directors, together with periodic loans from the directors.

In order to strengthen the company's position and improve liquidity, under pressure due to the nature of the business, an approach was made to their bankers for an additional increase in facility. Despite support from the local bank manager, this request was turned down at regional level on the grounds of an insufficient asset base. Reluctant to offer their own personal property as security, the directors were recommended to investigate the possibility of invoice discounting as a means of providing additional working capital, whilst allowing full control of the sale ledger to remain with the company.

Year 3 saw the commencement of an invoice discounting arrangement providing a 75 per cent prepayment facility. This allowed a reduction in the company's overdraft, the release of the directors' personal guarantees and a revolving facility geared to the turnover of the company, thereby allowing a ready cash flow despite the company's obligation to pay its staff promptly.

Financial Record (£,000)

	Year 1	Year 2	Year 3
Sales	£3,491	£5,003	£6,704
Retained Profit (Loss)	69	80	244
Simplified Balance Sheet			
Current Assets:			
Debtors	583	808	320
Stock and WIP	56	93	116
	639	901	436
Current Liabilities:			
Overdraft	250	472	70
Creditors	349	501	357
	599	973	427
Net Current Assets	40	(72)	9
Fixed Assets	174	366	560
Long Term Liabilities	(75)	(75)	(106)
	99	291	454
Net Assets	139	219	463
Issued Share Capital	55	55	55
P & L a/c	84	164	408
Net Worth	139	219	463

Insurance Premium Loans

For many Irish companies the annual insurance payment has become a heavy burden. Insurance in Ireland is expensive, particularly employer's liability, public liability, theft and motor cover. It would not be unusual for a company with fifty employees to pay £50,000 a year. Insurance must be paid; delays can void the policies.

To this end a number of institutions have developed insurance premium loans whereby the lender pays the insurance premium on the due date, and the borrower repays the loan usually in six payments at two monthly intervals. The security for the loan is often weak, but the lender can reserve the right to cancel the policies and recoup some of the funds.

CONCLUSION

One point to be taken from this chapter is that the raising of finance is fast becoming a complex and sophisticated job. The short-term sources of finance alone involve many different combinations of risk, income and control. The objective in raising short-term money is to minimise risk and possible loss of control at the lowest cost. Very often this means stretching short-term sources to the limit beyond which the image and/or reputation of the company becomes damaged. A generation ago bank overdraft and trade credit were the only short-term sources of note. A decade ago the range had expanded to include some factoring. Now the short-term money market offers even wider opportunities and inventory financing is becoming common.

In the final analysis the borrowing and payment schedule for short-term financing should be arranged to correspond to the expected swings in current assets. In this way, financing would be employed only when it is needed and is similar in approach to hedging in the commodities futures market.

Further Reading
J. C. Van Horne: *Financial Management & Policy, (7th Ed.),* Prentice Hall, London 1986.
T. G. Hutson & J. Butterworth: *The Management of Trade Credit*, Gower Press, London, 1984.
A. N. Cox & J. A. MacKenzie: *International Factoring,* Euromoney, London, 1986.
Susan Crichton & Charles Ferrier: *Understanding Factoring and Trade Credit,* Waterlow, London, 1986.
Louis A. Moskowitz: *Modern Factoring and Commercial Financing,* New York, 1977.
F. R. Salinger: *Factoring,* Tolley, London, 1984.

Chapter 10

Medium-Term Sources of Finance

The sources of finance identified in the previous chapter are best suited to investments in current assets. This means that the assets liquidate themselves in time to repay the funds raised. But not all investments are short term; some such as land or buildings are long term and are best financed by permanent or long-term sources of capital. Other investments have intermediate lives. Plant and machinery often have economic lives of between three and five years. A great many projects have paybacks of less than five years. To fund these intermediate-term investments a series of medium-term financial instruments have been developed. The principal instruments are leasing, hire purchase and term loans.

LEASING

Leasing can be traced back many years. It is reputed to have originated in the United States where in 1832 the firm of Cottrell and Leonard leased academic gowns, caps and hoods. In the twentieth century some firms specialised in leasing. Hertz pioneered car leasing, IBM leased computers while Xerox for many years would only lease copiers. Leases may be arranged in any of the four following ways:

(1) Maker to User. This provides control over the way equipment is used. It also facilitates maintenance. Leasing arrangements with IBM and Xerox are good examples.

(2) User to User. This system is rare, apart from contracting businesses where one user would not have full use for a machine. A number of individuals purchase different machines and lease them to each other.

(3) Leasing Company to User. Here a specialised company buys equipment from a maker and leases it to users. This is widespread in Ireland, particularly in the office equipment and car businesses.

(4) Finance House to User. In Ireland the associated banks, merchant banks and industrial banks have developed leasing divisions. A user decides on a piece of equipment. A financial institution purchases the equipment and leases it to the user.

Equipment leasing has grown rapidly. From a total figure of less than £12 million in 1972 it topped £200 million in 1986.

Very little information is available on maker-to-user or user-to-user leases in Ireland. The figures on leases between users and financial institutions are shown in Table 36.

Table 36   Leasing Agreement (£,000,000)

Years	Associated Banks	Non-Associated Banks	Other	Total
1982	—	20.5	163.5	184.0
1983	14.8	25.8	145.8	186.4
1984	20.2	30.1	174.1	224.4
1985	27.2	43.4	134.2	204.9
1986	37.1	71.5	109.9	218.5

Source: Central Bank of Ireland

From financing a narrow range of products such as office equipment, leasing has grown so that now it is possible to lease an entire factory plus all of the equipment in it.

To lease is to obtain use of an asset without ever gaining title to it. There are two types of leases. *Operating leases* are usually characterised by the following features:

(a) The lease can be cancelled by the lessee prior to its expiration, with options to review.
(b) The lessor provides service, maintenance and insurance.
(c) The sum of all the lease payments by the lessee does not necessarily fully provide for the recovery of the asset's cost. Subsequent lessees or the lease sale are required to recover the investment.

Typically operating lessors provide goods that are not peculiar to one kind of industry, that is, office space, computers, fleets of cars and trucks. *Financial leases* have the following features:

(a) The lease *cannot* be cancelled by the lessee prior to its expiry date.
(b) The lessor may or may not provide service, maintenance and insurance for the asset.
(c) The asset is fully amortised over the life of the asset.

A finance lease is now required by SSAP 21 to be shown on the balance sheet as an asset at fair value and as a liability for future lease payments. The key distinction is 'cancellability'.

Under a leasing agreement the 'lessee' obtains assets from the lessor, who maintains ownership of the assets. The lessee makes regular tax-deductible payments to the lessor for the use of the assets; these payments are a contractual liability and so failure to meet them could lead to bankruptcy.

A typical lease agreement covers four topics:

(a) The life of the lease.
(b) The timing and amount of payments.
(c) Agreements on renewing the lease or on purchasing the asset at the end of the lease period.
(d) Arrangements concerning repairs, insurance and other expenses.

There are two principal methods of obtaining leased assets. The first is a 'direct' lease where a user decides on an asset and then persuades a financial institution to buy the asset and lease it to him. On the other hand a 'sale and leaseback' lease is where a financial institution buys an asset already owned by a user and then leases the asset back to the user. The lessee receives cash and is able to continue to use the asset. This form of leasing is applied mainly to buildings and the leases tend to be for long periods. Chapter 11 examines 'sale and leaseback' in more detail. Direct leases in Ireland are usually for a period of between three and seven years; the total payment over the life of the lease amounts to the net cost of the asset plus a service charge and an interest charge. Leasing is a source of finance in that the only other way in which the user could obtain the asset would be by purchase. This would require finance.

The cost of leasing depends on the asset being leased, the creditworthiness of the lessee, the period of the primary lease, interest rates and service charges. The cost is somewhat reduced by the tax deductibility of leasing costs. However, these costs must be offset against the loss of depreciation allowances in computing taxable profits.

A firm considering a leasing arrangement should shop around to find the best leasing terms. It should then compare the cost of the leasing agreements with the costs and benefits that would arise through purchasing the asset using alternative sources of finance. In attempting a 'lease or buy' analysis it is particularly important to examine the availability of cash discounts, government grants and the initial and annual allowances granted by the tax authorities.

Leasing in Ireland differs somewhat from practice in the United States and United Kingdom due to the following:

(1) The availability of capital grants in Ireland, which are paid to the owner rather than to the user of the asset: hence the lessor and not the lessee gains an advantage.

(2) The liberal annual and initial allowances in Ireland. An Irish firm with taxable profits could write off the entire purchase price of an asset in one tax year. This provides a greater tax shield for purchasing an asset than leasing it.

(3) Tax relief on export profits, which means that many Irish manufacturing firms have no tax liability. Purchasing an asset in these circumstances provides no tax shield. Leasing an asset allows the lessor to gain a tax advantage, thus enabling the lessor to provide finance to the lessee on terms cheaper than that of purchasing the asset. Note that export tax relief applies only to firms exporting manufactured products prior to January 1981.

(4) A low 10 per cent tax rate on manufacturing company profits compared to 50 per cent on service company profits. As such a manufacturing company obtains a low tax shield on depreciation, plus interest payments should they buy the asset while a service company leasing the equipment to a user has a 50 per cent tax shield on depreciation plus interest. Savings can be passed on to the lessee.

The system of capital grants and taxation incentives available in Ireland are such that in theory certain lessees should be able to acquire the use of assets at absolutely minimal costs.

For example, Locscrew Limited are considering an investment in Nenagh, Co. Tipperary. The Shannon Free Airport Development Company have approved a 60 per cent capital grant to Locscrew. The management of Locscrew are considering leasing a £40,000 packaging machine. A leasing company has offered a three-year lease to Locscrew at a cost of £2,500 per year. At the end of the three-year period the bank will sell the machine to Locscrew for £5,000. The offer is very attractive to the management of Locscrew who are using all available cash to further expand export sales. Should Locscrew decide to buy the machine then they can borrow £16,000 from the same bank over a three-year period with repayments of £5,000 in each of the first two years and an interest rate of 16 per cent. The calculations in this extreme example are shown in Table 37. Remember that there is no effect on cash inflows, as revenues remain the same.

Table 37 Lease or Buy

A Cash Outflows on Buy Decision

Year	1	2	3
Interest on Loan	2,560	1,760	960
Capital Repayment	5,000	5,000	6,000
Total Outflows	£7,560	£6,760	£6,960

B Cash Outflows on Lease Decision

Year	1	2	3
Lease Payments	2,500	2,500	2,500
Purchase Price	—	—	5,000
	£2,500	£2,500	£7,500

Obviously in the case of Locscrew it is cheaper to lease than to buy. To understand the causes of the disparity examine Table 38.

Table 38 Cost of Purchasing Packaging Machine by Industrial Bank

Cost of Machine	£40,000
Less 60%	24,000
	16,000
Less tax shield of 50 per cent of net asset price offset against taxable profits	8,000
Net Cost of Asset	£8,000

Note that the tax shield is only a deferral of tax. If 100 per cent depreciation is taken in year 1 then none is available for subsequent years. However, a bank should be capable of having continuous tax shields, thus in effect getting a permanent saving.

What effectively happens is that the state pays 80 per cent of the purchase price of the asset. The example here is extreme in that grants are not paid immediately and depreciation allowances may also be taken in arrears.

In certain cases in Ireland businesses have been established with capital costs as low as those used in the above example. Prior to the passing of the 1986 Finance Act, the tax shield would have been allowed on the full cost of the machine.

Because it is the use of assets and not their ownership which is essential for profitable operations, leasing facilities offer several advantages. The major advantage is that the firm does not have to tie up scarce resources to obtain the use of assets. This can be of vital importance to the smaller business. A further advantage is that the most modern equipment can be obtained without the outlay of capital and should the asset become obsolete during the lease period the lessee has the option to trade in for the up-to-date model though a fine is levied for changing the lease.

The very rapid growth in leasing shown in Table 36 can be expected to continue. New specialist leasing firms have entered the market. They have little overhead, access to capital and skills and have a mix of business which ensures that little, if any, tax is payable, that is, they mix assets on which capital depreciation is free — such as industrial machines with cars.

These firms are cheaper, quicker and more flexible than the more traditional industrial banks. Because of increased competition costs are declining. Businesses can often lease assets cheaper than they can borrow or buy.

HIRE PURCHASE

Hire purchase in its widest meaning embraces two different systems for purchasing goods on an instalment basis; hire purchase agreements and credit sales agreements. The major difference between the two is the date of the transfer of ownership. Under hire purchase agreements ownership remains with the seller until the last payment. The agreement is for the rental of the goods with an option to purchase at a nominal price at the end of the hire purchase. Credit sales agreements transfer ownership immediately to the purchaser who agrees to pay for the goods over a specified period.

The range of goods that can be obtained through hire purchase is extensive. Motor vehicles form the largest category but other categories of importance to the businessman are industrial machinery, furniture and office equipment, and contractor's plant.

Hire purchase agreements are between three parties, the purchaser, the seller, and the financier, which is generally a company dealing exclusively with hire purchase transactions. Normally the financier is skilled in credit evaluation. Frequently, as in the case of television sales, the retailer enters into hire purchase agreements with the purchaser. A block of such agreements is sold to a finance house usually for 80 per cent of the face value. This process is known as 'block discounting'.

The objective in hire purchase or 'equipment financing' as it may be known, is to have the market value of the asset always above the sum owed to the financier. Hence only a percentage of the purchase price is advanced and the period of the agreement rarely goes over three years.

Hire purchase can be a very expensive form of finance. The rate of interest charged is calculated on the initial sum borrowed, not the amount outstanding at any one time. A simple method of calculating the true rate of interest being paid is as follows:

$$\frac{\text{Stated Interest Rate Per Annum} \times 2 \times \text{Number of Instalments}}{\text{Number of Instalments} + 1}$$

It can be seen from this formula that the true rate of interest is approximately twice the stated rate. In mid 1988 the true rate was almost $21\frac{1}{2}$ per cent per annum.

The advantages claimed for hire purchase as a source of finance are that (a) it enables a firm to obtain the use of assets without large outlay, (b) all costs are tax deductible and (c) annual depreciation allowances plus initial allowances on the full retail price of the goods can sometimes be claimed.

Relative to other sources, hire purchase finance is expensive. A further disadvantage is that total instalment due on hire purchase contracts will be detailed on the liability side of the balance sheet. If the amount is substantial, it will adversely affect the firm's efforts to raise further debt finance. Firms with no tax liability would be well advised to seek alternative sources of finance.

Despite the high cost of finance in early 1988 there was over £675 million extended under hire purchase and instalment credit agreements. Over 70 per cent of the total was advanced by industrial banks, 9 per cent by hire purchase companies and the balance by trading companies and state-sponsored bodies.

The principal users of hire purchase are private individuals and small firms who often find it the only source of finance available to them, though a surprising number of large companies hire car fleets, office equipment etc. The logic behind these apparently poor financial decisions is a desire to minimise investments on balance sheets.

TERM LOANS

One consequence of rapid economic growth in Ireland has been an increase in demands for capital. The banking system, which for many years had exported capital, now found internal demand greater than supply. Much of the new demand was for investment in fixed assets. The traditional bank overdraft form of lending was not suited to the demand and so term loans were introduced. A term loan is for a fixed period of time with repayments of principal and interest on an agreed periodic basis. While the average term loan is granted for periods between three and five years, in exceptional cases the term may be stretched to seven years.

Term loans are tailored to suit the requirements of the individual firm and consequently provisions are flexible, that is, there may be a remission of all repayments in the first year, large payments (balloon payments) may be permitted at the end of the term, and so on. The interest cost on term loans is higher than bank overdraft. The rate charged will depend on the source of the finance, the term of the loans, the creditworthiness of the firm seeking the loan and current interest rates. In general it will be at least one half of one per cent greater than bank overdraft rate but may be much higher depending on the risk of the venture. Interest is payable on the outstanding balance. As in the case of commercial bank loans, interest charges are tax deductible.

The term loan structure of interest rates in Ireland is shown in Table 39. Note the variation in interest rates between the associated and non-associated banks. In practice the non-associated banks arrange individual packages whereas the associated banks use the published interest rate tables.

Table 39   Selected Lending Rates in Ireland

Per cent per annum	1984	1985	1986	1987	1988
Central Bank					
Rediscount rate	13·90	10·85	13·30	13·10	12·5
Short-term facility	14·00	10·25	13·25	13·25	9·5
Licensed Banks					
Associated Banks					
Term loan categories					
Overdrafts and term loans					
up to 1 year					
AAA	14·75	10·25–10·50	11·75–14·00	11·75–14·00	10.5
AA	15·75	12·00–12·50	13·75–17·00	13·75–17·00	12.5
A	17·25	14·25–15·00	15·50–17·75	16·50–17·75	14.0
Over 1 year and up to 3 years					
AAA	14·00	10·50–10·75	12·25–13·75	12·25–13·75	11.0
AA	15·75	12·25–12·50	14·50–16·00	14·50–16·00	13.0
A	17·25	14·50–14·75	17·00–17·75	17·00–17·75	14.5
Over 3 years and up to 5 years					
AAA	14·50	11·00–11·25	12·75–14·00	12·75–14·00	11·5
AA	16·25	12·50–12·75	15·00–16·25	15·00–16·25	13·5
A	18·00	14·75	17·00–17·75	17·00–17·75	14·75
Over 5 years and up to 7 years					
AAA	15·00	11·50	13·25–14·50	13·25–14·50	12·0
AA	16·75	13·50	15·76–16·75	15·75–16·75	14·0
A	18·50	15·00	17·00–17·75	17·00–17·75	15·75
Loan accounts					
AAA	15·00	12·50	14·25–15·50	14·25–15·50	13·0
AA	17·25	14·25	16·50–17·50	16·50–17·50	15·0
A	19·25	15·00	17·00–17·75	17·00–17·75	16·0
World Bank Livestock Development Project					
Composite rate	12·50	11·25–12·00	12·25–12·50	12·25–12·50	12·0
House purchase loans scheme	14·75	11·25–11·50	12·50–12·75	12·50–13·75	10·5
Concessionary rates under export of capital goods scheme					
(a) To EEC member states	3·60	12·25	9·80	9·80	7·8
(b) To Non-EEC countries	10·70	9·85	7·40–9·55	7·40–9·55	7·4
Non-Associated banks					
Overdrafts	14·00–20·00	11·75–16·50	14·00–16·75	14·00–16·75	11·0 13·0
Term loans (1-5 years)	15·00–22·00	11·75–17·75	14·75–18·25	14·75–18·00	14·75 16·0
Instalment credit (incl. personal loans gross of tax)					
Flat rate	12·00–19·50	11·50–18·50	12·00–18·50	12·00–18·50	12·0
Annual effective rate	23·30–38·20	22·30–36·20	23·30–36·20	23·30–36·20	23·20
Building Societies					
Mortgage loans	11·75	9·75	12·50	12.50	10·25

Source: Central Bank of Ireland

The actual term loan agreement is a legal contract often stretching to many pages. Borrowers would be well advised to read carefully each line of the contract and to have lawyers explain any complex provision. The contract usually covers the following:

(a) The amount of the loan.
(b) The term of the loan.
(c) The purpose of the loan.
(d) Repayment dates.
(e) Interest rate and how it may vary.
(f) Commitment fees and drawdown fees.
(g) Restrictive covenants on working capital, dividends, salaries.
(h) The security being pledged.
(i) Guarantee of the principals behind the borrowing firm. The guarantees are usually joint and several guarantees.
(j) Provisions relating to default.
(k) Stock option schemes.
(l) Prepayment penalties and provisions.
(m) Life insurance on essential executives.

Many of the above provisions may bear hard on management, so it is wise to be fully aware of the implications of all the provisions of the contract. Frequently term lenders require fixed and floating charges over all the assets of a business, thus restricting asset management. Restrictive covenants may place limits on borrowings and/or ceilings on salaries/dividends.

The most common restrictive covenants relate to working capital levels and to capital expenditure limitations. Often an absolute net current asset figure is stipulated in the agreement. The purpose of this is to preserve liquidity, thus minimising any risk of default. Capital expenditure decisions are often limited to an agreed figure.

Stock option schemes can prove expensive if the business does grow. Lenders argue that they are entitled to share in the success of a business if they provide 'finance for growth'. This point is debatable but usually the borrower is in a weak position since the funds are required. Commitment, legal and other fees are usually charged by term-lenders. Though small, these fees increase the effective interest rate. Joint and several guarantees are onerous since each individual bears full responsibility for all the debt. In the event of business failure the investor will probably be ruined. Possibly of greater concern, other lenders will be less willing to advance funds to individuals with outstanding guarantees.

Borrowers would be well advised to seek funds from their commercial bank prior to approaching other banks. Non-associated banks are very flexible in their approach to lending while the commercial banks are more rigid. Increasing competition among banks makes it essential to shop around. A difference of 1 or 2 per cent in interest rates is often found between banks. This can make an important difference in the rate of return on the equity investment.

It is important to negotiate a term loan. That does not mean asking for the money and signing the contract. Each provision in the contract should be negotiated. It is possible that certain provisions can be deleted or adapted. Particularly in growing companies restrictions on capital expenditure may prove unwise.

PREPARING A TERM LOAN APPLICATION

Practically every business will require medium-term finance at some time or other. Before seeking a term loan, management would be well advised to prepare a detailed package for submission to the bank. The package should include the following:

(a) The audited accounts for the company for recent years.
(b) An outline of the proposed project including markets, capital cost and some operational details.
(c) A financial analysis, as outlined in previous chapters, which examines projected cash inflows and outflows and estimates the return on investment.
(d) A proposed repayment schedule.
(e) The nature of the security, if any, being offered as collateral for the loan.

While some of the above requirements seem onerous it should be remembered that cautious management will already have prepared most of the data for their own purposes. Furthermore, submissions for capital grants or assistance from the government must be accompanied by detailed figures on any proposed project.

Term loans are particularly useful to firms not wanting to raise permanent or long-term finance, and to those businesses expanding rapidly with a time lag between expenditure and the resultant cash inflows. Managements short of the cash necessary to make profitable investments or those with large semi-permanent bank overdrafts should examine the possibilities of putting their businesses on a stronger financial footing by raising a term loan. It is equally important for management to maintain a continuing relationship with the lender during the period of the loan. The lender has funds at risk in the business so he/she should be given up-to-date, candid information on the state of the business. Having accepted the terms of the loan contract, management must live up to the provisions and not attempt to circumvent them. The purpose of these provisions is to safeguard the interest and capital repayments of the term loan. It is important to remember that these provisions are negotiable both before the term loan is accepted and during the life of the loan. The lender will be quite willing to reconsider the provisions if management can show that they are restricting the profitable expansion of the business.

CONCLUSION

Medium-term financing covers those financial instruments with lives of between one and seven years. Such instruments have developed rapidly in Ireland. This chapter has covered the three principal forms of inter-mediate term financing — leasing, hire purchase and term loans. The explosive growth in leasing was explained. Indeed for export-oriented companies in business prior to 1981 and for all manufacturing firms established after 31 December 1980, leasing may be second only to state grants as a cheap source of finance. Hire purchase was shown to be a widely used but very expensive source. Term loans, which have become the stable source of business finance, are useful but expensive. In terms of risk, leasing and term loans have contractual obligations which if defaulted upon can lead to loss of the business. With hire purchase, default normally means the repossession of the asset. Term loans have the most restrictive control effect. Unless negotiated carefully, term loan agreements can dilute the control of the owners. This does not apply to leasing or to hire purchase.

Further Reading
J. H. Arnold: 'How to Negotiate a Term Loan', *Harvard Business Review,* **60** (March-April 1982), pp. 131-138.
J. Bates: *The Financing of Small Business,* Sweet & Maxwell, London 1982.
R. Robinson: *Financing The Dynamic Small Firm,* Wadsworth, Belmont, California 1968.

Chapter 11

Long-Term Loan Finance

Most businesses are going concerns. This means that they have no definable life. Some live for centuries. The Rathbone candle business in Dublin has lasted for five hundred years while the Smyth clothing company in Balbriggan was a relative youngster of around two hundred and fifty years experience when it died in 1980. Few if any businessmen look centuries into the future but many do expect to be in business for decades. Some investments, such as land, buildings and even some plant have very long lives. Less clear perhaps is the long-term element in working capital. Though all working capital should turn over rapidly, a part is a long-term or permanent investment.

Short- and medium-term sources of finance are not suited for long-term investment. Using them would raise the risk of liquidation. Financial institutions have developed financial instruments to meet the demand for long-term funds. This chapter examines long term debt instruments while the following chapter examines the sources of ownership finance.

The sources of finance examined in this chapter are:
(a) Sale and Leaseback.
(b) Debentures.
(c) Section 84 Loans.
(d) Indexed Bonds.
(e) Project Financing.

The above sources are generally available only to substantial, profitable businesses. Most privately-owned Irish-based companies would not be in a position to raise substantial long-term loans. Project financing is a very particular type of finance available only to large resource-based projects.

SALE AND LEASEBACK
Many businesses have substantial investments in property. Older firms often find themselves the owners of prime property. It is possible to sell

property to financial institutions who are seeking outlets for their funds and thereby 'unlock' frozen equity in real estate assets. This would give the vendor cash but no premises. The buying institution usually wishes to rent or lease the property. Who better to lease it to than the original owner?

Leases are usually for a period of thirty-five years with renewal options. Because of rapid inflation in rents, the leases normally carry a provision allowing revisions of rent every five or seven years. Insurance, maintenance and rates are generally paid by the lessee.

The cost of this source of finance depends not only on the annual lease payments, but also on the frequency of rent reviews. Management should press for as few rent reviews as possible during the lease period. A further factor in estimating the cost of sale and leaseback is the fact that the firm loses the capital appreciation on property. In times of inflation and/or heavy demand, the value of property can increase rapidly. It is equally true to say that in deflationary times property prices can decline. However, it may be valid to say that commercial firms are not property developers and therefore should not employ their resources in property. This is logical only if a firm can more profitably use resources released from property.

It is important that the premises be marketable. The lessee must also be a tenant of substance as the lessor does not want problems during the period of the lease. These two reasons have restricted sale and leaseback to prime properties in large towns and cities and restricted leases to well-known businesses. In isolated cases large foreign firms in Ireland have managed a sale and leaseback on their premises. These may involve parent company guarantees.

In recent years the technique has developed to the stage that it is now possible for a user to design a totally new building, have an insurance company finance its construction and then lease the premises. Jacobs Limited did just that with their factory at Tallaght. As a general rule, sale and leaseback is effected through insurance companies and institutional investors, such as pension funds, more often than commercial banks. A firm should answer carefully the following questions before it uses sale and leaseback:

(a) Does it need the funds that will be provided?
(b) Will the cost of leasing the building back exceed the return anticipated from the capital created through the sale and leaseback technique?

Sale and leaseback may be a particularly costly source of finance. In an inflationary era property prices tend to rise rapidly. The companies who sold their premises in the 1970s lost capital appreciation and so paid a high price for the funds. However, property prices fell through the first seven years of the 1980s, so firms who sold in the late 1970s would have a very cheap sort of finance. Selling a premises loses an asset widely acceptable as security and lenders tend to view premises as good collateral.

DEBENTURES

A debenture is a long-term loan with specific maturity, interest and repayment provisions. The average life of a debenture is between ten and twenty years. The lenders of long-term funds are creditors of the borrowing company. Generally, the relationship between borrower and lender is covered by a legal contract known as 'an indenture'. This contract is similar to the term-loan contract. As long as the borrower operates within the confines of the indenture the lenders have no control over the business. Should the terms of the contract be breached then the lenders may obtain a voice in management and in extreme cases they or their representatives may end up running the business.

Debentures are also known as fixed income securities. This is because long-term loans offer a fixed annual rate of interest to the lender. The interest rate is known as the 'coupon rate'. Apart from having fixed maturities and interest payments, debentures have preferential rights to repayment in the event of a corporate liquidation.

Types of Debentures

A firm can raise long-term debt in a number of ways.

(1) Unsecured or Naked Debentures. The lender of a naked debenture has no security apart from the profitability of the business. Such instruments are used when the business in question is either very strong or so weak as to have no security to offer. Generally naked debentures are issued only by extremely strong firms. Examples of unsecured loan stocks are the $7\frac{3}{4}$ per cent Unsecured Loan Stock issued by Guinness and redeemable in 2001, the 8 per cent Debenture Stock redeemable between 1986 and 1991 issued by Cement-Roadstone Holdings and 11 per cent Unsecured Loan Stock issued by Seafield Gentex Limited redeemable between 1976 and 1996. This latter issue is an interesting example of the dangers of being unsecured. When the debentures were issued Seafield was a strong company. By the mid 1980s successive annual losses had weakened it. The loan stock was selling in 1988 at £33 per £100 of stock, thus giving a yield of over 30 per cent.

(2) Mortgage Debentures. This is the most common method of long-term debt financing. The lender obtains a lien on specific assets, usually buildings and/or land. Often the lender takes a 'floating charge' over all

present and future assets of the business. The details of the mortgage must be registered with the Registrar of Companies. Where more than one mortgage exists debentures will be ranked by number.

(3) Guaranteed Debentures. Some businesses in Ireland are able to raise long-term money because their debts are guaranteed, usually by their parent companies. The subsidiaries of large American based multi-nationals find it easy to raise finance on foot of the guarantee of their parents. So too do state-sponsored companies such as the Electricity Supply Board and Bord na Mona who have state guarantees supporting them.

(4) Convertible Debentures. This method of raising long-term loans has grown in recent years. The lender is given the right to convert the debt into ordinary shares of the firm at specific prices on or before specified dates. In this way, the lender is allowed to share in the fortunes of the firm. If the business is a publicly-quoted company and share prices rise rapidly, the loan holder has the right to buy shares at fixed prices. If the business does not do well and/or share prices do not rise on the stock market, the lender can continue to hold his loan and receive interest payments plus eventual capital repayment. Debentures such as these may or may not be protected by a mortgage. There are a few examples of convertible debentures on the Irish Stock Exchange. The Bank of Ireland has a 10 per cent Convertible Loan Stock.

(5) Debentures with an equity 'sweetener'. Sometimes the debenture holder may be allowed to buy shares in a firm at a special valuation. If the firm expands to the stage that it can 'go public' then the loan holder may sell his shares and realise a profit. This type of financing is used mainly for small- to medium-sized private firms with good potential. Merchant banks are the usual lenders of this type of debenture. In return for their risk, they buy a proportion of the total shareholding — anything from fifteen per cent to about thirty per cent. They may also insist on the appointment of a director to assist the firm and to safeguard their interest. Merchant banks prefer to see ahead to the 'take out' point when they will have the opportunity to realise their investment. They may be content to see the shares grow in value and receive dividends for a long period. The logic of a sweetener is that the debenture holder is putting funds into a risky venture. All he receives is his interest, plus his original investment. The downside risk is the loss of all his investment. On the other hand, the holder of equity has the same downside risk but has far greater potential for profit. Should the venture succeed then the holders of shares will make handsome returns.

(6) Subordinated Debentures. A subordinated debenture is an unsecured debt which is junior to all other debts, that is, other debtholders

must be fully paid before the subordinated debenture holder receives anything. This type of debt will have a higher interest rate than more senior debt and will often have rights of conversion into ordinary shares. It is a very useful means of finance in that it does not restrict further issues of debt because it is subordinated. From the owner's point of view it is as good as debt because it will not affect control.

Subordinated debt is known as mezzanine finance because it ranks between equity and standard debt. It became very popular in the 1980s. The phenomenon known as the *Junk Bond* became a widely used source of finance in takeovers and 'leveraged buyouts'. Ireland has had very little use of this form of finance.

Many United States companies establishing subsidiaries in Ireland use subordinated debt in their capital structure. If profits are generated in Ireland instead of being repatriated to the United States where they will be taxed the subordinated debenture is repaid. Since this is a repayment of capital no tax is due. Hence the parent receives the full repatriation of cash. Independent Newspapers Limited has a 10 per cent Subordinated Loan Stock repayable in 1993. The coupon rate on a subordinated debenture should be higher than average to allow for the higher risk borne by the lender. Junk Bonds became a popular source of finance when it was shown that the higher interest rates more than compensated for the additional risk. There is concern among experts that in an economic recession there will be major defaults in subordinated bonds. Chapter 15 returns to this topic.

(7) Perpetual Debentures. This is a very rare animal. The only example in existence in Ireland was the 4 per cent Perpetual Debenture Stock of the Alliance and Dublin Consumers Gas Company. In 1866 when the stock was issued individuals thought that the right to receive 4 per cent interest in perpetuity was a good investment. In 1985 the company went into liquidation. The debenture holders were repaid in full.

Characteristics of Debentures

The characteristics of debentures can be evaluated by means of risk income and control effects. The risk to the borrower of using debentures is the inability to meet annual fixed commitments. Every increase in borrowed funds increases this risk known as the 'financial risk'. The income effect arises from the possibility of investing fixed interests funds to produce a return higher than the cost.

Debt financing involves the firm in fixed annual commitments as to interest and perhaps capital repayments. This is both the great advantage of this source and the great disadvantage: each is related to the concept of leverage or gearing. If a firm raises a loan at, say, nine per cent and invests this money to yield fifteen per cent, the difference is an extra profit to the owners. However, if the firm is unable to get any return from the investment of borrowed money and cannot pay the nine per cent annual interest the debenture holders are entitled to foreclose on the firm. This may best be explained by a short example:

Two firms, A and B, have investments of £50,000 each but firm A financed £20,000 of this investment by means of a debenture with net interest payment of £1,200 per annum. Both firms earn £5,000 after taxes which equals an earnings yield of 10 per cent for firm B, that is, £5,000 ÷ £50,000. However, after paying out interest of £1,200 the owners of firm A have £3,800 left which represents a yield of 12.6 per cent on their investment of £30,000.

Table 40   Gearing Effect

	Firm A		Firm B	
Year	1988	1989	1988	1989
After tax earnings	£5,000	£1,000	£5,000	£1,000
Interest on £20,000 at a rate equal to 6 per cent after tax	1,200	1,200	—	—
Net earnings on owner's investment	£3,800	(200)	£5,000	1,000
Owner's investment	30,000	30,000	50,000	50,000
Earnings yield	12.6%	–0.65%	10.0%	2%

Now consider the effect of an 80 per cent drop in after-tax earnings, that is, earnings of each firm drops to £1,000. Firm B now yields 2 per cent on owner's investment. Firm A is unable to pay its interest. The debenture holders may foreclose on firm A and sell off the assets to receive their £20,000. Because of the fixed charge commitment of long-term debt the risk to the owners and creditors is automatically increased.

In most countries debentures are a cheap source of finance. This is because interest rates are tax deductible. In Ireland, the 10 per cent manufacturing profits tax rate means that the tax shield on interest rates is small. An estimate of the cost of a debenture is as follows:

$$\text{Net Cost} = \frac{\text{Annual Interest}}{\text{Net Proceeds of the Issue}} \times (1 - \text{tax rate})$$

For Irish manufacturing industry the tax rate is often zero but rarely more than 10 per cent so that the net cost approximates the gross cost. This compares to a net cost of half the gross cost in most countries.

Straight debenture issues are rare in Ireland. Service industries such as banking and insurance use them but they are costly for many firms and unattractive to most investors. Inflation can make a nonsense of debentures. Anyone buying £100 of debentures knowing that they will be repaid £100 in twenty years time would need a very high rate of interest to compensate for the time value of the money, the risk of not being repaid and the loss in real value caused by inflation.

Deciding the amount of long-term debt to raise involves the balancing of the risk, income and control aspects of the firm. However, certain guidelines can be applied to the firm's operations to discover the debt capacity of the business.

In evaluating a debenture, a lender will tend to examine three measures of business worth. These have previously been mentioned in Chapter 3 but are worth repeating.

(1) Debt/Equity Ratio. This is the ratio of the amount of long-term debt to the amount of permanent or ownership capital in the business. The lower the proportion of debt to equity, the less risky a firm appears. The rule of thumb applied to the average firm with average earnings is an optimum debt equity ratio of twenty-five to thirty-five per cent. Two investigations of the proportion of debt to equity in Irish business revealed that long-term debt made up less than ten per cent of the long-term capital structure. This would appear to indicate that Irish businessmen are conservative in their approach to introducing fixed charge capital, or that long-term funds are not readily available.

(2) Times Interest Covered. This measures the cushion of earnings available to a prospective lender, for example for Ardmore Limited in 1986.

Earnings after tax	£78,700
Interest	£35,700
Times interest covered	2.2

(3) Times burden covered. It is common for debentures to be repaid by annual instalments rather than on a lump payment at the end of the term. The total of interest and annual capital repayments is called the burden. A cover of two, that is, earnings twice the annual burden, is a commonly required figure.

SECTION 84 LOANS

An innovation in Ireland is 'Section 84' loans. Arising from Section 84 of the 1976 Corporation Tax Act, where a payment can be classified as a distribution, it is regarded as franked income and not liable to tax in the hands of the receiving company. In effect this means that a bank loans funds to a company. Instead of paying an annual interest rate on the loan the company declares a dividend. In theory this dividend is at risk whereas interest *must* be paid. However, to enable a distribution to be made, all that is required is a reserve of undistributed profits. In order to persuade the Revenue Commissioners that the loan is a section 84 loan the interest on the loan must be related to the profitability of the company. The method in common use is to state that the lender will receive .001 per cent of the profits of the borrower over a certain agreed figure.

Because the lender is not paying tax on his income he can charge a lower interest rate. A useful formula for estimating the rate of interest on Section 84 loans is as follows:

Cost of Section 84 Loan = (1 – bank tax rate) × Dublin Interbank Rate + banks margin.

This type of financing is particularly advantageous to businesses with no tax liability due to export tax relief or to losses carried forward. The advent of the 10 per cent corporate tax rate increased the demand for this type of loan.

A particular aspect of Section 84 loans arises in the Shannon Export Zone where a 10 per cent corporation tax rate is in force until the year 2000 for manufacturing and internationally traded services. In order to assist foreign investment in Ireland, the State negotiated double taxation agreements with numerous countries whereby tax advantages arising in Ireland could be passed back to the country of origin of the investors. In many countries dividends paid by an Irish company are exempt from tax in the hands of the recipient. In certain countries the double taxation treaty requires a minimum shareholding in the Irish venture. Examples are shown in Table 41..

The investor in Shannon — provided he is a resident in one of the above countries — obtains tax relief on funds borrowed to invest in Shannon. Income from Shannon is tax free.

The higher the rate of corporation tax in the investor's country, the greater the tax benefit. A German company pays corporation tax of 60 per cent; therefore a 10 per cent cost of borrowed funds has a net after-tax cost of 4 per cent.

Table 41   Minimum Shareholding Required to Obtain Tax
Shelter on Irish Dividends Percentage of Equity

Country of Origin	Percentage Holding in Irish Companies
Austria	25
Denmark	25
France	10
Canada	25
Belgium	0
Finland	0
Germany	10

By investing these funds in Shannon and loaning them on, a German investor can obtain a tax-free source of income while at the same time offering significantly lower interest rates to borrowers. A simplistic example is worked below:

Stage A

German company borrows funds at 10%	=	10%
Tax shelter at 60%	=	6%
Net cost		4%
Funds invested in Shannon associate		

Stage B

Shannon term loans or leases to customer nominated by German investor at 8%	=	8%
Shannon tax rate 10%	=	0.8%
Net return to Shannon company	=	7.2%

Stage C

Dividends declared to German company by Shannon associate	=	7%
Tax on Irish dividends received by German company	=	0
Net return	=	7%

Result
Everyone happy except the German tax authorities who subsidise the exercise.

INDEXED BONDS

Inflation has already been mentioned as having a very damaging effect on debentures. Fixed income and fixed sum repayments are uneconomic in times of rapid inflation. Numerous attempts have been made to develop a financial instrument which retains the security and fixed income of the debenture but which also provides some safeguard against inflation.

Club Mediterranée, in early 1980, launched a sixteen-year debenture with an 8.5 per cent coupon rate but with two additional bonuses: (a) an increased payout to debenture holders if occupancy of a new holiday resort rose above 60 per cent and (b) a bonus related to rises in the prices of vacations. The very low interest rate on the debentures and the fact that the issue was heavily over-subscribed suggests that the new financial instrument may finally bridge the gap between debt and equity. The first bonus, on occupancy, offers a participation in profits while the second bonus, on prices, makes an allowance for inflation.

The benefit to the borrower is the low rate of interest and the fact that higher rates will not be paid until the venture in which the funds are being invested is successful.

It is thought that this type of finance will be attractive to any business which can identify the breakeven threshold and whose prices match or exceed inflation. In Ireland organisations such as the Electricity Supply Board and Ryans Hotels may find this type of finance efficient.

PROJECT FINANCING

Two events coincided in recent years to make the financing of many projects virtually impossible. Technology in many industries changed so that efficient production required massive capital-intensive projects. At the same time inflation caused capital costs to soar. The net result was that many large projects, particularly in natural resources, became virtually impossible to finance. New instruments had to be and were developed. Now huge capital projects are financed by means of a custom-tailored package. This package is known as project finance. In Ireland project finance has been used on the £450 million Alcan project on the Shannon Estuary, the £105 million Tara zinc/lead mine at Navan and the £100 million Marathon gas field off Kinsale. In the United Kingdom a special package of over £1,000 million was raised to finance British Petroleum's Ninian oil field in the North Sea.

Large capital intensive projects cause additional problems:

(1) Often construction and development take years. During that period the parent company would have to fund interest and other carrying costs with no revenue arising from the project.

(2) Attempting to consolidate huge debt sums on a balance sheet would totally distort the apparent financial strength of the company, for example, up to the day the Ninian field came on stream, British Petroleum had little to show for their investment, but debts of £1,000 million.

(3) Any one financial institution could hardly afford the risk attaching to such loans. Few banks would survive a £1,000 million write-off. Remember the Bank of Ireland Group with £8,000 million of assets produced £50 million in profits in the year ended March 1987.

Although the term project financing has been used to describe all types and kinds of financing of projects, both with and without recourse, the term has evolved in recent years to allow a more precise definition:

A financing of a particular economic unit in which a lender is satisfied to look initially to the cash flows and earnings of that economic unit as the source of funds from which a loan will be repaid and to the assets of the economic unit as collateral for the loan.

Boards of directors are receptive to proceeding with projects which can be financed entirely or substantially on their own merits.

Industries engaged in the production, processing, transportation or use of metals and energy have been particularly attracted to project financing techniques because of the needs of such companies for new capital sources to provide new sources.

The ultimate in project financing is to arrange borrowing for a project which will benefit the sponsor and at the same time be completely non-recourse to the sponsor, not in any way affecting its credit standing or balance sheet. Indeed, project financing is sometimes called off balance sheet financing. This can be accomplished by using the credit of a third party to support the transaction. However, rarely are projects constructed or financed themselves without credit support from sponsors or interested third parties.

There is considerable room for discussion between lenders and borrowers as to what constitutes a feasible project financing. Borrowers prefer their projects to be financed independently off balance sheet. Lenders, on the other hand, are not in the venture capital business. They are not equity risk takers. Lenders want to feel secure that they are going to be repaid either by the project, the sponsor or an interested third party. Therefore, *the key to successful project financing is structuring the financing of a project with as little recourse as possible to the sponsor while at the same time providing sufficient credit support through guarantees or undertakings of the sponsor or third party so lenders will be satisfied with the credit risk.*

An independent economic unit which qualifies as a viable credit for a project financing will usually have all of the following characteristics:

(1) The project must be backed by strong supporters. This backing may be provided by the sponsor or by a third party. The backing may be limited to the critical construction and start-up period rather than for the

life of the project. It may take the form of direct or indirect guarantees, take-or-pay contracts, or economic necessity. These types of supports can often be structured so they do not have the same impact as debt on the sponsor's balance sheet. They may be off balance sheet for the sponsor if support is provided by a third party.

(2) A credit risk is involved rather than an equity risk or a venture capital risk. As noted previously, lenders are lenders. They are not in the business of taking equity risks even if compensated as equity risk takers.

(3) The financial viability of the project must be shown. Conservative projections of assured internally generated cash flows must be prepared and justified by appropriate independent feasibility and engineering studies. The cash flow projections must be sufficient to service any debt contemplated, provide for cash needs, pay operating expenses and still provide an adequate cushion for contingencies.

(4) Supply contracts for product and/or energy to the project must be assured at a cost consistent with the financial projections.

(5) A market for the product or service must be assured at a price consistent with the financial projections. If take-or-pay contracts are being relied upon, they must be tight.

(6) Transportation for product into the project and product produced by the project must be assured at a cost consistent with the financial projections.

(7) The expertise of the contractor who is to construct the project facility must be well established.

(8) The financial capability and the technical expertise must be available to cover cost overruns and complete the project so that it operates in accordance with cost and production specifications.

(9) The project is not a new technology. The reliability of the process and the equipment to be used must be well established. The technical reliability and commercial viability of the project must be clear. If a new technology is involved, more than a lending risk is involved.

(10) The principal or the beneficiary of the sponsorship must have available the expertise to operate such a facility. In other words, the project cannot be a start-up situation dependent upon going to the outside to hire the expertise to operate the new facilities.

(11) In addition to operating expertise, management personnel must be available to manage the project. If the sponsor is already short on management personnel, the project is suspect.

(12) The properties and facilities being financed must have value as collateral.

(13) The political environment for the location of the project and the type of project must be reasonably friendly and stable.

(14) The sponsor must make an equity contribution consistent with its capability, interest in the project, and risk of the project.

(15) An adequate insurance programme must be available both during construction and operations.

(16) Government approvals must be obtained.

To overcome the problems a series of steps are followed:

(1) The project is developed by a subsidiary company; thus the parent can in many cases simply consolidate the equity investment in the subsidiary.

(2) One bank agrees to become the 'lead bank'. The lead bank attempts to organise a consortium of banks willing to take part in financing the project. The consortium might be as large as forty. Depending on the nature of the projects certain banks are likely to be interested, Texan banks in oil, New York banks in iron ore mining and Toronto banks in base metal mining.

(3) The banks commission a feasibility study which examines the physical and commercial viability of the project.

(4) Assuming it to be viable the consortium designs a set of loans with repayments based on the cash flow of the project. The repayment schedules are related to a percentage of revenue, say 20 per cent, or on a percentage of net cash flow, say 80 per cent. The repayments will vary with the level of production and the price of the output. Due to high depreciation write-offs in the early years tax is rarely paid so cash flows tend to be large.

(5) Shareholders rarely receive any dividends until all of the debt is repaid. This is not as harsh as it first appears since shareholders usually put up only a small percentage of the capital cost. The debt package may run as high as 90 per cent of the total cost.

(6) The lending consortium appoints one or more experts to monitor the capital expenditure, the operation of the projects and the loan repayments.

(7) A detailed contract, often running to numerous volumes, spells out the relationship between the consortium and the principal.

(8) The package of debt finance often involves subsidised loans for capital exports, loans from international organisations such as the World Bank, or European Investment Bank.

(9) The cost of the funds provided by the banks themselves is based on London Interbank rates or on Eurodollar rates.

As the search for natural resources spreads into more remote areas the costs of development rise. It is expected that the continuing rise in capital costs will mean that financing consortia in the future will broaden to include joint venture equity partners, governments and international agencies.

Causes of Project Failures

The best way to appreciate the concerns of lenders to a project is to review causes for project failures, which are as follows:

(1) Delays in completion with consequent delay in the contemplated revenue flow.

(2) Capital cost overrun.

(3) Technical failure.

(4) Financial failure of the contractor.

(5) Government interference.

(6) Uninsured casualty losses.

(7) Increased price or shortages of raw materials.

(8) Technical obsolescence of the plant.

(9) Loss of competitive position in the market place.

(10) Expropriation.

(11) Poor management.

In order for a project financing to be viable, these risks must be properly addressed and avoided.

Credit Impact Objective

While the sponsor or the beneficiary of a project financing ideally would prefer a non-recourse borrowing which does not in any way effect its credit standing or balance sheet, many project financings are aimed at achieving some particular objective such as any one or several of the following:

(1) Avoid being shown on the face of the balance sheet.

(2) Avoid being shown as debt on the face of the balance sheet so as not to impact financial ratios.

(3) Avoid being shown in a particular footnote to the balance sheet.

(4) Avoid being within the scope of restrictive covenants in an indenture or loan agreement which preclude direct debt financing or leases for the project.

(5) Avoid an open-end first mortgage.

· Any one or a combination of these objectives may be sufficient reason for a borrower to seek the structure of a project financing. Where a sponsor or a beneficiary of a project cannot initially arrange non-recourse borrowings which will not impact his balance sheet, the project may still be feasible if the sponsor is willing to assume the credit risk during the construction and start-up phase and provided lenders are willing to shift the credit risk to the project after the project facility is completed and operating. Under such an arrangement, most of the objectives of an off balance sheet project financing can be achieved after the initial risk period of construction and start-up. In some instances, the lenders may be satisfied to look to unconditional take-or-pay contracts from users of the product or services to be provided by the project. In other instances, the condition of the market for the product or service may be such that sufficient revenues are assured after completion of construction and start-up so as to convince lenders to rely on such revenues for repayment of their debts.

CONCLUSION

This chapter has broadened the sources of finance to include long-term sources of borrowed funds. Over time a wide variety of long-term debt sources have evolved to meet the needs of investors who want security but who also want participation. Inflation has pushed debentures out of favour. Recent new products include convertibles, equity sweeteners and profit-linked interest rates.

Traditionally long-term debt is a cheap source of finance. This arises due to the tax deductibility of interest rates. Low levels of corporate tax in Ireland mean that ordinary debentures are very expensive. The Section 84 loan employs a technique to reduce interest rates at the expense of the tax liability of the lender. The scope and size of many modern projects render obsolete traditional methods of finance. Project financing using a consortium of lenders, custom-tailored finance and repayments related to cash flow is the response of the financial community to the new needs.

Chapter 12

Ownership Sources of Finance

The sources of finance discussed to date have two things in common—they are all other people's money and they have to be repaid. These two features mean that a business should not be solely financed by debt sources of finance. A business venture, no matter how good, has an element of risk. Lenders are paid for the use of their funds. They may receive a risk premium but it is usually only a token payment. A business has an indeterminable life. It should outlive all of the debt sources of finance. This leads logically to owners' funds as a source of finance—the risk capital which is invested by people. This capital is usually permanent. It bears the financial and business risk of the venture. In the event of a liquidation all other sources of finance are repaid before the owners receive anything. Offsetting the risk disadvantages of ownership funds are the income and control advantages. Debt capital has a fixed return. After interest is paid the remainder of the profit is available to the owners. In successful ventures the profits can be very substantial. Borrowed funds rarely gives any control to the lenders. The investors in equity own and run the business.

This chapter examines ownership funds. The ownership sources of finance examined are preference shares, ordinary share capital and retained earnings. A mention is made of the evolution of venture capital in Ireland and the development of business expansion schemes.

PREFERENCE SHARES

Some investors are not willing to take the full risk which attaches to owners' funds. Instead, for a lower expected rate of return they seek a lower risk. Preference shares are designed to meet such needs. Preference shares usually have preferential rights to dividends and, in the event of liquidation, to repayment of capital. They participate in risk and profits but not to the same extent as ordinary shares. They combine some of the characteristics of both debt and equity. Owners tend to regard preference shares as similar to debt while lenders regard such issues as equity.

From the ordinary shareholder's point of view, apart from the cost, there is little to choose between preference shares and long-term debt, particularly if the firm has a stable earnings record. An ordinary shareholder will not receive a dividend as long as either interest or preference dividend payments remain unpaid. An ordinary shareholder expecting to receive dividend payments will regard the preference share dividend as much as a fixed charge as interest payments on debt. Looked at in this light, preference shares are an expensive form of long-term debt. The expense arises from the fact that dividends on preference shares are distributions of profits, not an expense, and as such they are not tax deductible.

Control of a firm is rarely affected by issuing preference shares. Generally the shares are non-voting except where the dividend has been passed. Control may be affected to the extent that an arrears of preference dividends may restrict management's actions.

Types of Preference Shares

Over time a number of variations on the basic form of preference share has evolved. The variations are designed to meet the varying needs of investors.

(1) Cumulative Preference Shares. Practically all preference issues are cumulative. This means that dividends not paid accumulate. All arrears must be cleared prior to paying dividends to the ordinary shareholders. There are many examples of cumulative preference share issues on the Irish stock exchange. Examples include Jacobs $6\frac{1}{2}$ per cent Cum. Pref., Arnott 6 per cent Cum. Pref.

(2) Redeemable Preference Shares. Many investors do not wish to make a perpetual investment at a fixed rate of return. To cater for such investors a finite life is given to certain preference shares—usually twenty years or longer. Some firms quoted on the Irish Stock Exchange have issued Redeemable Preference Shares. Examples include the 7 per cent Red Cum. Pref. issued by Unidare Limited.

(3) Participating Preference Shares. Some investors want the security of an annual dividend but they also want the chance to participate in the profitability of the business. To cater for such needs participating preference shares were developed. These shares are entitled to a fixed dividend coupon and to a further dividend which is related to the dividend paid on ordinary shares. An example is the 15 per cent Redeemable Participating Preference shares issued by Seafield.

(4) Convertible Preference Shares. In recent years a number of preference share issues have attracted subscribers by offering conversion rights into ordinary shares. Waterford Glass have a 10 per cent Conv. Red. Cum. Pref. share. In the mid 1980s Heitons issued a 6 per cent Con-

vertible Preference issue. One of the most complicated issues is a Convertible Cumulative Redeemable Participating Preference share issued by Youghal Carpets.

(5) Export Preference Shares. The 1970s/1980s saw an increase in the number of preference shares issued in Ireland. These shares are generally redeemable preference shares with a life of less than ten years, though twenty-year redeemable preference shares have been issued. Few of these issues have been through the stock market. The normal channel is an institution which purchases the entire issue. The cause of this resurgence in preference share issues is the tax relief granted on exports. This tax relief is granted not only for corporation tax but also for income tax. A firm exporting a large part of its output will pay a greatly reduced rate of tax. The dividends declared by this firm qualify also for tax relief. Consequently, export-oriented firms are able to issue preference shares at lower rates than long-term debentures. The net after-tax income to the holders of the shares may be greater than the net income resulting from a higher interest rate. The greater the proportion of exports in a firm's total output the greater the advantage of preference shares over long-term debt. Firms in the export field would be well advised to investigate fully the possibility of raising medium- or long-term finance through an issue of preference shares. This facility does not exist for firms beginning to export on or after 1 January 1981.

Preference share financing worldwide has declined as a source of new finance. Investors faced with inflation and a fixed dividend object to taking a higher level of risk than do debenture holders.

From the viewpoint of an Irish manufacturing company preference shares have attractions. Few manufacturing companies will have a substantial tax bill, therefore the lack of tax deductibility is not serious. Furthermore, preference share financing is flexible in that the dividend does not have to be paid and the average preference issue, being irredeemable, is in fact a permanent loan. Preference shares expand the equity base of the company and make it more attractive to lenders.

ORDINARY SHARE CAPITAL—COMMON EQUITY

Investors in ordinary shares are the real owners of a business. They invest in hope and expectation. If hopes are realised then a stream of earnings and dividends will accrue to the owners. If the venture is unsuccessful then the owners will in all probability lose their total investment. Mining provides the best possible examples. Between the revival of Irish mining in 1954 and 1988 over 150 exploration companies spent £80 million prospecting in Ireland. Four economic deposits were discovered. One hundred and forty-six companies lost their entire investment in Irish mining while four mines, Tynagh, Gortdrum, Silvermines and Tara, were developed. While the shareholders in the successful companies could look forward to an income, those in the unsuccessful companies were, at best, lucky not to see their businesses go bankrupt.

The ordinary shareholder is the risk-taker who controls the company. The objective of every business must be the maximisation of the long-term wealth of the ordinary shareholder. Ordinary shares differ from all other sources of finance,for depending on the success of the company, the value of ordinary shares can rise or fall spectacularly. In general, debentures and preference shares have a maximum redemption price. The price of these securities will hardly rise above their redemption prices no matter how well the business does but they can and do fall if the company is doing poorly.

Ordinary shares carry with them no right to repayment or no right to a dividend but they almost invariably possess the right of ownership. The ordinary shareholders must have regular opportunities, usually annual, to elect a board of directors and to vote on issues such as whether or not a dividend is to be paid.

The ordinary shareholders have the right to the income remaining after all commitments to other sources of finance have been met. The remaining income can all be paid out as a dividend of so much per share but more often the directors propose, and the shareholders usually accept, that a percentage of the income be retained in the business. The expectation is that retained income or 'retained earnings' will be used to generate even more profits for the ordinary shareholders.

The option to declare a dividend or not is a major advantage of ownership funds. When multiple investment opportunities exist management can reduce or forego dividend payments. The type of investor who purchases ordinary shares is one prepared to take the risk of an uncertain income flow. In return he gets the opportunity of capital appreciation and/or higher income plus a voice in control.

In large publicly-quoted companies the risk and control aspects of investing in ordinary shares is more apparent than real. Companies such as Smurfit, Cement Roadstone and the banking groups have a perfect record of paying dividends. The average shareholder with his few votes can attend the annual general meeting of these companies but he will wield no power. Nevertheless, the underlying theory holds true. In the 1970s Youghal Carpets was the darling of the exchange. Investors could see only rising dividends and a rising share price. By 1988 a series of setbacks had left the company virtually insolvent. The rising equity stars of one decade may be the disasters of another.

One of the most important financial judgments made by management is the decision to issue new equity shares. It is important for two reasons: new shares carry rights to vote and as such they may affect the control of the firm; except in special circumstances ordinary shares are irredeemable and consequently share in all future profits and dividends of the firm.

The admittance of new shareholders is likely to be considered in every business from the small one-man private firm to the large public company. In the small private firm the owner/manager may find that his talents are in one particular field, say, marketing. He may seek a partner experienced in production or financial matters who would invest in the business. If the firm grows, the partnership may discover that extra ownership finance is required. This can be raised by admitting more partners or by forming a limited company and admitting more share-holders. A further expansion of the business may be partially financed by retained earnings with additions of short-, medium- and long-term debt but ultimately the firm may require a stronger ownership interest. The owners of a profitable growing firm may wish to release some of the capital tied up in the business and may elect to sell shares to the public through the stock market. Finally, public companies often require extra ownership finance either to finance expansions or to secure and consolidate their existing position.

In general it can be stated that each ordinary share carries a vote and is entitled to a proportional share of earnings and dividends. Non-voting ordinary shares have been issued but they tend to be frowned upon as they place owners in the unenviable position of being forced to accept decisions affecting their interest without a say in the matter.

Deferred ordinary shares are another form of equity which have been issued in special circumstances. Shares such as these would not qualify for dividends except where abnormally large profits are made and may not have voting rights until a specified date or until annual earnings have reached a certain figure. Deferred ordinary shares may arise on a recon-struction of a company where new equity capital is required and the original ordinary shareholders become 'deferred' in order to attract new shareholders.

Risk Levels of Equity Capital

It may surprise some to know that all equity issues are not of equal risk. Though all ordinary shares face the same financial risk insofar as they get repaid only after everyone else is paid the level of business risk varies enormously. Investors seek the type of investment which best suits their own personal risk profile. The risk classes of equity capital can be categorised as (a) seed capital, (b) venture capital, (c) development capital and (d) ongoing equity capital.

Seed Capital. Usually the first source of capital raised is equity. Very often this 'seed capital', as it is known, is the most difficult source to tap. The individual with the good idea frequently has no cash; he/she is often at an age where capital has not been accumulated; there is no history of success, that is, the so-called track record. In practically every new venture the first moneys spent are equity funds. These funds are the capital at most risk. Many ventures never get off the ground. A business is most at risk in the first year of life. It is during this period that any weaknesses emerge. Over 50 per cent of all IDA-assisted firms which close do so in the first two years. The nature of seed capital is such that few organisations or individuals apart from friends or family of the entrepreneur are prepared to take the risk. Certain exceptions do exist. Brave souls invested seed money in exploration companies such as Aran Energy, Kenmare and Ovoca. These investors took a high level of risk but at least had the option of selling their stakes. Few new ventures are publicly quoted, most are private firms.

Seed capital is notoriously difficult to come by in Ireland. Apart from friends and relatives the only likely sources are wealthy individuals.

Venture Capital. Venture Capital is generally thought to be equity capital, but it should be emphasised that it can take the following forms; equity debt and convertible debt. The term is also confusing in that there is no one precise definition for venture capital, having different connotations to different individuals. Webster defines a venture as 'an undertaking involving chance, risk of danger, especially a speculative business enterprise.' Some may interpret this as being limited to start-up businesses, while others would see it as being more inclusive. This text assumes the former.

Once a project takes shape then the level of risk decreases. The individual who spends money to build a prototype has a tangible product instead of a vague idea. Turning ideas into products has sounded the death knell for many entrepreneurs. The project has more attraction if the market potential has been surveyed and likely customers identified. With a market survey, a product and even a limited history of production, investors will examine the potential. A review of the venture capital market in Ireland is included below.

Development Capital. Projects which get into production either grow or fold. Growing projects usually require additional cash. The original investors find that their own resources and any profits emanating from the venture are insufficient to allow for rapid expansion. Development capital is required. Development capital often comes in the form of a term loan and an equity investment. To be of interest to any potential investor a company would need a track record of production, sound management, profits of at least £50,000 per annum and substantial potential.

Ongoing Equity Capital. The final type of equity arises from the needs of large companies who find that their equity base is becoming too small in relation to the size of the business. Very often a new investment or a diversification opportunity requires some additional equity. Such finance can be called Ongoing Equity Capital. It is usually raised from existing shareholders by means of a rights issue. Alternatively, expansion can be an acquisition paid for by an issue of shares. This expands the equity base. Previous chapters have pointed out the deleterious effect of high inflation on capital needs. Should profits prove insufficient to meet inflating working capital needs then in the long run an equity issue needs to be considered.

VENTURE CAPITAL MARKET IN IRELAND

The United States is generally recognised as a world leader in the area of venture capital and has the most open environment for general investor participation in private enterprise. In the first half of the 1980s, the United States venture capital business witnessed spectacular growth and success. In 1988 the funds pool amounted to $16 billion with investments of over £3 billion. Annual rates of return of 30 per cent to 40 per cent were by no means uncommon with the average over the ten year period to 1988 estimated to be 25 per cent.

While risk equity was available in Ireland from private sources for many years, the development of the venture capital industry dates no further back than the mid-1970s. During the early years the industry concentrated almost solely on investment in established companies but in recent years there is growing evidence that the industry is investing more money in start-up situations.

The main objective of the venture capital company is to have a minority shareholding in its investee companies. The venture capital investor will normally insist on a shareholder's agreement ensuring him of certain minimum rights despite his minority status. The required rate of return will depend on the individual assessment of the risk attaching to each specific proposal. In Ireland, an overall rate of 30 per cent per annum is, generally speaking, required.

The Irish Venture Capital Association (IVCA) was set up in January 1985, in order to provide a forum for, and a stimulus to, the venture capital industry in Ireland. According to the IVCA the number of companies in which their members have equity shareholdings amounts to approximately 200. These companies have a combined turnover in excess of IR£500 million, export 30 per cent of their goods and provide employment for over 8,000 people. The funds pool is estimated to be in the order of £60 million.

Table 42 Venture Capital Companies

	Range of Individual Investments Preferred		Shareholding Level
	Min.	Max.	
	£'000		
Allied Combined Trust Limited Allied Irish Venture Capital Limited First Venture Fund Limited	50—3,000		10%—40%
Development Capital Corporation Limited	50—400		20%—40%
Food Venture Fund	120—200		20%—30%
ICC Corporate Finance Limited	100—500		Up to 49%
The National Development Corporation Limited	50—2,500		Up to 49%
Equitas	100—300		Up to 20%
Finance for Growth Limited	150—700		Up to 40%

METHODS OF RAISING NEW EQUITY CAPITAL

The major means of raising new funds are:

(1) Owners increasing their investment. This method is frequently used where the firm is very small and the owners have outside sources of funds. It involves no change in the control of the firm, if each owner can supply his share of the new investment.

(2) Introducing new partners or members. Small private firms starved for capital may accept funds from private individuals wishing to become involved in the business. In many cases, the new members are willing to forego all control in return for the opportunity to invest. This method is occasionally adopted by the new investor providing a high interest term loan in return for the right to buy a certain percentage of the issued shares.

(3) Institutions providing term loans and accepting equity interest. Small-and medium-sized firms with good potential are often able to secure badly needed capital from financial institutions. These institutions provide a term loan and usually take a proportion of the total equity capital. The shares would be bought at par or at a valuation rather less than current value.

(4) Selling shares to suppliers or customers. If a firm is an important supplier to or purchaser from a company, the management of the company may consider it worthwhile to provide some equity capital for it.

(5) 'Going public'. A firm with a strong earnings record and good potential may benefit from 'going public', for example, obtaining a stock exchange quotation and selling shares through the market. The mechanics of obtaining a quotation were dealt with in Chapter 8.

Basically, therefore, equity financing can be increased in two ways. A firm can retain and reinvest some or all of the net earnings, or it can sell new stock. Conceptually there is no difference between the two from the point of view of the cost of equity, except that issuing new equity involves flotation costs that make it more expensive than using retained earnings.

CONSIDERATIONS IN RAISING NEW EQUITY

In considering new equity sources of capital, management should consider the control, risk and cost effects. These should be related to the capital structure required to provide the necessary base for the firm's future activities.

New equity is very much a long-term source of funds and it should be considered in conjunction with the long-term future of the business. One important consideration relating to new equity issues, particularly public issues, is the time factor involved. Negotiating and issuing new capital may take many months and therefore management must anticipate the need and plan well in advance.

In summary the principal considerations are that:

(a) The issue of equity capital to outside interests can result in changes in control, that is, dilution of control.

(b) Equity issues will tend to lower the financial risk of the firm and will thereby enable the firm to raise more debt.

(c) The cost of equity issues is difficult to define but it may be excessive. The cost is related to the fact that each new share qualifies for a proportion of all future earnings of the firm, that is, dilution of earnings may arise.

BUSINESS EXPANSION SCHEME (BES)

A major development in Irish corporate finance was the creation of tax incentives for equity investment.

Under approved schemes an investor can invest up to £25,000 per annum in equity investments and write this sum off against taxable income. At the high rates of personal income tax in existence in the late 1980s (58 per cent) the net cost to an investor of a £25,000 investment is £10,500.

To further encourage private equity investment in Irish industry, tax incentives on dividends have been introduced. On approved investments shareholders pay half the rate of income tax on the first £14,000 of dividends received.

There are restrictions on these schemes. The primary restriction on BES investment is that shares must be held for five years otherwise the tax authorities may clawback some or all of the tax write-off. The second restriction was on the nature of approved investments. Initially, only manufacturing firms were included. Subsequent relaxations allowed the scheme to apply to software companies and to tourist developments. A third restriction related to promoters and executive directors interests. Initially, working directors were not entitled to tax relief but this has subsequently been relaxed.

It is particularly important that investors and companies wishing to take advantage of BES incentives use competent advisors at an early stage.

After a very slow start the BES scheme flowered. A number of BES funds have been established whereby professional investment advisors seek out and manage BES investments on behalf of clients. Certain of the accounting firms actively match investors with companies.

The development of the Smaller Company Market (SCM Chapter 8) has greatly enhanced the scheme. One of the great problems in equity investment in private companies is that the minority investor is 'locked in', that is, there is virtually no way in which he can realise his investment. The SCM offers investors an out. Companies which have raised money under BES schemes can float their shares on the SCM without loss of tax relief unless shares are sold. Investors can now see the value of their investments on a daily basis and have the option of selling if needs be.

The main impact of the BES scheme is twofold:

(1) An expansion in the range of seed capital and venture capital available.

(2) A reduction in the cost of equity capital to companies. The tax incentives mean that promoters can finance equity issues at a higher price, thus reducing both the cost of equity and the loss of control.

RETAINED EARNINGS

Each year the directors of the firm make a dividend decision whereby they pay to the ordinary shareholders part, all or none of the profits earned during the year. Most firms do not pay out all their earnings all the time but prefer to keep some in the business either as reserves or for investment projects.

In deciding on the dividend the board of directors are also deciding for the shareholders how much they should invest. The following explains the procedure. Tax complications are ignored.

Net earnings	£7,000	This belongs to the shareholders.
Dividends declared	£2,000	The shareholders receive this in cash.
Retained earnings	£5,000	The directors have decided to keep this amount of the shareholders' money in the business.

Had the £5,000 retained earnings been paid to the shareholders they would have been able to use the money as they wished. The directors, by keeping the money in the business, have decided that the shareholders will derive greater benefit by increasing their investment in the firm. By retaining earnings the directors are providing funds for further investment. They should be quite certain that the return on the proposed investment will be higher than the return which the shareholders could achieve if they had received the funds.

Retained earnings provide industry with much of the funds needed for investment. Very often these funds are retained without considering the implications of the decision. In a private firm the directors are normally the owners and consequently there is no possibility of an incorrect decision being reached. In a public company the directors may only represent a part of the total ownership and so they must be very careful to make decisions in the best financial interests of the shareholders.

The advantages of retained earnings as a source of funds are that:

(a) There is no change in the control pattern of the firm.
(b) Retained earnings, being equity capital, reduce the financial risk of the firm, that is, lower the debt/equity ratio.
(c) The funds are readily available and do not involve expensive issuing costs.
(d) There are no fixed charges.
(e) There is no fixed maturity, as equity capital is a perpetuity.
(f) There is no increase in the number of shares, so even a small return on the investment of retained earnings will increase the earnings per share to all existing shareholders.

The disadvantages of retained earnings are that:

(a) Management may not be as careful with retained earnings as they would be with an alternative source of capital.

(b) Retained earnings may not be the most suitable source of capital, that is, a firm with no debt and stable earnings may be able to raise debt capital more efficiently than using retained earnings.

(c) The 'cost' of retained earnings may be high.

The last disadvantage is often difficult to explain to managements who look on retained earnings as a costless source of funds. They point out that retained earnings have no issuing costs, and that no new dividends arise. This serious error has led many a management into a serious trap. If retained earnings are viewed as a costless source of finance management is tempted to reduce dividends. Paying out low dividends often causes share prices to remain low. High levels of retained earnings, if properly invested, increase assets per share. Over time, assets per share may greatly exceed the share price. This makes the company vulnerable to a takeover bid which can result in management personnel losing their jobs.

Since retained earnings are equity their cost is the same cost as that of raising new shares with the exception of the issuing costs attaching to new shares.

DIVIDEND POLICY

As stated already the amount of earnings retained is a function of the dividend policy followed by a business. In practically every case the dividend is a cash payment to shareholders. A dividend payment reduces the value of the business. The power to declare a dividend rests with the board of directors of a company. Dividends are usually declared twice yearly. An 'interim' dividend is declared when the half-yearly results are announced and a 'final' is declared with the annual results. The dividend decision is voted on at the annual general meeting. Dividends need not and cannot be declared unless profits have been made or unless reserves of undistributed profits exist. It is illegal to declare a dividend out of subscribed capital.

In attempting to define a policy on dividends the directors must remember that the objective of the business is the maximisation of the long-run wealth of the owner. In practice this means maximising the share price in the long term. The effect of dividends or the lack of dividends on the share price has been the subject of much theoretical debate. In the early 1960s Modigliani and Miller put forward a well-argued thesis that the value of a business was defined totally by the earning power of the firm. It therefore did not matter whether a firm paid dividends or not; in terms of net worth to shareholders, there could be no difference between paying dividends on the one hand or allowing retained earnings to reflect themselves in share price rises on the other. The model used by the individuals concerned assumed a world of perfect certainty and no taxes. Modigliani and Miller suggested further that investors would invest in firms with dividend policies which suited their own needs.

Other researchers take a very different view. In a world of uncertainty, dividends are relevant because investors are receiving cash now instead of an uncertain gain in the future. The evidence available tends to support the view that firms paying dividends are in general more highly valued than firms retaining all earnings.

Differing taxation policies also affect the issue. In Ireland capital gains tax at 30 per cent is lower than the average income tax rate paid by investors on dividend income. This suggests that many investors would prefer lower rather than higher dividends. Offsetting this to some extent is the tax relief available on dividends paid out by many companies.

The factors that influence a dividend policy can be outlined as follows:

(1) The informational content of dividends. Paying regular cash dividends leads investors to expect that they will continue. Changing dividends either upward or downward provides information to the shareholders. The new information is likely to lead to a change in expectations. This in turn leads to a change in the share price.

(2) Industry 'norms'. Over time, the financial community comes to expect firms in certain industries to perform in certain ways. A maverick company may worry the financial community. This can lead to a flight of investors.

(3) Reinvestment opportunities. Firms may have or, equally important, be perceived to have, certain investment opportunities. If opportunities are limited as they might be in mature businesses such as brewing or tobacco, investors would expect profits to be paid out as dividends. Other companies such as high technology communications or information processing firms will have many potentially profitable investments. Investors might expect such companies to retain some or all of their profits.

(4) Restrictive covenants in lending agreements might place a limit on dividends.

(5) The tax status of the shareholders should influence the proposed policy.

(6) Revenue Service regulations on the dividend policy in private firms will affect policy. The Revenue Commissioners are keen to prevent owners retaining earnings which would be taxed as income if declared as dividends. They will on occasion tax retained earnings as if they were declared as dividends.

(7) The availability of cash. Irrespective of all other considerations, a business may lack the ready cash with which to pay dividends. Lenders rarely like to see their funds being paid out as dividends.

In practice companies tend to follow a stable, conservative dividend policy. Investors are assumed to prefer a stable level of cash income rather than a fixed percentage of earnings. The fixed percentage formula would mean a drop in income in poor years. Studies of dividend policy in Ireland have shown that management only changes the level of dividends when it is expected to be able to maintain the revised payout levels.

It is important to note the distorting effect of taxation on Irish dividend policies. Profits arising from export sales in companies exporting prior to 1981 are tax free both for corporation tax and income tax. This creates a bias in favour of paying dividends against retaining earnings. The halving of income tax on the first £14,000 of dividends in a private manufacturing company also creates a bias in favour of dividends. This is exacerbated by the tax deductibility of sums invested in new shares.

It is possible that Irish management has been too conservative in dividend policies. Increasing the level of dividends has been shown repeatedly to increase the value of the company though in fact the net worth of the business is reduced by the payout. Higher dividends lead investors to expect higher income. Discounting a future stream of expected dividends leads to a higher price unless the discount factor is also increased. Evidence suggests that this does not occur.

In early 1988 the average Irish dividend-paying, publicly-quoted firm was paying out 33 per cent of its profits as dividends.

CONCLUSION

This chapter has discussed ownership sources of finance. It was suggested that preference share financing, though related to equity financing, had many characteristics in common with debt financing. New equity finance is an area fraught with complexity. Equity reduces risk and relieves the burden on management but it is costly and may result in dilution or loss of management control. New equity enhances the future borrowing capacity of the firm. Creditors prefer to lend to firms with a substantial equity base. Equity finance is needed at various stages of a company's life. It is usually the most difficult to find when it is most needed—at times like start-up and in times of financial difficulties. The Business Expansion Scheme in Ireland greatly enhances the attraction of issuing new equity.

Retained earnings are a widely used and substantial source of finance. They are not, as is commonly held, costless since they are, in fact, only slightly cheaper than issues of new equity. The amount of earnings retained is a function of dividend policy. In deciding on that policy, the firms must take into consideration a number of factors such as legal constraints, investment opportunities, earnings stability, taxes and the fact that management uses dividends as a way of sending signals to investors about current financial strength and future profit potential.

Decisions regarding ownership finance, particularly new issues of ordinary shares, are taken only after serious soul-searching. Practically every other source has a finite life, so even if a mistake is made it will disappear some day. Not so with ordinary shares: they are a permanent feature of the company.

In Ireland ownership finance has been very difficult to raise. The amount of new equity raised on the Irish Stock Exchange pre 1980 was meagre. Indeed, between 1973 and 1985 no new business went public on the Irish exchange. The 1980s saw a major increase in activity with over £300 million raised in the five-year period ended 1985. For private firms new financing institutions have developed but it remains true to say that the bulk of risk money must be provided by the risk takers—that is the entrepreneurs who establish the venture.

Further Reading
See readings at the end of Chapters 9, 10.

Chapter 13

State Aid in Financing Business

The history and structure of the Irish economy have left Irish business at a disadvantage relative to business in more developed countries. As a province of a larger economic unit Ireland, until 1922, developed few businesses apart from agriculture and service industries. Agriculture, mainly based on cattle, supplied the raw materials for processing in the United Kingdom. Service industries, such as retailing, banking and insurance, reflected the structure existing throughout the United Kingdom and so were relatively advanced.

A priority of the first Irish government was to promote agricultural development on the premise that prosperity in farming would filter through to the rest of the economy. It was quickly realised that development required capital. Existing financial institutions were reluctant to lend to farmers. In 1923 the state established the Agricultural Credit Corporation to provide capital for agricultural development.

In the early 1930s there was a change in policy. A new administration believed that the future prosperity of Ireland lay in industrial development. It was believed that manufacturing industry offered the best solution to the twin problems of emigration and poverty. The thinking of the time was that imported goods could be made in Ireland. Tariffs and quotas were placed on a host of imported products. Investment capital was in short supply, so the state established the Industrial Credit Corporation (ICC). The ICC was to provide finance which would complement the various sources of finance then available.

After World War II a further policy change evolved. The strategy of economic development by means of import substitution was seen to have limitations. In a market as tiny as Ireland there were few products with a market demand sufficient to enable economic production. Small production runs produced high-cost items, often of inferior quality. After the first rush of establishments during the 1930s, few other firms set up. There was insufficient demand to create any noticeable backward linkage. This meant that the demand for machines to make sweets, knit vests and roll cigarettes was not large enough to lead to the setting up of a machinery business, all of which in turn meant little or no demand for the output of a steel plant.

The new economic strategy which evolved during the 1950s was based on export markets. If Irish business was to grow it needed to export; the Irish Export Board, Coras Trachtala, was established. It was realised that Ireland lacked four ingredients essential to success: technology, access to markets, management and capital.

The easiest way to acquire all of the essentials was to attract overseas companies to establish manufacturing operations in Ireland. This strategy became known as development by means of export-oriented foreign direct investment.

In order to attract investors to a poorly located island with a limited infrastructure, a series of agencies and incentives were created, among them the Shannon Free Airport Development Company (SFADCo), the Industrial Development Authority and Udaras na Gaeltachta. Capital grants, tax incentives and liberal depreciation policies were introduced. During the 1960s and 1970s, economic development policy extended the range of assistance and incentives available. Agencies such as Bord Failte, Bord Iascaigh Mhara and AnCO (now FAS), to name but three, grew rapidly and developed a range of subsidised financial instruments.

In the late 1970s policy changed again. The native Irish entrepreneur was being recognised as an essential part of the development process. Schemes and incentives were made available to promote Irish-owned businesses. In 1987 after 40 years of capital incentives there was a change of emphasis onto employment grants.

The main agencies which offer support to Irish business are:
(a) The Industrial Development Authority.
(b) The Shannon Free Airport Development Company.
(c) Udaras na Gaeltachta.
(d) The Industrial Credit Corporation.
(e) Foir Teoranta.
(f) FAS.
(g) Coras Trachtala.
(h) The Agricultural Credit Corporation.
(i) Bord Failte.
(j) Bord Iascaigh Mhara.
(k) Custom House Docks.

The main forms of financial assistance offered are:
(a) Labour grants.   (d) Low taxation levels.
(b) Capital grants.   (e) Liberal depreciation policies.
(c) Training grants   (f) Interest and/or rent subsidies.

THE INDUSTRIAL DEVELOPMENT AUTHORITY (IDA)

Formed in 1949, the IDA became a potent force during the 1960s. As the main agency attracting overseas investment the IDA had to combat many false views of Ireland. Time and experience was necessary to hone the financial incentives offered. The success of the IDA can be measured by the fact that by 1988 over 80 per cent of all new private capital investment in the period 1960–88 was made by foreign interests. Manufactured exports in 1987 were predominantly from foreign-owned firms. Of the 150,000 people in manufacturing industry, over 80,000 were employed in IDA-assisted companies. On the debit side are the facts that manufacturing employment dropped in the period to 1988 while imports grew as fast as exports.

IDA Incentives and Services

IDA incentives and services are provided under the headings of:
(a) New manufacturing and service industries or a major expansion of existing ones.
(b) Re-equipment of existing manufacturing industries.
(c) New or existing small industries, defined as manufacturing firms with up to fifty employees and fixed assets of £300,000.
(d) Enterprise development which provides IDA guarantees for loans raised towards working capital needed for a project as well as grants towards the reduction of interest payable on loans raised to provide working capital in addition to normal financial assistance.

New Industries or Major Expansions. A wide range of financial incentives are available to Irish or overseas projects. In 1987 a new scheme was introduced to eventually replace the existing systems. The main elements of the new incentive are;

(1) Every new job created will be eligible for a once off grant of £5,000.

(2) Corporation Profits Tax for all manufacturing industry at 10 per cent from 1 January 1981 until 31 December 2000.

(3) 100 per cent tax depreciation allowances, including accelerated depreciation, will continue to be available to manufacturing industry for buildings, plant and machinery. This was modified to 50 per cent in the 1988 Finance Bill.

(4) Dividends paid to overseas shareholders, both corporate and individual, will be fully exempt from Irish income taxes and there will continue to be no withholding taxes.

Non-repayable cash grants towards the cost of fixed assets—defined as site, site development, buildings, new machinery and most equipment—are negotiable in certain circumstances in designated areas. The designated areas are counties Donegal, Sligo, Leitrim, Roscommon, Longford, Cavan, Monaghan, Galway, Mayo, Clare, Kerry and parts of counties Cork and Limerick.

Non-repayable cash grants are available towards approved capital costs of product and process development facilities, including R and D units on IDA research parks. The grants are negotiable up to a maximum of 40 per cent of eligible costs in designated areas and 25 per cent of eligible costs in non-designated areas.

Training grants of up to 100 per cent are available towards the costs of wages, travel and subsistence in Ireland or to parent companies abroad; salaries, travel and subsistence of training personnel; management training; and where necessary, the cost of hiring training consultants.

Grants towards factory rent reduction in IDA industrial estates, IDA advance factories or commercially operated estates are made available, as are loan guarantee and interest subsidies and IDA equity participation, where desired and possible.

IDA development services to new industrial projects comprise:
- (a) Assistance with project development and financing including expert advice on taxation and legal aspects.
- (b) Provision of advance factories on IDA industrial estates and other locations.
- (c) Advisory service on site selection, factory building cost control, and planning and pollution-control requirements.
- (d) Manpower information and advisory services.
- (e) After-care services in initial production stages.

Re-Equipment/Modernisation of Existing Industries. Re-equipment grants may be available towards the cost of modernisation of plant and machinery in existing industries. The grants are payable up to a maximum of 35 per cent of eligible costs in designated areas and 25 per cent elsewhere. They are administered selectively on the basis of defined criteria for different sectors of industry. The IDA provides rescue and developments services to existing manufacturing firms as follows:

(1) It assists certain firms in commercial difficulties to organise appropriate packages of financial aid. In each case, assistance is given where there are prospects of commercial viability without continuing subsidy.

(2) Restructuring of sensitive sectors. Certain sectors of Irish industry have been experiencing serious trading difficulties following the introduction of free trade. The IDA encourages mergers or acquisitions within selected industries through the provision of grants towards the reduction of the interest payable on a loan raised in connection with an acquisition

or merger and may also act as guarantor for the repayment of money borrowed for the same purpose.

(3) Promotion of joint ventures between Irish and overseas industrial companies.

(4) Promotion of product licensing and sub-contracting opportunities for existing industrial companies.

(5) Assistance with identification of product development opportunities.

(6) Grants towards current costs of R and D projects negotiable up to a maximum of 50 per cent of such costs or £50,000 per project, whichever is least.

(7) The IDA assist in-house feasibility studies which assess the viability of new project possibilities by means of grants. Up to 50 per cent of eligible costs will be grant-aided. Expenditure eligible for the assistance includes executives' salaries, travel costs and expenses. The studies must involve the normal commercial and technical considerations, provided the work is related to products not already being manufactured by the company. It must also lead, if positive, to a new investment in fixed assets or an R and D project.

Small Industries. Under the Small Industries Programme of the IDA, capital grants are available to new and existing small manufacturing firms up to a maximum of 60 per cent of fixed asset costs in designated areas and 45 per cent in non-designated areas (with the exception of Dublin where the maximum grant on a building is 45 per cent and 35 per cent for new machinery). Training grants, product development grants, rent subsidies for up to five years and a recent innovation, employment grants of £5,000 per job instead of capital grants are also approved under the programme.

Enterprise Development Programme. The IDA's normal range of grant incentives for new projects is supplemented under the Enterprise Development Programme by additional benefits including: an IDA guarantee for loans raised towards the working capital needs for a project, grants towards the reduction of interest payable on loans raised to provide working capital and equity participation by the IDA, if necessary.

The normal incentives cover capital grants on fixed assets, loan guarantees for fixed assets, rent reduction grants and training grants.

The capital incentives are available for service companies as well as manufacturing companies.

In recent years the IDA has become one of the principal financial institutions in Ireland. In 1987 alone the IDA offered over £560 million in capital grants to new projects and created over 11,000 first time jobs.

Since 1982 the IDA has introduced new policies and programmes in keeping with the Government White Paper on Industrial Policy.

These new policies have culminated in a greater focus by the decision-making boards of the IDA on the realism of market, profit and job projections; an assessment of the 'value added' to the Irish economy as well as direct jobs within the firm; the totality of the IDA's financing commitments compared with the promoting firms and the linking of the IDA's payments closely to performance. The days of new capital equipment expenditure giving rise to 'automatic' grants are over.

The core change is that the IDA will seek to ensure that the agreements it negotiates guarantee the State value for money from the IDA's investment. The principal methods used are:

(1) Performance clauses.

(2) Explicit parent company guarantees of the subsidiary's liabilities.

For some years now the IDA has been using financial appraisal techniques to assess proposals submitted to it. These systems were of a standard sort and ensured that the proposal was coherently structured and did not lay the promoter open to a cash shortage over the period of the project or, indeed, an unwarranted cash surplus.

More recently it has been using an economic appraisal system designed to calculate the anticipated return to the State on its investment. The investment is calculated by calculating the total cost to the State, expressed in terms of Net Present Value, of grants and tax foregone on any leasing. This is then compared to the benefits in terms of the NPV of the stream of value-added created during the life of the project or seven years if that is shorter. The three principal components of value-added are direct wages and salaries, Irish raw materials and Irish services. These elements are not necessarily taken at full value but may be downweighted because of 'leakage', that it, one local raw material is not as local as another. In order to ensure a positive return to the State it is understood that the IDA requires a benefit: cost ratio of the order of 4:1 for a project to receive approval.

Obviously, all of this sophisticated appraisal process is so much wasted effort if the project does not proceed in the way outlined. Thus it is a natural development of this process that the IDA should seek to ensure that it gets what it has agreed to pay for, by an extension of the value-for-money principle. Specific assurances are sought from industrialists as to the accuracy of their proposals in the areas of job creation and/or other key aspects of their project on the basis of which IDA grants are approved. As a corollary to this, specific provisions are being inserted in grant agreements whereby the company will be liable, on demand, to repay a proportionate part of capital grants where projects are not met within an agreed time scale—normally 3-5 years (the 'clawback approach'). A variation of this principle is to withhold payment of part of the grants pending achievement of the projections (the 'holdback approach'). The middle course, which is the course now most usually followed, is to review progress of the project at the end of each year and to withhold subsequent payments until prior projections have been met (the 'annual review approach').

Whilst the IDA has said it is conscious of a need for flexibility in handling these performance clauses when they come up for review, considering that the most carefully prepared business plan may require amendment through its development stages, it must be understood by the investor that the level of grant to be paid has been approved on the basis of the performance targets submitted by him and agreed by the IDA; the grant has been approved (in the case of capital grants) both against proposed investment expenditure and against anticipated returns to Ireland in the form of achievement of performance targets. Therefore, if the key targets are not met the basis upon which the grants were approved has changed and the level of grants which should be paid in total is, therefore, in question. In other words performance by the IDA in paying out on foot of the approved grant package is conditional upon performance by the company in delivering upon its committed targets.

THE SHANNON FREE AIRPORT DEVELOPMENT COMPANY (SFADCo)

In 1947 the Shannon Airport area was designated a 'free port', thus becoming the first such zone in the world. Companies were encouraged to establish there. They could import products without custom duties, tariffs or quota as long as they were later exported. Tax at 10 per cent is levied on any profits made in the zone irrespective of the nature of the business. Shannon seeks high-technology manufacturing industries as well as commercial and trading companies serving overseas markets.

The incentives available at Shannon are:

(1) Non-repayable cash grants towards the cost of new fixed assets, that is, site cost (including site development), buildings and new production machinery and equipment. The maximum grant level for new projects establishing at Shannon is 60 per cent. The actual amount is a matter for negotiation in each case and depends on the overall attractiveness of the particular project to Shannon.

(2) Training grants of up to 100 per cent of the cost of approved training programmes for workers in new industries. Included are the cost of

training overseas, travel and subsistence expenses incurred during training, management training expenses and the cost of hiring training consultants.

(3) Research and development grants towards new or improved industrial processes or products. Grants range up to 50 per cent of the approved cost of a project, subject to a maximum grant of £50,000. Grants are also available towards the cost of fixed assets for research and development projects linked to a manufacturing unit, and in-house feasibility studies on the viability of new projects qualify for grants of up to one-third of the cost.

(4) In addition to the above incentives, Shannon Development can, in certain cases, guarantee loans, subsidise interest charges and take equity stakes in new ventures.

Small Industries Programme

Beginning in 1977 SFADCo undertook responsibility for developing small enterprises in the mid-west region of Ireland. The Shannon Development Small Industries Programme applies to manufacturing or export service firms which employ fifty people or less and have fixed assets of less than £500,000.

Apart from the range of services outlined above, Shannon Development has developed a comprehensive package of aids and supports designed to promote and foster existing small firms and especially to help those starting up. They include:

(1) Enterprise Centres, Workspace Centres, Innovation Centres, Craft Centres.

(2) Matchmaker Service, Business Advisory Service, Community Enterprise Schemes.

(3) In conjunction with a number of other State agencies and the National Institute for Higher Education, the establishment of a Technological Park at Plassey, Limerick.

Shannon Development is also engaged in the development, marketing and operation of specific tourist products aimed at international markets such as castle banquets, the Craggannowen Museum Project and the Bunratty Folk Park. One of the most successful developments in Shannon has been the creation of a number of service businesses. The legislation for Shannon offered a 10 per cent corporation tax rate on approved service industries.

One well known result has been the growth of a series of export oriented financial services companies. Among them are Guinness Peat Aviation (GPA) which has become the largest aircraft leasing company in the world, Irish Air Services (IAS) providing aircraft on a worldwide rental lease basis, a number of large leasing companies and some rein-surance firms.

The attraction of Shannon is based on low tax, inexpensive accom-modation and available competitively-priced white collar labour. The success of financial services in Shannon led to the creation of the Custom House Dock Scheme in Dublin (see below).

UDARAS NA GAELTACHTA

Udaras na Gaeltachta, The Gaeltacht Authority, is responsible for the economic, social and cultural development of the Gaeltacht (Irish speaking) regions in Counties Donegal, Mayo, Galway, Cork, Kerry, Waterford and Meath. These scattered Gaeltacht areas have a total popu-lation of under 80,000.

The Udaras was established by the Government in 1979 and took over the functions of its predecessor Gaeltarra Eireann which had been established in 1956. Udaras na Gaeltachta has a thirteen-member board, seven of whom are elected democratically by the people of the Gaeltacht regions. The remaining six, including the Chairman, are appointed by the Minister for the Gaeltacht. Udaras is the only state-sponsored body in Ireland which has members of its Board elected directly by popular vote.

Udaras na Gaeltachta offers a special range of services including con-struction, legal, financial and recruitment to businesses and grant aid of up to 60 per cent. To date it has developed a wide range of indigenous industries while at the same time attracting new enterprises and skills into the Gaeltacht regions from other parts of Ireland and from the UK, Europe and the USA. There are now some 4,700 people employed in industry in the Gaeltacht regions.

Udaras na Gaeltachta, in cooperation with University College Galway, has helped to pioneer the Research and Development of Mariculture in Ireland. As a result of this work there are now fourteen salmon farms and forty shellfish farms along the sheltered Gaeltacht coastline. Over 70 per cent of all salmon farmed in Ireland presently comes from salmon farms on the Gaeltacht coastline.

Since 1979 Udaras has administered a Community Development Scheme and this has encouraged many small Gaeltacht Communities to take a more active part in shaping the future of their own areas, with a strong emphasis on Community Education.

Distinct from other Development Agencies, the Udaras has 13 wholly-owned subsidiary companies trading in textiles, knitwear, food pro-cessing, electronics, plastics, information technology and hotels. The long term economic success has been difficult to attain. The isolation of many areas has played a significant role in the lack of success.

Udaras na Gaeltachta's headquarters are at Furbo in Co. Galway and there are regional offices in Bunbeg, Co. Donegal, Belmullet, Co. Mayo and Dingle, Co. Kerry.

THE INDUSTRIAL CREDIT CORPORATION (ICC)

The Industrial Credit Corporation was established in 1933 to provide finance for the many new businesses being established behind the high tariff walls then being erected. Ireland at that time had underdeveloped financial institutions. Hence ICC had to play multiple financial roles such as issuing house, term lender and development bank. During the 1940s and 1950s it floated many new issues on the Irish Stock Exchange. In the 1960s and 1970s ICC developed a full range of financial services. It has four subsidiary companies: Mergers Limited, which provides financial advice; Shipping Finance Limited, which was established to provide subsidised loans for the purchase of ships constructed in Ireland; ICC Fund Management Limited which provides investment management for pension funds, life assurance funds and private client portfolio as well as money management for corporate funds; ICC Corporate Finance Limited which has responsibility for equity investment.

The Industrial Credit Corporation provides capital to Irish Industry and distribution services in the following ways,

(a) Term loans of up to 12 years.
(b) Machinery leasing and hire purchase.
(c) Finance for under-capitalised industrial concerns.
(d) Issuing house services.
(e) Underwriting services.
(f) European Investment Bank loans at fixed rates of interest.
(g) Working capital for exporters.
(h) Hire purchase and leasing.
(i) Equity investment.

Of particular interest is a package whereby finance is provided for under-capitalised companies. This usually involves two loans, one a normal term loan at commercial rates, followed by a junior loan which can have any or all of the following provisions; deferred interest, deferred capital repayment, conversion or subscription rights into equity.

Table 43 shows the growth and pattern of investments made by the Industrial Credit Corporation.

Because of poor demand for fixed asset investment and growing demand for short-term working capital finance and foreign currency export credit, ICC has entered into a number of new financial service areas over the past years such as foreign exchange, fund management and the provision of mortgage lending for the purchase of commercial property. These developments reflect the bank's overall strategy of establishing a broader base in the financial services sector.

ICC is involved in ongoing discussions with the Department of Finance with a view to revising the legislative provisions under which the bank operates. In the future the degree of State control is likely to be reduced and ICC will be allowed more scope to develop as an industrial bank offering a wide range of financial services to business customers. An increasing proportion of ICC's income will be generated from its agency services while the volume of lending is likely to remain static.

Table 43   ICC Investment Activity 1982-86

As at 31 October	1982	1983	1984	1985	1986
Investments	£000s	£000s	£000s	£000s	£000s
Loans	299,329	348,362	381,596	386,001	377,858
Investments	3,976	4,085	3,868	4,235	4,585
Hire-purchase	14,714	12,170	9,230	9,627	10,991
Property and equipment on lease	26,787	35,474	35,524	34,432	34,981
Other assets	66,597	76,314	87,235	92,478	84,762
Total	411,403	476,405	517,453	526,773	513,177
Financed by:					
Share capital and reserves	27,599	28,942	28,416	29,659	34,025
Loans and deposits	363,675	426,985	470,054	476,441	459,666
Other liabilities	20,129	20,478	18,983	20,673	19,486
Total	411,403	476,405	517,453	526,773	513,177

Source: ICC Annual Reports

FOIR TEORANTA

The ICC has always attempted to operate as a commercial merchant bank. This is not the same as being a development bank. Development banks are subject to political pressures to provide 'soft money' to projects which otherwise might not exist. Over the years ICC was forced to make advances to companies which on normal conservative banking criteria might have been rejected. In 1963 Taisce Stait Teoranta was established to relieve ICC of some of the conflicts between providing development finance and bankable finance and to supplement grants provided by the IDA. Though not established as a lender of last resort Taisce Stait became the vehicle whereby ICC could make soft loans to risky ventures without adversely affecting its own image as a merchant bank. In 1972 the situation was regularised when the state established Foir Teoranta (Help Limited) as an independent company with the power to offer finance to firms meeting the following criteria of eligibility:

(a) Engaged in manufacturing activity.
(b) Having significant employment or invested capital.
(c) Having a reasonable equity base.
(d) Having a reasonable hope of permanent profitability.
(e) Having an inability to survive due to difficulties in obtaining finance from commercial sources.
(f) That the failure of the company would have serious repercussions either nationally or locally.

Sectors such as clothing, textiles, footwear and structural steel have been major recipients of Foir Teo. aid. Foir Teo. will not investigate a company until all commercial sources of finance have been exhausted. If Foir agrees to provide finance it usually attaches a number of prior conditions such as the following:

(a) Management changes. This is becoming more common; Foir may install management.
(b) Stricter financial controls. This is a certainty if good procedures do not already exist.
(c) Foir Teo. nominees on the board. This is a normal request.
(d) Provision that the existing lenders continue to finance the firm on an agreed basis. This is to avoid other lenders cashing in on Foir Teo. money.
(e) Conversion and/or subscription rights into equity.

Considering the nature of the business in which Foir Teo. invests, a large number of failures are to be expected. Current levels of redundancy and high social welfare payments combined with the high cost of new IDA-created jobs makes Foir Teo. an efficient user of state finances.

The list of companies which have used Foir Teoranta include many of the largest firms in Ireland as well as publicly quoted companies such as Youghal, Seafield and Irish Wire Products.

FAS

In 1988 the state established FAS to co-ordinate the activities of AnCO, the Youth Employment Agency (YEA) and National Manpower Service. FAS has a general responsibility for training and job placement.

FAS runs six main programmes:

(a) Company-based training, where FAS works on development programmes with company training personnel.
(b) Skills training, which mainly consists of apprenticeship schemes.
(c) Individual training programmes in nine regional centres. Training courses are related to the skills required in the locality. Trainees are paid training allowances and where necessary travelling and accommodation allowances.

(d) Management and supervisory training. In close consultation with the Irish Management Institute, FAS offers grants of up to 50 per cent of the cost of attendance at courses for further training in supervisory and management skills.

(e) National Manpower Agency which attempts to match employers and employees.

(f) A range of educational training and employment programmes for school leavers.

FAS is funded by the EEC, the state, a training levy on employers and a 1 per cent charge on incomes. FAS is one of the largest employers in the state with over 3,000 employees. Employers should note that 90 per cent of the levy is returnable if the company has an approved training programme.

CORAS TRACHTALA (CTT)

Coras Trachtala was established on 1 September 1959 by the Export Promotions Act 1959. Its functions have been regulated from time to time by the Export Promotions Acts 1959 to 1983. It provides a wide range of support and advisory services and grant-aid to exporters. These services include market research, overseas office facilities, trade missions and retail promotions, introductions to overseas contacts and the resources of a large trade information centre.

The successful development of Ireland's export trade can be seen from Tables 44 and 45 where over £9,000 million was exported in 1986. The other dominant features to be noted are the reducing dependence on the UK market with a consequent increase in exports to the other EEC countries and the continued growth in manufactured goods despite reducing employees numbers in that sector.

Table 44   Irish Exports by Category

	1986		1976		1966	
	Value IR£m	% of Total	Value IR£m	% of Total	Value IR£m	% of Total
Manufactured Goods	6,369.8	67.9	983.5	52.9	98.9	36.2
Food, Drink and Tobacco	2,168.0	23.1	664.8	35.8	84.4	30.9
Live Animals	255.1	2.7	108.3	5.8	54.7	20.0
Raw Materials and Fuels	480.6	5.1	90.3	4.9	18.9	6.9
Other Exports	113.3	1.2	11.0	0.6	16.5	6.0
Total	9,386.8	100.0	1,857.9	100.0	273.4	100.0

Source: CTT

Table 45   Irish Exports by Market

	1986 Value IR£m	1986 % of Total	1976 Value IR£m	1976 % of Total	1966 Value IR£m	1966 % of Total
UK	3,201.5	34.1	905.0	48.7	169.3	61.9
EEC (excl. UK)	3,546.7	37.8	527.5	28.4	26.7	9.8
North America	938.6	10.0	149.1	8.0	18.7	6.8
EFTA	546.9	5.8	55.5	3.0	3.0	1.1
Other	1,153.1	12.3	220.8	11.9	55.7	20.4
Total	9,386.8	100.0	1,857.9	100.0	273.4	100.0

Source: CTT

In discharging its functions CTT spent in excess of £26 million in 1986 (Table 46) and made available a wide range of grants.

Table 46   CTT Budget 1986

Market Development (Market research, product design, consultancy etc.)	£2.8m
Building Marketing Strengths in Firms (Employment Support Scheme)	1.5m
Support Services (Incentive grants for travel, advertising, promotion etc.)	2.1m
Marketing Information (Research, library publications etc.)	0.9m
Group Selling and Promotion (Trade fairs, exhibitions, missions etc.)	4.2m
Technical Assistance Programme	1.0m
General Operating Expenses	13.5m
	£26.0m

The range of grants available are as follows:
(a) Up to 50 per cent of an overseas advertising programme, maximum £20,000.
(b) Up to 50 per cent, or £10,000 maximum, of the cost of participating in exhibition and fairs.
(c) Up to 50 per cent of the cost of engaging designers to upgrade design.
(d) Grants to assist foreign buyers to visit Ireland. The grant is 50 per cent of costs or 100 per cent of airfare, whichever is the lesser.
(e) Overseas marketing research projects qualify for a 50 per cent grant subject to a maximum of £8,000.

(f) The costs of translating packaging and sales literature is fully grant eligible.

(g) A full-time sales representative located in overseas markets may qualify for a 100 per cent grant for one year.

(h) Travel grants of 100 per cent are available to senior executives travelling abroad for the purpose of sales promotion.

A review of CTT activities in the mid 1980s led to the disturbing discovery that the growth in Irish exports was due almost entirely to a small number of foreign-owned firms in a small number of industries; computers, electronics, drugs and chemicals. Native Irish firms had, in general, not developed an export business. Less than 20 per cent of their exports went to countries other than Northern Ireland and the United Kingdom.

A major staff reorganisation followed a change in policy. A new market entry scheme for Irish-owned companies was launched whereby such firms could qualify for loan guarantees on loans of up to £450,000 plus priority in CTT grant approvals. This scheme which is available to only a small number of firms is particularly attractive to businesses needing some years to develop a presence in overseas markets.

THE AGRICULTURAL CREDIT CORPORATION (ACC)

The ACC was formed in 1923 to assist farmers to improve their farms by investing in modern equipment and machinery. The company's financial services include loans repayable over periods ranging from one to sixteen years. Loans are available for a wide variety of purposes including:

(a) Purchase of livestock, feeding stuff, fertiliser, seeds.

(b) Purchase of machinery and equipment.

(c) Erection and repair of farmhouses and farm buildings.

(d) Installing water supplies.

(e) Land drainage and reclamation.

(f) Fruit farming and horticulture.

(g) Working capital.

(h) Purchase of land and implementation of family settlements.

Loans are granted usually against the security of lands. Loans up to two-thirds of the market value of the land may be approved.

Loans at preferential rates of interest may be offered to the following:

(a) Owners of small farms.

(b) Farmers participating in the World Bank Livestock Project to develop herds of beef and pigs.

(c) Small loans to members of Macra na Feirme.

Loan repayment schedules are designed to suit the cash flow of the average farmer. On non-preferential loans the interest rates would be competitive with alternative term loans. In certain instances, particularly loans for land purchase, preference is given to full-time farmers.

A farm development loan package has been designed to facilitate planned expansion. The scheme offers a repayment arrangement tailored to suit the borrower's individual requirements.

In 1986 ACC became one of the first major banking institutions to offer farmers the option of repaying their loans by the Endowment Method. Instead of paying a loan gradually over time, a borrower can contribute to an insurance policy, which will mature at the end of the loan term. The proceeds of the policy should be sufficient not only to repay the loan but to provide a surplus.

Loans may be granted for any combination of the following purposes: fertilisers, stock, drainage, reclamation, fencing, farm buildings or working capital as set out in a simple development plan.

The repayment period depends on the purpose for which the loan is required. The usual security is a charge on the lands.

A repayment period of up to sixteen years is available, including one year in which no repayment of either principal or interest will be required and a further three years in which interest only may be paid. The year in which no repayment of principal or interest need be made will always be the first year. One of the years in which no repayment of principal is required may, at the borrower's option, be held in reserve to provide him with a cushion should he experience a difficult year during the currency of the loan. The sixteen-year repayment period is a maximum and the actual period and length of moratorium allowed will depend on the project being financed.

Businessmen considering investing in agriculture would be well advised to examine the wide range of capital grants available from the Irish Government and from the European Economic Community. Significant capital grants or an equivalent interest rate subsidy are available for:

(a) Land improvement.
(b) Fixed assets.
(c) Purchase of extra stock.
(d) Mobile equipment.
(e) Group water supply schemes.
(f) Land improvement in mountain areas.
(g) Cattle incentive schemes.
(h) Housing grants.
(i) A host of other minor schemes.

At the beginning of 1987 the ACC had over £460 million loaned to Irish agribusiness. The pattern of loans is outlined in Table 47.

Table 47   Pattern of ACC Loans %

	1984	1985	1986
Land Purchases	8	8	6
Buildings	7	7	5
Livestock	19	17	10
Grains, Feeds and Fertilisers	19	19	9
Food Processing	25	27	48
Working Capital and Other Short Term Facilities	22	22	22
	100%	100%	100%

Source: ACC

After spectacular growth in the 1960s and 1970s ACC has suffered from the decline in agriculture. Many farmers simply could not repay loans borrowed to buy land at inflated prices or to invest in non-productive assets.

Subsequent losses in ACC have all but wiped out the capital base. The State will have to decide future strategy for ACC. It is unlikely to remain an independent entity.

BORD FAILTE

In 1986 the Irish Tourist Industry earned £865.6 million of which £649.0 million came from out-of-state visitors and £216.6 million was domestic tourism spending. Tourism is the second largest industry in the country.

Tourism was one of the first industries to be formally recognised by the State for the potential it possessed for bringing benefits to less developed areas of the country. In the 1920s the Irish Tourist Association and the Hotel Proprietors' Association were set up. The ITA opened the first tourist information offices at major centres and also produced guide booklets and maps.

In 1939 Bord Cuartaiochta na hÉireann, the first Irish Tourist Board, was set up and was given statutory powers for the registration of hotels. In 1952, An Bord Failte, which had responsibility for development work and Fogra Failte, which was charged with the promotion of Ireland overseas, were established. They were amalgamated in 1955 into the new Bord Failte Eireann, literally the Welcome Board of Ireland.

The national objective of tourism, set out by the Government in their White Paper on Tourism Policy, is to optimise the economic and social benefits of tourism both to and within the country, consistent with ensuring an acceptable economic rate of return on the resources employed and taking account of:

(a) Tourism's potential for job creation.
(b) The quality of life and development of the community.
(c) The enhancement and preservation of the nation's cultural heritage.
(d) The conservation of the physical resources of the country.
(e) Tourism's contribution to regional development.

In addition to offering an extensive range of services the Bord offers grants for the following when finance permits:

(a) Providing new bedrooms.
(b) Improving bedrooms.
(c) Supplementary Holiday Accommodation. The grant scheme is intended to assist in the development of rural supplementary accommodation in farmhouses, town and country homes and self-catering houses for visitors and is operated by the regional tourism organisations.

    The grant is given on structural work and/or furniture and equipment either in respect of new premises or existing premises to bring them to the required standard for listing.

Board Failte is mainly financed by annual State grant and in 1986 its budget of £27.3 million was allocated as follows:

Marketing (including Advertising, Print, Publicity and Promotions)	61.0%
Development (including Product, Capital and Accommodation Development)	17.4%
Corporate Services (including Administration, Personnel, Financial Services, Computerisation)	10.9%
Subvention to Regional Tourism Organisations	8.0%
Superannuation	1.6%
Board/Directorate/Secretariat/Planning	1.1%
	100%

This agency in common with other state-sponsored bodies has been through a rigorous examination resulting in staff cutbacks, reorganisations and new directions. The approval in late 1987 of Business Expansion Scheme status for tourism schemes approved by Bord Failte will revitalise the capital expenditure side of the industry.

BORD IASCAIGH MHARA (BIM)

Bord Iascaigh Mhara was established in 1952 to promote sea fisheries. The Bord has many activities such as market development, fish processing and the promotion of boat owning through capital incentives.

The package of capital incentives consists usually of a capital grant ranging from 25 per cent to 50 per cent, subsidised term loans, and discretionary grants to assist exporters and processors with packaging and promotional material, participation in international food fairs and exhibitions, advertising and travel incentive schemes.

On the home market the objective is to increase the domestic market for fish and fish products, increase per capita consumption and effect import substitution. Discretionary grants are available on the same basis as that which applies in export development.

The Bord spent over £11 million in 1987 with almost half of its grant-in-aid being capital development.

CUSTOM HOUSE DOCKS FINANCIAL SERVICES DEVELOPMENT

In 1987 the government introduced legislation offering significant tax incentives for financial service firms located in a designated area of Dublin docks. A thirty-acre site downriver from the Custom House has been designated a financial services zone. Firms locating in this area and conducting their business outside of Ireland qualify for a 10 per cent rate of corporation tax. A £200 million redevelopment scheme on the dock site will provide modern high-tech offices and communications.

The attractions of the Custom House Dock area include:

(1) Low tax rate on profits.

(2) Good double taxation agreements with many countries, so that the tax savings in Ireland can be maintained in investors' home countries.

(3) EEC membership.

(4) Well-educated English-speaking workforce available at relatively low cost.

(5) Attractive time zone between Tokyo and New York.

It is hoped that 10,000 white collar jobs will be created by this scheme.

RANGE OF BUSINESS INCENTIVES

As outlined above the spectrum of state agencies provides a wide range of subsidies which can be grouped as follows:

(1) Labour grants.

(2) Capital grants.

(3) Training grants.

(4) Low taxation levels.

(5) Liberal depreciation.

(6) Interest subsidies.

Labour Grants

Ireland has a large surplus of labour. In the late 1980s the IDA and other agencies recognised this fact and began offering labour incentives. Companies taking on employees may qualify for a once-off grant of £5,000 per employee.

Capital Grants

Many of the agencies examined above offer capital grants. The grants are normally permanent finance but in the event of liquidation part or all of the grant becomes repayable. Grants are normally given on new machinery or plant.

Capital grants are available on a wide range of fixed assets including office equipment. Service industries which are not eligible for taxation incentives are eligible for grants.

Grants are paid after the installation and subsequent certification of the asset. It may be some months before the cash is received, so bridging finance is often required. Capital grants will decline in importance in the coming years.

Training Grants

Many modern projects require skilled staff. Training a workforce can require huge inputs of both capital and time. In a business such as diamond cutting, glass blowing or entertainment the biggest capital investment may be in the staff. Recognising the cost involved, the state established grants to enable manufacturers to train their workforce. Grants cover not only the direct wages cost but also the costs of materials used and managerial costs associated with training. A training programme must be drawn up and approved in advance by the IDA and FAS.

Low Taxation Levels

To maintain the attraction of Ireland as a base for manufacture, corporate tax on manufacturing profits was reduced to 10 per cent. This is one of the lowest levels of corporate tax in the world.

Liberal Depreciation

For many years the state has provided for liberal depreciation allowances. Free depreciation or the ability to write off assets against taxable profits has been available to manufacturing industry for many years. This facility reduces the financial risk of new projects. Expanding businesses will have continuous write-offs against profits and so they should pay little or no tax. In line with the bias towards labour grants there has been a reduction in the liberal depreciation allowances in the 1988 Finance Bill to 50 per cent.

Interest and/or Rent Subsidies

A high interest charge burdens a company with costly fixed expenses. This is particularly relevant to small businesses which often have a high proportion of borrowed funds in their capital structure. To reduce the cost, interest subsidies are available through the IDA, SFADCo, Udaras na Gaeltachta and, for fishery assets, BIM. Interest subsidies may be as high as two-fifths of the cost. They may last for five years or the life of the loan, whichever is the shorter. Rent subsidies are often offered to businesses moving to new premises.

CONCLUSION

Grants are undoubtedly a most attractive form of finance. Apart from being costless to the individual firm they are non-repayable under normal circumstances, involve no risk to the business and do not affect control. Grants reduce the investors' risk as they can put up less capital. They reduce the lender's risk in that grants rank behind all sources of borrowed funds and they do not affect annual cash flows.

Apart from capital grants a bewildering range of incentives exist, liberal depreciation allowances, subsidised loans, low taxes and a host of specialised grants for training and marketing.

The range of loans available complements that available from the private sector. Many of the state agencies such as ICC, ACC and BIM are interested in development as much as profit and security so they may view a loan application in a manner different from private financiers.

As if the above range was not enough the state has provided a financial rescue service for those in difficulty. Foir Teo., as a lender of last resort, has saved many jobs and businesses.

Every businessman should be fully aware of the range of state assistance to business. Contacts should be opened and maintained with the relevant state organisations.

Further Reading
1. Annual Reports of each organisation examined.
2. Information package on the services offered by each organisation.

Chapter 14

The Cost of Capital and Capital Structure

Chapter 6 examined methods of evaluating investment proposals in some detail. The output from each technique examined is a rate of return which measures the profit from the venture against the capital cost of undertaking the venture. This rate of return is meaningless unless it is compared with the cost of obtaining the funds to make the investment. The cost of funds is known as the cost of capital. The cost of capital has been defined as 'the rate of return a firm must earn on its investments for the market value of the firm to remain unchanged'. Accepting investments with a return below the cost of capital will reduce the value of the firm whereas accepting projects with a rate of return above the cost of capital adds to the value of the firm.

The cost of capital is usually an amalgam of several costs, because a project will seldom be financed from a single source. Usually capital projects have debt, equity and grant sources of finance. Taken together, these sources are known as the capital structure of the firm. The effect of changes in the capital structure on the value of a business has been the subject of much learned debate. Some of the arguments put forward will be examined later but for the present it is sufficient to note that the capital structure of a firm determines the level of financial risk in the firm.

A business faces two classes of risk, business risk and financial risk. Business risk is the chance that the investments undertaken by the firm will prove unsatisfactory. Financial risk measures the danger that the fixed charge sources of finance will force the business into insolvency. The greater the percentage of fixed charge sources in a capital structure then the higher the financial risk. Financial risk is, therefore, a function of the proportion of debt in the total financing of the firm. The word 'gearing' is used for this proportion, though the American term 'leverage' is also used in practice. Chapter 3, under the heading Debt Ratios, covers gearing. Consider what happens as a consequence of a firm borrowing funds. Annual interest and capital repayments are fixed. These charges must be met irrespective of the profitability of the firm. Should a downturn in business occur than there may be insufficient cash to meet fixed charges and so the business slips into liquidation. As the financial risk of a business increases so too does the cost of capital. Lenders note the level of borrowings and so charge a higher rate of interest and/or exact more onerous repayment provisions.

The cost of capital can be defined as follows:

$$k \quad = \quad f(r,b,f)$$

where

$$
\begin{aligned}
k &= \text{cost of capital} \\
r &= \text{the pure rate of interest} \\
b &= \text{a business risk premium} \\
f &= \text{a financial risk premium}
\end{aligned}
$$

A lender or consortium of lenders examining a request for capital must consider three elements in evaluating the price to charge. The first element is the pure time value of money or the riskless rate of interest. In addition lenders must evaluate the possibility that the business to which they are lending funds will collapse. The higher the probability the greater the premium. Finally, lenders look at the capital structure of the firm. The greater the proportion of fixed-charge funds the greater the financial risk and so the higher the risk premium.

In practice this means that the cost of capital varies substantially across business. At one extreme, high-risk mineral exploration is such a risky business that no lender will provide funds. Only risk-seeking equity investors are prepared to balance the high level of business risk with the prospects of high returns.

At the other extreme investors in government bonds feel that there is virtually no business or financial risk and so they accept a rate of return close to the riskless rate of return. Many manufacturing firms in Ireland have found themselves facing ruin because commercial lenders have refused to loan additional funds. The state, to protect employment, created Foir Teo. as a lender of last resort. This lender is prepared to accept financial risks unacceptable to other financial institutions.

Capital costs arise usually in relation to long-term sources of capital. Sections below examine the costs of the following sources of capital: debentures, grants, preference share capital and ordinary share capital.

THE COST OF DEBENTURES

The costs attaching to long-term loans are easily identified. They are:
(1) Fixed interest payments.
(2) Issuing costs such as legal fees, underwriting fees.
(3) Commitment fees.

(4) All premiums on repayment.

Item 1 represents a periodic cost over the life of the loan, items 2 and 3 represent a reduction in the actual amount received, while item 4 represents any excess to be paid on maturity.

An example would be a £100,000 sixteen-year term loan from the Industrial Credit Company. The borrower has to pay costs of £4,000 to obtain the funds therefore the net proceeds are £96,000. The rate of interest payable semi-annually is 12 per cent. A lump sum of £100,000 is repayable in sixteen years.

It should be noted that interest is usually a tax-deductible expense. The formula for calculating the cost of a debenture is

$$k_i = \frac{I + \left(\dfrac{FV - N}{n}\right)}{\left(\dfrac{N + FV}{2}\right)} (1 - t).$$

where

$$
\begin{aligned}
k_i &= \text{net after tax cost of the loan} \\
I &= \text{annual interest payment in punts} \\
FV &= \text{face value of the loan} \\
N &= \text{net proceeds received by the firm} \\
t &= \text{tax rate} \\
n &= \text{period of the loan.}
\end{aligned}
$$

Assuming that the ICC loan above was negotiated in 1987 by a manufacturing firm then the cost is

$$k_i = \frac{12,000 + \left(\dfrac{100,000 - 96,000}{16}\right)}{\left(\dfrac{96,000 + 100,000}{2}\right)} (1 - .10)$$

$$= \frac{12,000 + 250}{98,000} (.9)$$

$$= 11.25\%$$

Note carefully that the borrower has only a 10 per cent tax shield. A service industry concern with a 50 per cent tax rate would have a net cost of 6.25 per cent.

In theory a lender examines each loan application and applies business and financial risk premiums to the company. In practice lenders tend to categorise businesses. The commercial banks use three categories:

AAA   Which encompasses the state, semi-state organisations, local authorities, schools, churches and a few large public companies.

AA   Stable well-financed businesses.

A   Small businesses and personal borrowers.

An A borrower might expect to pay 5 per cent or more of a risk premium compared to an AAA borrower. Differences within categories tend to be nullified by the taking of collateral and by insisting on personal guarantees from the owners and/or directors.

THE COST OF GRANTS

Grants from organisations such as the IDA and SFADCo are a vital source of long-term finance to modern business. Apart from being available, grants are also costless. Should the business cease within ten years of grants being paid, then a portion may be repayable. There is a sliding scale rate of repayment tied to the period which has elapsed since the grant was obtained.

In the purely theoretical sense grants do have costs:

(1) Since many grants are normally payable only on new assets the business might be forced to use new higher-cost equipment instead of adequate second-hand and cheaper equipment. This has often been claimed in Ireland.

(2) The availability of labour grants may result in more labour intensive activities and possibly higher costs of production.

(3) The state normally insists on a certain equity contribution by the promoters of the project. If this is higher than would be required were no grant obtained then it is possible that obtaining grants leads to higher costs on the remainder of the capital structure. Equally relevant is the likelihood that the presence of grants reduces not only the financial risk, in that no fixed charges apply, but also the business risk in that lenders know that the grantor has examined the proposed project and is satisfied with the viability. These effects could reduce the cost of debt capital.

In general it is safe to assume that capital grants have no cost to the individual company.

THE COST OF PREFERENCE SHARE CAPITAL

Preference share capital has some of the characteristics of debt, such as fixed annual charges, and some of the characteristics of ordinary share capital. For example, preference dividends rank behind debentures in terms of obtaining annual fixed payments.

It is theoretically incorrect to state that preference dividends are fixed. Firstly, directors must declare the payment of the dividends annually. Secondly, dividends can only be declared out of profits—either current profits or distributable earnings. From the viewpoint of the ordinary shareholder preferred payments are fixed in that no distribution can be made on the ordinary shares until the preferred shareholders are paid. Since dividends are a distribution of after-tax profits no tax shield arises.

The cost of preference share issues is as follows:

$$kp = \frac{dp}{Np}$$

where

$$
\begin{aligned}
kp &= \text{cost of preferred share capital} \\
dp &= \text{annual dividend in punts per share} \\
Np &= \text{net proceeds received from selling one share.}
\end{aligned}
$$

Where a firm has a corporation tax liability preference shares are more expensive than debentures. The system which obtained in Ireland, where many export oriented manufacturing firms enjoyed complete tax exemption on export profits, led to a large number of preferred share issues. Export tax relief extends to the taxation liability on dividends declared out of export profits, hence preferred shareholders receiving dividends from a totally export oriented company would pay no income tax. The effect is shown in Table 48.

Table 48

	Domestic Service Industry Company	Manufacturing 100% Export Company (Exporting Prior to 1981)
15 per cent preference dividend declared on £100,000 of capital:	£15,000	£15,000
Income tax liability of bank receiving dividend:	50%	0
Net income of bank:	£7,500	£15,000

If it is assumed that a bank is satisfied with a net tax income of 7.5 per cent then they will be prepared to accept a coupon of 7.5 per cent on preference shares issued to wholly exporting companies as against a 15 per cent coupon to companies with no tax exemption.

Export preference share issues are made almost exclusively by banks. There is almost no difference between such issues and terms loans. The cost to a borrower is:

kp = (1 – tax rate) 3 months interbank rate plus a spread of between $1\frac{1}{2}$ and $2\frac{1}{2}$ per cent.

Export tax relief ceases in 1990 but certain firms may continue to pay dividends out of tax-relieved reserves.

THE COST OF EQUITY

There are two types of equity, new funds raised by an issue of shares and retained earnings representing owner's funds not paid out as dividends but reinvested in the business. Estimating the cost of equity capital is extremely difficult in practice. Every ordinary share has the right to a proportion of all future dividends declared by the board of directors of a company. Investors examining the company make up their own mind as to the likely pattern of future dividends. Depending on the level of expectations, investors will be either buyers or sellers. If the future flow of dividends was known with certainty, the cost of equity could be found by discovering the discount rate, which would equate the flow of future dividends to the current market price.

A Professor Gordon developed a dividend price model based on the above suggestions. The model is shown below.

$$MP = \frac{D_1}{(1 + k_e)^1} + \frac{D_2}{(1 + k_e)^2} \cdots \frac{D_n}{(1 + k_e)^n}$$

where

MP = current market price
D = dividend per share
k_e = the cost of equity

For the sake of simplicity rather than theoretical accuracy many observers suggest that investors expect dividends to grow at a constant rate. Using this parameter the model can be rewritten as follows:

$$MP = \frac{Do (1 + g)^1}{(1 + k_e)^1} + \frac{Do (1 + g)^2}{(1 + k_e)^2} \cdots \frac{Do (1 + g)^n}{(1 + k_e)^n}$$

where

Do = the current dividend rate
g = the expected annual growth rate in dividends.

From this the cost of equity capital can be estimated as

$$k_e = \frac{D_1}{MP} + g$$

This means that the cost of equity is the expected dividend yield, using next year's dividend plus a growth factor. The above method of costing equity is most appropriate to retained earnings. Very often management assume that retained earnings are costless. This is untrue. Retained earnings are, in fact, dividends foregone. Shareholders could have had the use of this money but instead the directors chose to retain it. In theory the cost of retained earnings must be calculated by assuming that the full sum was paid out to shareholders who then decided to reinvest the sum. As was shown in Chapter 12 taxation policies in Ireland distort the value of dividends versus new equity investment. The differences between (a) retaining earnings and (b) issuing new shares to the same amount are issuing costs such as underwriting, advertising, and printing and price discounts. New equity is usually issued at a discount against the existing market price. Therefore the cost of new equity is

$$k_{ne} = \frac{D_1}{NP} + g$$

where

k_{ne} = the cost of new equity capital
D_1 = expected dividends per share next year
NP = net proceeds per share
g = expected annual growth rate in dividends.

Note that the cost of new equity is almost always above the cost of retained earnings since the net proceeds per share will be below the market price of the share.

In general, new equity is thought to be the most costly source of finance. This may not be true in Ireland where tax exemptions on export profits and a 20 per cent abatement of income tax on dividends declared by certain publicly quoted companies and tax deductibility on approved equity investments increase the attractiveness of equity as an investment. Consequently the cost is lower.

THE OVERALL COST OF CAPITAL

Having identified the cost of each specific source of finance it is now possible to develop a means for determining the overall cost of capital. This figure can then be used as the cutoff rate for investment evaluation. Two methods are presented below. They are the weighted average cost method and the marginal cost method.

The Weighted Average Cost of Capital

Most investment projects use a mixture of grant, debt and equity capital. A weighted average cost is found by weighting the cost of individual sources of capital by the proportion of each source used. The weights may be either the historical proportions in the capital structure of the firm or the actual proportions of each source used to finance a particular project. Traditionally the historical weights are used.

Table 49 shows the weighted average cost of capital of financing the Ardmore Limited stainless steel tank project. To recap, Ardmore Limited was considering an investment of £183,000 to establish a stainless steel tank engineering project. The capital was being subscribed by the IDA, a bank and by the owners.

Table 49   Weighted Average Cost of Capital

Source	Quantity	Weight	Cost	Weighted Cost
	£			
IDA Grant	32,000	17.5%	0	0
Bank Loan	100,000	54.5%	13.5	7.35
New Equity	51,000	28.0%	59.0	16.5
	183,000	100.0%		23.85

The following are the assumptions:

(1) IDA grant has no cost.

(2) The cost of the bank loan is $(15.0)(1-.1)=13.5$ per cent. The loan has a seven-year term and a 15 per cent interest rate. There is a tax shield of 10 per cent.

(3) The owners intend to begin paying dividends at the end of the current year. The amount of dividends attributable to the £51,000 of equity will be £20,000 in Year 1. This is expected to grow at the rate of 20 per cent per annum. The cost of equity in this case where there are negligible issuing costs is

$$\frac{£20,000}{£51,000} + 20\% = 59\%$$

The weighted average cost of capital of 23.85 per cent is very close to the rough estimate of 25 per cent used to evaluate the investment proposal in Chapter 6.

If a company has publicly quoted ordinary shares then it is preferable to use the market value of equity rather than its book value.

The Marginal Cost of Capital

This method takes into account the fact that raising additional funds may change the overall cost of funds to the firm. This can best be understood by considering a situation where a company borrows 100 per cent of the funds required to undertake a project. Existing lenders looking at the new fixed cost funds are concerned with the rising level of financial risk so they increase the financial risk premium on existing funds.

At the opposite extreme a company with a high level of equity may find it possible to fund a project with only grant and debt finance. Equity holders may view this decision as improving dividend prospects and so they may pay a higher price for the share.

VALUATION AND CAPITAL STRUCTURE

For many years now a heated debate has raged among financial theorists. One group, the traditionalists, believe that there is an optimum capital structure. By this they mean that one particular combination of all long-term sources of finance provides the least expensive cost of capital to the firm. On the other hand a group of researchers support the Modigliani-Miller approach which states that changing the mix of capital sources does not affect the valuation of the business.

The Traditional Approach to Capital Structure

At the simplest level the traditional approach suggests that using cheap fixed interest debt will provide higher earnings for the ordinary shareholders. Investors seeing a higher rate of profitability will be prepared to pay more for the shares of the company and so the total value of the company will rise. Since the objective of the business is to maximise the long-run wealth of the shareholders it is therefore correct for management to manipulate the capital structure. The approach is presented graphically in Figure 7 below.

In this example a firm is considering financing a project with 100 per cent equity. As an alternative the managers consider obtaining a grant for part of the cost. The effect of the grant-equity mixture is to reduce the overall cost. As the ratio of no-cost grant to high-cost equity increases the average cost decreases. Once all available grants are used debentures are substituted. Since debentures are often cheaper than equity the average cost continues to decrease. Sooner or later lenders become worried about fixed costs so they charge a risk premium which rises rapidly as the percentage of debt increases. Likewise preference share capital can be used to bring down the average cost. At point x in Figure 7 the company has an optimum capital structure.

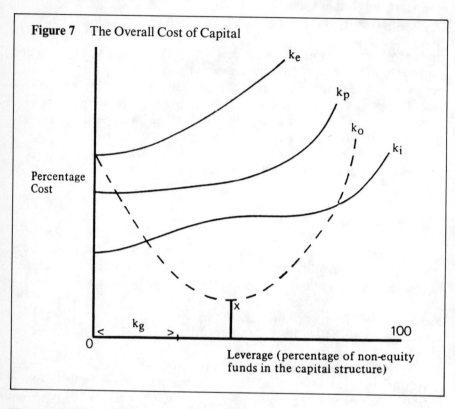

Figure 7   The Overall Cost of Capital

Percentage Cost

Leverage (percentage of non-equity funds in the capital structure)

The Modigliani-Miller Approach

The MM approach as it is known has two basic elements:

(a) That the market value of a firm and its cost of capital are totally independent of the capital structure of the firm.

(b) That as cheaper debt funds are used in a structure the cost of equity rises proportionally.

Figure 8 shows the MM approach using only two sources of funds, debt and equity.

If the market for capital were perfect, no taxation anomalies, if all relevant information were free and available to all investors and if there were no transactions costs then there would be truth in the MM thesis. In a perfect capital market investors can substitute personal leverage for corporate leverage. The net effects is that the capital structure could not affect the market value of the business.

Figure 8   Modigliani-Miller Approach to the Cost of Capital

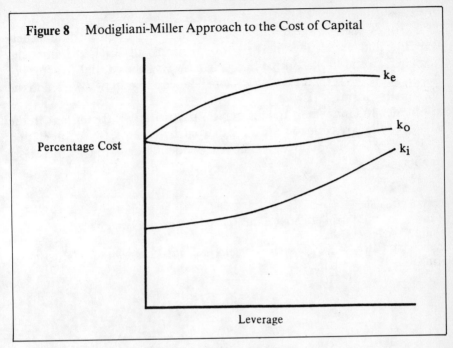

Within the many restrictive assumptions of the MM model the conclusion is logical. However, this argument cannot be supported in a practical world, for it is extremely doubtful that personal investors would substitute personal leverage for corporate leverage, since they do not have the same risk characteristics. In a world of uncertainty, imperfect capital markets, poor diffusion of information and a battery of tax incentives, the proposition does not stand up. Nevertheless, the propositions and their criticisms should be carefully studied since they will aid in understanding capital structure theory.

CONCLUSION

This chapter has discussed two important topics, the cost of capital and capital structure. Calculating the cost of capital is essential if a firm is to have a realistic cost against which returns on investments can be compared. Methods of calculating the cost of debt, preference and ordinary share capital were presented. The importance and zero cost of grant capital was noted.

Capital structure and the changes in financial risk as leverage changes were examined. The weighted average cost of capital was calculated. Finally, the thorny question of capital structure and the valuation of the firm was examined. Whilst the theoretical Modigliani-Miller model has its merits, a successful capital structure policy must be based on understanding and exploiting market imperfections. In brief, the financial manager should look at three things in assessing the capital structure of the firm: the tax rate; the degree of dependence on tangible assets; and the amount of business risk.

Financial managers in Ireland have a particularly difficult task in the cost of capital area due to state incentives such as grants, free depreciation and exemption from income tax for dividends declared from export profits.

Further Reading

Keown, Scott, Martin & Petty, *Basic Financial Management,* (3rd Ed.), Prentice Hall, New Jersey 1985.
Wilkes and Brayshaw, *Company Finance and its Management,* VNR, United Kingdom 1986.

Chapter 15

Mergers and Takeovers

The decade of the 1980s saw an unprecented growth in the number and size of corporate mergers and acquisitions. Business megastars such as T. Boone Pickens, Carl Icahn, James Hanson and James Goldsmith caught the imagination of the public as they 'wheeled and dealed' in billions, on a world stage. Terms such as 'Dawn Raider', 'White Knight', 'Leveraged Buyout' and 'Junk Bonds' were used by people far removed from the centre of financial takeovers. Ireland, too, experienced significant takeover activity. A number of top quality Irish companies—CRH, Smurfits and Waterford became significant multinational entities by means of international acquisitions.

This chapter provides an introduction to the takeover arena.

TYPES OF MERGERS AND ACQUISITIONS

Growth in income is a fundamental objective of all private enterprise businesses. Such growth usually requires an increase in the activities of the firm. Very often increasing activity means expanding the product range of the company, expanding the market served by the business or diversifying into totally new businesses. Expansion can be internal or external. This chapter examines external growth, that is, growth by acquisition.

The amalgamation of one firm with another through a merger or acquisition is now an established and well-accepted part of commercial life. Legally, mergers may be distinguished from acquisitions but from a financial viewpoint there is rarely a significant difference. A merger or acquisition is defined here as an amalgamation of two or more firms into one organisation with common ownership and management. Reasons for amalgamation are many, but it is important to remember that there are at least two sides to a merger and the reasons for acquiring a firm may differ substantially from the reasons for disposing of a firm. There are a number of motivations and corresponding strategies involved in acquisitions. The following are major categories of acquisition activity:

(1) Conglomerate Takeover.
(2) Diversification Takeover.
(3) Horizontal Takeover.
(4) Vertical Takeover.
(5) Leveraged Buyout/Management Buyouts.
(6) Shell Operations.

Conglomerate

Conglomerate takeover occurs when a firm acquires another firm in an unrelated industry. The logic centres on financial/management skills in the acquiring firm being used in the acquired firm. The golden era of conglomerates was the late 1960s/early 1970s. In Ireland, conglomerates such as Fitzwilton, Brooks Watson, Moore Holdings, James Crean and Ferrier Pollock were formed.

Conglomerates grow through five stages of development:

(1) Creating a management group which will appeal to the investing public. This usually involves managers with proven track records.

(2) Getting the backing of a financial group.

(3) Obtaining a quotation by injecting large amounts of cash into a small moribund publicly quoted company. By taking shares in return for the cash injection the promoting group gets control of the original company.

(4) Using the cash in the public company to take over high-earning privately-held companies. This explains the tendency of Irish conglomerates to purchase builders and distribution operations. Both of these industries were expanding rapidly in the 1970s. Neither were capital intensive. By purchasing earnings with cash, the earnings per share of the original company rise. If investors value a company on the basis of earnings per share, then the share price will rise as earnings are purchased.

(5) The final stage is to buy assets. Ideally the group is by now composed of high income earners with little asset backing. By merging the high earnings/low asset company with a low earnings/high asset company a more stable operation is supposed to ensue. In addition, making the group larger widens the number of shares issued and is supposed to diffuse ownership. This should allow the initial investors to sell off part of their shareholding if they desire.

Conglomerates fared badly in the bear markets of the 1970s. Many were dismembered and some went bankrupt. In Ireland, Ferrier Pollock, Moore Holdings and Braids closed, while Brooks Watson and Fitzwilton were reduced to shells. Ultimately Brooks Watson was acquired.

Unrelated activities based on high levels of borrowing did not survive economic recession.

Diversification by Takeover

Diversified companies operate in more than one country and/or business. A strategy of diversification is often followed when a firm has proprietory technology, specialised skills, efficient distribution networks, or strong brand names. A company may have a combination of strengths which lead it toward a diversification strategy.

Certain Irish companies have followed such a diversification strategy. Smurfits have diversified internationally within the packaging industry. CRH have expanded abroad in related activities. Clondalkin Group has purchased printing operations in both the United Kingdom and United States.

To date related diversification by takeover has been successful for Irish companies. CRH and Smurfits now make the bulk of their profits from acquired activities.

Horizontal Takeovers

Horizontal takeovers are undertaken to capture specific markets, to increase market share, or to eliminate competitors. Capital intensive industries with high breakeven points often find it cheaper to buy market share than to develop new sales. In the 1970s major horizontal waves of takeover activity took place in the Irish printing and packaging industry and in the concrete trade.

The retail grocery trade in Ireland provides a good example of horizontal takeover activity. Over a twenty year period literally hundreds of acquisitions have led to the creation of two dominant forces in Irish grocery retailing—Dunnes Stores and Quinnsworth. Over the years these two firms have bought market share which enabled them to bulk purchase thus giving lower costs. They also bought geographic advantage to consolidate their position. The battle which began in Dublin has spread throughout the country and has seen the demise of many hundreds of small retailers and a number of large chains such as Five Star, Tesco and H. Williams.

Vertical Takeovers

Vertical buyers are seeking acquisitions that will enable them to gain greater efficiencies through integration, either forward by buying distributors and/or outlets, or backward by acquiring supply and/or manufacturing capability. An example of a vertical takeover was that of Dakota by P.J. Carroll. This company produced all of the packets for

Carrolls. Agribusiness in Ireland has seen a number of forward integration takeovers.

Internationally, resource producers have strong reasons to integrate forward to protect sales of their raw materials. The international oil producers acquired transport, refineries, petrol stations, and chemical companies in their drive for survival and profit. An Irish example was the acquisition of Dublin Gas by Bord Gais Eireann.

Leveraged Buyouts/Management Buyouts

The most spectacular development in the takeover arena has been the growth in 'leveraged buyouts'. A leveraged buyout (LBO) is any acquisition of a company which leaves the acquired operating entity with a greater than traditional debt-to-equity ratio. The structure of the debt will always fall into one of the following quadrants:

	Type of debt financing	
	Secured	Unsecured
Asset acquisition		
Share acquisition		

Type of transaction

Secured financing occurs when the assets of the acquired operation are used to collateralise the debt. The difference between the secured debt and the purchase price is normally covered by a combination of equity contribution of the investing group and by subordinated debt.

Unsecured financing normally involves some combination of venture capital, 'mezzanine debt' (subordinated debt), generally with an equity kicker, and senior debt (generally owing to banks), aggregating to the total purchase price.

Asset acquisitions involve the formation of a new corporation (or utilisation of an existing corporation), which acquires the assets of the target company. If the acquired operation is a corporate division rather than a separate corporation, an asset acquisition is the only available type of transaction.

Share acquisitions take many forms: they can include stock redemptions, tender offers, pure stock acquisitions, and reverse mergers. They generally involve the most complex structuring and the greatest number of legal issues. They are most commonly used if the target company is publicly held or if an asset acquisition will result in significant tax issues.

The corporate culture of the 1980s believed in 'sticking to the knitting' so a range of businesses which no longer met the long term strategic needs of diversified firms came onto the market.

In the early 1980s investment banks moved aggressively into the business of organising management buyouts using the assets of the company being acquired as collateral for the deal.

An LBO involves borrowing from a financial source to acquire a target company. The proceeds are used to pay the seller. Internal cash flow and sales of assets are used to repay the lender.

Table 50 and Table 51 show the growth of LBOs in the United States and United Kingdom.

Table 50 Total Number and Value of United Kingdom Buyouts 1967-1986

Year	No.	Value (£m)	Year	No.	Value (£m)
1967-76	43	n/a	1982	170	265
1977	13	n/a	1983	205	315
1978	23	n/a	1984	210	415
1979	52	26	1985	229	1,150
1980	107	50	1986	261	1,210
1981	124	114	1987	125	1,360
			(9 months)		

Source: Financial Times, 14 October, 1987.

Table 51 US Leveraged Buyouts

Year	Total deals	Known prices $billion	Year	Total deals	Known prices $billion
1981	99	3.1	1984	251	18.6
1982	164	3.5	1985	253	19.3
1983	230	4.5	1986	329	44.7
			*1987	136	13.2

*First six months of 1987 (not included are companies with unregistered prices and the unreported private market).
Source: Financial Times 14 October 1987.

Shell Operations

In the mid 1980s a new takeover phenomenon appeared on the Irish scene. A number of Irish publicly quoted companies were partially acquired by UK based investors to be used as vehicles or shells in the United Kingdom.

The causes of this development lay in exchange control regulations between Ireland and the United Kingdom. Irish institutional investors were restricted to investing 15 per cent of their funds outside Ireland but they could buy shares in Irish companies which were investing abroad. Private Irish investors were largely forbidden to invest outside of Ireland. Investment opportunities for companies as well as private individuals were limited in the depressed Irish economy of the 1980s. Certain publicly quoted Irish firms, generally those in low technology mature industries, were declining.

The final variable in the equation was the fact that companies publicly quoted in Ireland are part of the London Stock Exchange so acquiring an Irish company was a means to a quotation on London.

In 1986 and 1987 a number of Irish companies were sold in part to UK investors, who in turn were expected to introduce a number of UK acquisitions mainly in properties. The companies involved were: Dwyers, Glen Abbey, Irish Wire Products, Edenderry Shoe, Rohan Group, Woodingtons. Seafield, Irish Ropes, Milford Bakery and Green Group were expected to follow the shell route.

The collapse in stock market values in 1987 saw share prices in shell companies drop by up to 80 per cent.

CAUSES OF MERGERS AND TAKEOVERS

The previous section has identified categories of takeover activity. While the causes and reasons for such activity are visible in the categories the following lists specific causes:

(1) The desire of a company to obtain the scarce technology controlled by another.

(2) The desire of a company to acquire the management or special skills of another company.

(3) To safeguard a source of supply. Examples of this include the acquisition of small private oil companies with North Sea interests by large multinational oil firms.

(4) To reduce or eliminate competition. Alternatively the acquisition may be simply to stop a competitor from increasing his strength.

(5) To obtain economies of scale. This can be by horizontal integration where one firm buys up competitors.

(6) To obtain growth by diversification due to maturity in the existing product range of the company. Diversification out of tobacco by Carrolls Industries is an example.

(7) To improve the spread of investment risk. It may be possible to purchase a contracyclical or contraseasonal business. An illustration

would be a snow ski manufacturing company purchasing a tennis equipment manufacturer.

(8) A need for rapid increase in capacity. Increasingly roundabout methods of production mean that adding new capacity can take years. It is often quicker to buy existing capacity.

(9) The discovery that it is cheaper to buy rather than to build. Share prices were low for many years particularly in relation to net asset value.

(10) To obtain synergy. An example is adding a sportswear company to a sports equipment company.

On the sellers side there may be numerous reasons for merging such as:

(11) Tax or estate planning.

(12) Lack of management succession.

(13) Lack of technical know how.

(14) To avoid being acquired by unwelcome suitors.

(15) Lack of fit with current or future strategic direction.

(16) Need to be part of a larger entity to maintain a competitive edge.

(17) Availability of a 'good price'.

FINANCIAL EVALUATION: DETERMINING THE PURCHASE PRICE

Value is the process whereby the worth of the target company is established. Purchase price is not always equal to value.

The price which one company is prepared to pay for the shares of another is a matter of bargaining and negotiation—there is no one perfect theoretical method of determining the value of a firm but there are certain guidelines which may be of assistance in the bargaining process.

Five methods are used to value the equity of a publicly-quoted firm: (a) the market price, (b) the net book value, (c) the fair value, (d) the present value of future net cash flows, (e) comparative values.

Market Value. Theoretically the price of a share represents the market's appraisal of the future earnings and dividends attributable to the share. Prices over a previous period should be averaged, as fluctuations in price may have taken place due to speculation or rumours of a possible takeover bid. The price on the stock exchange is based on a price/earnings (P/E) ratio. This is simply a relationship between the price of an individual share and the earnings of the company divided by the number of shares. A company which is in a growth industry and which is increasing profits each year might be on a price ratio of 20, while a firm in a declining industry with a poor profit record might be valued at five times earnings. This would mean that the price of the share of the company was twenty times the earnings attributable to one share. If the stock exchange is used as a guide to valuation the total equity worth of the company would be valued at twenty times its current earnings. P/E ratios are regularly calculated and are available in newspapers for all public companies. The problem with using the P/E ratio as a basis for valuing a firm is that historical earnings may be a very imperfect indicator of future earnings. The bidders for a firm are likely to understate anticipated increases in earnings while the owners are likely to project a very rosy picture of future earnings.

Net Book Value. This method values the firm by taking the stated balance sheet value of current and fixed assets. A company acquiring another as a going concern is not interested in the asset value of the business but in its earning ability. This method therefore is of little use even if the balance sheet figures are realistic appraisals of worth.

Fair Value. Instead of accepting the balance sheet figures a firm may examine each asset individually to get an idea of the realistic value of the assets. This method is of particular importance if the balance sheet has fully written-down property and land assets. In situations where property makes up a large percentage of a firm's assets it is not uncommon for the fair value to be many times the book value of the balance sheet.

Present Value of Future Cash Flows. This method examines the future cash flows and the terminal value of the company at the end of the projection period. The difficulties in estimating future cash flows and discount rates have been dealt with in Chapter 6.

Comparative Value. This involves comparing the prices paid in recent acquisitions, for companies operating in the same or similar industries. The difficulties again are obvious; few comparable deals in Ireland; each deal is unique.

The suggested procedure of valuation is to use all five methods. A worked example is shown below.

Example: A publicly quoted Irish company has decided to invest in the United States. After prolonged examination a potential acquisition has been identified. The mergers and takeover team has put together a study for the board of the Irish parent which includes:
- (a) A detailed description of the company's products and services.
- (b) Its organisational structure, with biographical information on senior management.
- (c) Financial results.
- (d) Sources of raw materials.
- (e) Distribution patterns.
- (f) Customers.
- (g) Marketing policies.
- (h) Patents.
- (i) Sales force.
- (j) List of physical locations.
- (k) List of equipment.
- (l) Employees.
- (m) Competitive position.

The section on financial results includes historical operating results and balance sheets for five years. Explanatory statements are included to describe unusual features or events that have affected the financial statements, including salaries and bonuses that would not be continued under new ownership, assets that are understated, or excess assets that are not necessary to the conduct of the business.

Table 52 shows the balance sheet value of the proposed acquisition together with a fair market value and liquidation value.

Table 52   Market value of XYZ Corporation ($'000)

Assets	Balance Sheet December 31, 1987	Fair Market Value	Liquidation Value
Current Assets:			
Cash	$2,000	$2,000	$2,000
Accounts Receivable	5,000	4,500	3,500
Inventories			
Finished Goods	2,250	1,500	1,000
Work in Process	2,500	1,250	500
Raw Materials	3,000	2,250	2,000
	14,750	11,500	9,000
Other Current Assets	250	—	—
Total Current Assets	15,000	11,500	9,000
Property, Plant and Equipment:			
Land	2,500	6,000	6,000
Buildings	10,000	9,000	9,000
Equipment	14,000	10,000	7,500
	26,500	25,000	22,500
Less Accumulated Depreciation	(13,500)	—	—
	13,000	25,000	22,500
Other Assets	500	—	—
	$28,500	$36,500	$31,500
Liabilities and Stockholders' equity			
Current Liabilities:			
Accounts Payable and Accrued Charges	$5,650	$5,650	$5,650
Bank	1,350	1,350	1,350
Total Current Liabilities	7,000	7,000	7,000
Long-Term Debt	500	500	500
Shareholders' Equity	21,000	29,000	24,000
	$28,500	$36,500	$31,500

The market price of the company is $35,000,000, that is $5.00 per share for each of the seven million outstanding shares. In this case the market price is misleading as there is a very thin market in the shares. Takeover interest has focussed on the company in recent times causing the share price to double.

Comparative prices are available for a range of businesses in similar industries. A number of recent acquisitions have taken place at P/E ratios of between 12 and 16 times after tax earnings. XYZ Corporation had 1987 after tax earnings of $2.2 million thereby placing a comparative value of between $26.4 million and $35.2 million on the company.

Table 53 shows the data required for the last valuation method, the Net Present Value of cash flow. Discount factors of 12 per cent, 14 per cent and 16 per cent are used.

Table 53   Net Present Value of XYZ Corporation ($'000)

Years	XYS Corp's Projected Cash Flows	Present Value at 12%	Present Value at 14%	Present Value at 16%
1988	$3.33	$2.97	$2.92	$2.87
1989	3.46	2.76	2.66	2.57
1990	3.60	2.56	2.43	2.30
1991	3.74	2.38	2.21	2.06
1992	3.89	2.21	2.02	1.85
1993	4.05	2.05	1.85	1.66
1994	4.21	1.90	1.68	1.40
1995	4.38	1.77	1.54	1.34
1996	4.55	1.64	1.40	1.20
1997	4.74	1.53	1.28	1.08
Present Value of Cash Flows		$21.77	$19.99	$18.33
Present Value of Terminal Value		12.40	10.40	8.74
Present Value of XYZ Corp		$34.17	£30.39	$27.17

The estimated terminal value of XYZ Corporation is $38.5 million.

Table 54 Shows a summary of valuations.

Table 54   Valuations of XYZ Corporation

Method	Value ($million)
Balance Sheet Value	21
Fair Value	29
Liquidation Value	24
Market Value	35
Comparative Value	26.4—35.2
Cash Flow Value	
at 12%	34.17
at 14%	30.39
at 16%	27.17

After long negotiations a deal was agreed whereby the Irish company paid $32 million cash for the company.

Valuation of a Private Company

The methods used to value a public company can also be used to value a private company but they must be adapted. The major adaptation lies in the use of net profits as a basis for valuation. A private firm has no market price valuation on its shares and consequently it is impossible to use a P/E ratio. A times earnings method is used.

Here a profit figure, usually an average over a period of years, is taken. The bidder will tend to average the next few years' projected earnings. Usually the valuation is on a pre-tax basis. The next step is to decide on a multiple, that is, how many times earnings will be paid. One way of getting an approximation on this is to examine the multiple being paid on earnings of a public firm in the same industry, for example, a quoted textile firm is selling at a P/E of six, a private textile firm might be valued at five.

Almost without exception multiples in private companies will be less than those in public companies because (a) shares in a public company are more marketable and (b) the advantages of a public quotation discussed in Chapter 8 make the public firm less risky than a private firm. In deciding on the multiple the bidder is taking into account projected earnings without the merger, projected earnings after the merger, the quality of the earnings, that is, how risky they are, and an implicit measure of the opportunity cost of investing money in this particular venture rather than in another project.

Methods of Payment

There are a number of wellknown ways of paying for takeovers. They can be categorised as:

(a) A total cash acquisition.

(b) A cash purchase of a majority stake.

(c) An instalment cash purchase.

(d) Payment by shares.

(e) Payment by issuing new fixed-charge securities.

(f) Part cash and part paper payment schemes.

Cash Acquisitions

The simplest method of acquisition is where one company acquires the total ordinary share capital of another with the total payment being made in cash, that is, Company X pays cash to the shareholders of Company Y to acquire the total ordinary share capital. From that moment it controls the appointment of the directors of Company Y and therefore controls policy and operations. If Company Y has other classes of voting shares it may also be necessary to acquire them. If Company Y has preference shares which carry no voting rights, the ordinary shares can simply be acquired, leaving the preference shares in the hands of their existing owners.

Cash Purchase of a Majority Stake

In this case 51 per cent of the shares of the company are acquired. This is sufficient to gain and continue control. In a case where a majority of the shares is acquired and the payment is for cash, the minority shareholders in the company acquired have certain well-defined rights. These rights can be found set out in the relevant Companies Acts. If the company which is being partly acquired is a public company, that is, with shares quoted on a stock exchange, it is necessary to make an offer for the bidding percentage (that is, 51 per cent of the shares) to all the holders in the acquired company. This is a requirement of the City Code on Takeovers and Mergers which is operated by the stock exchange and it effectively stops an acquiring company gaining a majority percentage while not making a similar offer to all the shareholders. In certain instances the resolution of the shareholders agreeing to a proposed merger may have to be a 'special' resolution requiring a 75 per cent majority.

In the case of a publicly-quoted company it may be possible to gain control by purchasing less than 51 per cent. Where a large number of shareholders each hold small blocks of shares it may be possible to obtain effective control with between 20 and 30 per cent of voting shares. To protect small shareholders against effective loss of control the City Code on Takeovers and Mergers requires a full bid if one buyer purchases 30 per cent or more of the stock.

Acquisition for Cash on an Instalment Basis

An acquisition of shares may be made for cash but the cash may be paid in instalments, with or without interest, over a period. Sometimes the level of the instalments is related to the profitability of the company being acquired during a particular period, that is, one or two years after the date of acquisition. This method of paying cash by instalments can be validly used where there is doubt about the reality of the profits shown as earned or where the profits earned are increasing so rapidly as to make the price, paid immediately in cash, seem unrelated to the value of the company.

This method of paying for acquisitions is used extensively by publicly-quoted companies buying rapidly growing private firms.

Payment by an Issue of Shares

In the previous examples, acquisition for cash was assumed, and it is obviously necessary for the acquiring company to have a reserve of cash to meet the payment. If this is not the case the acquiring company may exchange some of its own shares for the shares in the company being acquired. This raises the problem of valuing the shares of the acquiring company and those of the company being acquired. Where the acquiring company is a public company a market price is available on the stock exchange. This is frequently used to exchange the shares between the acquired and acquiring firm. It is possible then for those shareholders, who have received shares, to sell them on the stock exchange but this has the possible disadvantage that if a great number of shares are placed on the market, at any one time, the price of the shares may fall due to the normal operation of supply and demand. It may, therefore, be more desirable for the shareholders who are gaining the public company shares either to hold these and sell them gradually over a period, or to place their block of shares with an institution, normally an insurance company or pension fund. If this placing is carried out, the price obtained is less than the quoted market price of the share as the institution will buy 'at a discount'.

If the acquiring company is a private company the value of the shares which it is proposing to offer for acquisition must be worked out in relation to the results of that private company in the same way as the value of the shares in the company being acquired is calculated.

Purchasing by means of a share issue can be very expensive. As Chapter 14 pointed out, new equity carries rights to dividends. If new shares are issued it is virtually impossible to estimate the cost being paid for the acquisition since each share will participate in all future earnings of the company as a whole.

Payment by Means of New Fixed Charge Securities

The acquiring company may pay for an acquisition by issuing either preference shares or loan stock. The dividend rate or interest rate attaching to the new issues will be determined by existing market conditions. It will be priced to allow the sale of the preference shares or loan stock in the market at par. Alternatively the shares or loan stock may be placed with an institution. In this way the shareholders in the company being acquired are in receipt of a cash equivalent. The calculation of price is carried out in the same way as in any ordinary cash deal. If the acquiring company is paying by means of its own ordinary shares then the new shareholders decide on the growth prospects of the acquiring company, particularly after the acquisition of their old company and on this basis decide whether to dispose of or hold the new securities. Leveraged buyouts almost always use fixed interest securities.

Part Cash and Part Paper Payments

Very often the purchase of a business involves both a cash payment and the issue of new shares. This method is used by publicly-quoted companies who are acquiring private firms. Sellers obtain cash plus an interest in the new business.

One further method of acquisition deserves comment—the reverse takeover. In such a situation a company purchases a larger company but the shareholders in the acquired company end up with control of the entire operation. This method was used widely by the promoters of conglomerates in Ireland in the 1970s.

Occasionally two companies will come together and form a holding company to hold the shares of each. The shareholding in the holding company will depend on the valuation of each company. In effect there is not much difference between this and the case where one company acquires the shares of another. The formation of the company, however, may be cleaner structurally in that it may leave these two existing companies operating in a semi-independent state.

One factor which must be kept in mind by the acquiring firm in the cases quoted above, is the danger of diluting the equity by the acquisition. This means that if a company is making an acquisition and paying for it by an issue of new ordinary shares, it may not make enough in net profits from the acquired company to service the new shares, that is, the dividend declared on the new shares is not covered by the net profits due from the acquired firm. The dividends to the new shareholders would, in effect, be paid out of the profit which would normally have accrued to the old shareholders; their shares would therefore be reduced in value because either the dividend cover or the total amount of the dividend would have been reduced by the presence of the new shares.

Numerous research studies have shown that the danger of dilution is real. Many acquisitions do not pay for themselves.

NEGOTIATING THE DEAL

'Every deal dies nine times.' This is the rule of thumb used by experienced negotiators in the takeover field. Successful negotiation requires two things: one, keeping in mind objectives to be achieved during the discussions and, secondly, being well-prepared for negotiations.

Both sides should recognise that the closer the two parties come to an agreement, factors about which there are strong feelings will emerge—some very trivial—that could keep them apart. At this time no problem is too small to merit the full attention of the selling and the acquiring chief executives.

Negotiations include discussions not only on price, but also on terms and conditions including representations and warranties, tax, accounting and legal considerations, series of payments, employment contracts, reporting functions and other post-merger integration problems.

Negotiation is a team effort and requires the involvement of many participants at different points in the process such as:

(a) Principal Shareholders.
(b) Officers.
(c) Directors.
(d) Accountants.
(e) Lawyers.
(f) Investment Bankers.
(g) Operating Management.

The negotiating process cannot be reduced to a precisely calculated formula. Still, there are a few guidelines, basically common sense, that can facilitate negotiations and increase the chances of getting what you want. Some of the most important are discussed below. Keep in mind that the person across the table is following some of these same guidelines. The notes below assume the seller's side.

(1) Know what you want. Even before you begin negotiating, you should have a clear idea of what you want and of what's important to you. For example, what is the minimum price you will accept? Is the form of payment—cash, stock in the acquiring company, long-term debt, and so

on—important? Do you want to retain some control in the new organization? How much?

(2) Try to determine what the other side really wants. Is the buyer interested in the technology, patents, fixed assets, market outlets, customer base? Knowing what the other side wants will save time and effort in offering useless concessions.

(3) Consider the use of an experienced negotiator. Negotiating is an art. It is a delicate process, one that often benefits from the use of an experienced, tactful, disinterested third party. Your own intimate knowledge of your business, certainly an advantage during the course of negotiations, may be offset by an inability to deal unemotionally and dispassionately with some aspects of the give-and-take of negotiating. It is sometimes difficult for many owners to remain objective during discussions that seem to undervalue their creations.

An experienced negotiator, with no direct interest in the outcome, is open to all ideas and is willing to give them a fair hearing. Also, the negotiator is often better able to develop ideas and float 'trial balloons' that may advance the negotiations.

(4) Focus on particular issues. Separate the issues and deal with them on an individual basis.

(5) Do not back the other side into a corner. You should always leave a face-saving way out.

(6) Get something for each compromise.

(7) Listen carefully to what people say during negotiations. The negotiating process is complex. Words are merely one indication of what people mean. Gestures, facial expressions, and voice inflections are other important signals of what is taking place. 'Yes, I want that', for example, can mean a whole host of things, depending on the way it is said —including: 'I don't care about that one way or the other.'

Similarly, be aware of what you say and how you say it. Words can be taken out of context; they can be subtly redefined and come back to haunt you. Think before you speak, and monitor carefully the nuances of what you say.

(8) Think ahead; have a response prepared for what the other side might say. Try to anticipate what the prospective buyer will say —objections, counterproposals, and so on. The more you are able to do this, the less chance you have of being caught off guard and, by default, agreeing to an unfavourable proposition.

(9) Don't allow yourself to be rushed. You don't have to respond to everything the other side says. And when you do respond, take enough time so that your response is well thought out. However, it is important to be aware of time constraints that may have an effect on the

negotiations—the approaching end of a reporting year, for example.

On the other hand, a false sense of urgency is a tactic that can lead to unwise shortcuts and concessions. Keep in mind what's truly important, and make your responses count.

The overall goal should be to obtain the highest price for your business. The goal of the buyer is to pay the lowest price. The actual price will undoubtedly be neither—failing somewhere in between the extreme expectations of both sides.

However, if you have done the ground work carefully—valued your business accurately, attracted the appropriate buyer, and negotiated the sale skillfully—the final price you obtain for your company will be a fair one. It will satisfy you and it will satisfy the purchaser.

REVIEW OF MERGER ACTIVITY

Mergers and acquisitions come in waves. Usually late in a cycle of prosperity merger activity increases. Very often a wave of mergers spreads across the developed world. Bursts of activity in the USA in the 1920s, 1940s, 1960s and 1980s were repeated within a short time lag in the United Kingdom and Ireland. Ireland experienced a significant increase in mergers in the period 1960-73 when in that period one hundred quoted securities were either taken over, merged or liquidated on the Irish exchange. In that period, fifty-three quoted companies had major ownership changes. This activity reached a peak in the first three years of the 1970s, due mainly to the growth of conglomerates. During this period certain industrial sectors were prone to takeovers and mergers. Shoes and leather, paper packaging and the builders' providers sectors were reduced to virtually one company each.

Beginning in early 1971 the Irish Stock Exchange experienced a wave of acquisitions which ultimately produced a number of industrial holding companies or conglomerates. This development had been preceded by similar occurrences in the United States and United Kingdom. The acquisition of Crowe Wilson, which is now part of the Fitzwilton Group, began the movement. This was followed in rapid succession by Braids, Brooks Watson Holdings, Barrow Milling, James Crean and Ferrier Pollock.

The development of conglomerates on the Irish Stock Exchange could be traced to five causes:

(1) The extremely limited nature of the exchange with less than seventy quoted companies, many of which had relatively small total capitalisations.

(2) Laxity in applying stock exchange rules in Dublin.

(3) The presence of a bull market.

(4) The developing financial scene in Ireland which provided facilities for acquisitions.

(5) Precedents in the United States and United Kingdom.

The rise of conglomerates was followed by a spectacular fall which reduced share prices to a fraction of their high. One conglomerate, Braids, had to have its quotation suspended. Fitzwilton was forced to sell off most of its profitable companies. By the end of the 1970s Fitzwilton was not very different from the Gouldings of 1970. Brooks Watson too was forced to divest itself of businesses. Many investors paid dearly for their experience.

In the 1980s a new merger wave was in progress. This wave was based on the philosophy that it was cheaper to buy than to build. The bear markets of the late 1970s had reduced share prices while inflation had in many cases increased the net assets per share. Divestment of unwanted assets was a major factor in the development of the merger wave of the 1980s—led by Leveraged Buy Outs (LBOs).

LBOs began in the United States. During the heavy conglomerate era of the 1960s, a number of entrepreneurs formed miniconglomerates through the use of leveraged buyouts. The lender was normally a commercial finance company; commercial banks were not yet in this business. The acquired company was normally a smaller company—generally with less than £10 million of sales volume. The underlying collateral for the loan was the accounts receivable, inventories, and fixed assets of the acquired company.

In many cases the investor had no equity risk; in some he was not even asked to personally guarantee the loan. For that reason, this type of financing was often called 'bootstrap' financing—the entrepreneur could lift himself by his own bootstraps into a position of wealth and success. The lender normally insisted on adequate security, measured in terms of distressed liquidation values, and the thrust of the lender's analysis was directed toward good security rather than toward cash flow. Because each transaction was relatively small, the flow of deals went virtually unnoticed except by those who were actively engaged in the business.

In the 1970s a second type of leveraged buyout began to emerge. This type involved situations where a lender would take an option on equity and subordinate its debt, rather than taking collateral. This combination of equity and subordinated debt would entice another group of unsecured lenders to lay on a level of senior debt, since the target company's cash flow could clearly service such senior debt. The subordinated debt holders, initially limited to a small group of aggressive insurance companies, were willing to take a significant downside risk for an even more significant upside gain. Because no one was secured in the transaction, however, the analytical emphasis by all financing sources was on cash flow rather than on collateral.

Both secured and unsecured lenders had certain common criteria. Since in both cases an additional layer of debt was being imposed on the target company, with additional debt-servicing requirements, a company that was incurring heavy losses would not normally be a target for a leveraged buyout unless the loss was clearly a short-term phenomenon that could be quickly reversed. Second, the leaders in both cases normally wanted to have continuity of management, and most leveraged buyouts involved the management group's continued involvement. To assure this, the management group would often be given some part of the equity. In many cases, in fact, the driver behind the leveraged buyout was the management group itself, although in a number of cases a third-party entrepreneur would promote the acquisition.

In early 1980s a small number of US investment houses organised large-scale LBOs. This led to one of the greatest takeover booms ever seen in the world.

Inflation which increased the value of fixed assets, a booming stock market and, most importantly, a wave of development decisions led to a rapid increase in takeover activity.

In the six year period 1982-1988 much of corporate America was re-structured. In 1987 alone over $200 billion of takeover deals were agreed. A breed of financier known as a 'Corporate Raider' was able to obtain vast financial backing by issuing debt, that is, 'Junk Bonds'. With 'war chests' in the billions T. Boone Pickens made numerous takeover attempts on some of the world's largest oil companies. Companies such as Gulf Oil, and Texaco were raided.

Carl Icahn raided and acquired TWA and forced a major restructuring of United States Steel and then went after Texaco.

Many of the largest companies in the world adopted anti-takeover pro-visions in their Articles of Association so called 'poison pill provisions' and/or restructured themselves by borrowing on the assets of the company and paying the cash out to shareholders. Leveraged buyouts grew in size up to the $6 billion acquisition of Beatrice Foods by the former management. 'Junk Bonds' were the principal weapons in this takeover frenzy.

In the 1970s a young student Michael Milken completed a study on second line debentures. He discovered that the additional interest rule paid on these debentures more than covered any additional risk. This discovery led to the introduction of a range of second line debentures at above market rates of interest. In the ten year period 1975-1985 there were few defaults on these debentures. From becoming a curiosity in the late

Table 55　　　　　　　　Major Acquisitions in Ireland 1987

No.	Company	Amount Paid (£million)	Target	Percentage Acquired
1.	CRH	63	Catalan (Spain)	100
2.	Bord Gais Eireann	62	Dublin Gas	100
3.	Phoenix (UK)	45	Rohan Group	Maj
4.	Nat. Aus. Bank	41	Northern Bank	100
5.	Aer Lingus	30	Copthorne Hotels	100
6.	FII-Fyffes	29.5	Irish Distillers	20
7.	Bank of Ireland	27.7	Bank of America Fin. (UK)	100
8.	Waterford Glass	26.5	Trent Sanitaryware	100
9.	CRH	25.6	NC/Prods/Adams Prads	100
10.	Appletree (UK)	20	Kildare Chilling	100
11.	Smurfit Group	19	CCA (US)	Balance
12.	CRH	14.6	Big River Industries (US)	100
13.	Smurfit	14	CCA (Europe)	Balance
14.	Aviette	14	H. Williams	100
15.	Fitzwilton	13.3	Keep Trust (UK)	30
16.	Clondalkin	12	Fortune Plastics (US)	100
17.	Woodchester	11.90	Lookers (UK)	28.4
18.	Irish Wire	11.4	Tiger Tim (UK)	100
19.	Woodchester	10.4	Bowmaker	100
20.	Express Dairies	10	MacCormack Products	100
21.	Goodman International	10	Minch Norton	100
22.	Management/Acq.	9.9	Cahill May Roberts	100
23.	Kenmare	7.7	Irish Marine Oil	100
24.	Bord Bainne	7.5	Voko Foods (UK)	70
25.	Tuskar Resources	7.2	Ardmore	100
26.	CRH	6	St. Francis Materials (US)	Maj
27.	Hoskyns Group (UK)	5.7	CBT Systems	100
28.	Stallion	5.1	Impshire	100
29.	Goodman International	5	Merchants Warehousing	66
30.	Institutions	4.64	Wardell Roberts	35

Source: *Irish Business* January 1988

1970s they became, by the mid-1980s, the principal form of takeover finance. In the process Michael Milken became one of the world's richest men and the firm which employed him, Drexel Burnham Lambert, became a world ranked investment house.

This gearing up, or leveraging of companies increased the financial risk. In the event of a prolonged economic recession it is likely that many companies would be unable to meet their interest and capital repayments.

RECENT MERGER AND TAKEOVER ACTIVITY IN IRELAND

The depressed state of the Irish economy during the 1980s placed a damper on takeover activity yet by 1985 there were signs of a pick up in activity. Irish financial institutions experienced major bad debts in the 1980s and so were very reluctant to finance any form of speculative activity.

The major takeover activity in the 1980s was the flight abroad by substantial Irish firms. Most of the top ten publicly quoted Irish firms acquired one or more overseas companies. Some like Smurfits and CRH became true multinationals.

The move to divest unwanted divisions led to the emergence of Leveraged Buy Outs in Ireland. Most of the leverage had to be supplied by the seller in the form of debentures. A number of US firms divested themselves of Irish divisions. Public companies to follow this route included: Smurfits, Glen Abbey and Irish Ropes.

By 1987 confidence in the economy was returning, the stock exchange was rising and takeovers were active. Table 55 shows the top 30 takeovers affecting Irish companies in 1987. The total amount involved was in excess of £550 million.

Major changes took place on the stock exchange with control of a number of shell companies changing hands.

By the end of the takeover wave in the 1980s it would be safe to say that a majority of the fully listed publicly quoted companies in Dublin will derive the bulk of their business from overseas activities.

Further Reading
William, Davis: *Merger Mania,* The Anchor Press, London 1975.
E. Hekfert: *Valuation: Concepts and Practice,* Wadsworth, Belmont, California 1966.
Issuing House Association: *The City Code on Takeovers and Mergers,* London 1986.
R. W. Moon: *Business Mergers and Takeover Bids,* (6th Ed.). Gee, London 1982.
M. A. Weinberg: *Takeovers and Amalgamations,* (5th Ed.). Sweet and Maxwell, London 1986.

Chapter 16

International Finance

Ireland has one of the most open economies in the world. This means that international trade plays a stronger role in the Irish economy than it does in most other economies. Total imports and exports in 1987 were in excess of £20,000 million as against gross national product for the year of almost £16,000 million. Belgium, Holland and Denmark rank alongside Ireland. Nations such as Japan, the United Kingdom and the United States derive a much smaller proportion of their economic income from foreign trade.

As a small island economy Ireland had little option but to become involved in overseas business. Many of the conveniences of modern life are not produced in Ireland; they must be imported. New industries establishing throughout the country require plant and machinery which can only be found abroad. Irish agriculture and manufacturing industries need overseas markets to enable efficient levels of production.

The rapid development of the Irish economy in the 1960s, 1970s and 1980s was based on a policy which depended on export markets. The success of the Industrial Development Authority in attracting export-oriented projects to Ireland resulted in a fifteen-fold growth in manufactured exports in the period 1962-87. Accession to the European Economic Community in 1973 led to a rapid growth in agricultural exports.

However, the country did not permanently improve its balance of payments position. A positive balance of trade was offset by capital outflows or *vice versa*. Increased exports were offset by rising imports. A reduction in tariffs led to substantial increases in consumer goods and in raw material imports. Small Irish manufacturers who traditionally purchased locally found themselves faced with a dazzling range of international sources of material.

Balance of payments deficits were financed by tourism inflows, by private capital inflows and by state borrowing overseas. By the end of 1987 the state had borrowed overseas over £10,000 million while state-sponsored enterprises had borrowed a further £2,000 million.

Reserves fund the trade of a country. Irish reserves rose smartly in the 1980s from £975 million in January 1980 to £2,700 million in January 1988. The figure at the beginning of the decade represented four months' imports, whereas the figure in January 1988 covered less than three months' imports.

International business adds complexity and uncertainty to the job of management. Modern business management is difficult enough without adding problems of language, culture and currency differences to the task. As long as the bulk of overseas business was with the United Kingdom then Irish businessmen muddled through. The United Kingdom had a similar language, culture and economic life. At least as important was the fact that parity existed between the British and Irish currencies. This meant that the same financial institutions operated in both countries.

During the 1970s and 1980s overseas trade expanded into new markets. Many businessmen found themselves, for the first time, dealing with unknown institutions and handling little understood currencies. The problems were magnified in the spring of 1979 when parity between sterling and the punt was dissolved. During the 1980s further difficulties arose as currencies experienced major swings in values.

An understanding of the rudiments of international finance is an essential feature of every businessman's skills. This text sets out to provide such an understanding by examining the following areas: (a) the world monetary scene, (b) managing foreign exchange risk, (c) foreign currency borrowing, (d) international financial institutions.

THE WORLD MONETARY SCENE

In late November 1987 an Irish exporter receiving dollars for a sale could have exchanged them for punts at the following rate:

$$IR£1 = \$1.46$$

Six months later the rate was

$$IR£1 = \$1.60$$

So what, you might say, a 9 per cent difference! Consider the effect on a textile exporter operating on a gross profit margin of maybe 5 per cent. The currency swing if favourable would more than double his profits. If negative his margin and business could be wiped out.

Background to the Current System

The story of the modern system of international finance goes back to the latter days of the Second World War. A group of eminent economists met, at Bretton Woods in the United States to decide on an international currency system for the post-war era. If every nation fixed their currency against one medium of value such as gold there would have been no need for this meeting. On a gold standard, countries running a balance of payments deficit would cover the deficit by gold payments. Over time countries running deficits would adopt economic policies to stop the outflow. Such a simple system was not acceptable to the economists at Bretton Woods because many countries had no gold, others required time to rebuild and adapt their economies and, more importantly, the discipline of a gold standard was too harsh.

Instead, the economists developed a system of fixed exchange rates, in reality not too unlike the gold standard system. The United States dollar has a price fixed in gold. $35 = 1 oz. gold. Every other country established a relationship with the dollar, for example, the United Kingdom initially established a rate of $4.00:£1. To allow flexibility, currencies could vary by 1 per cent on either side of the agreed parity, for example, the 1944 dollar/pound rate could vary between $3.96:£1 and $4.04:£1. Central banks were obliged to maintain the value of their currency within the agreed limits. Organisations were established to assist the process of currency value maintenance. The International Monetary Fund was set up to assist countries to weather short-term international difficulties. Structural or secular problems were to be handled by the International Bank for Reconstruction and Development (World Bank). These institutions are examined in later sections.

The system of fixed exchange rates appeared to work well in the 1950s and 1960s. Trade expanded rapidly. Cracks did appear but they were papered over. The United Kingdom consistently ran balance of payments deficits. Major political importance was attached to the defence of sterling with the result that the country lived with a consistently overvalued exchange rate. This resulted in expensive exports, cheap imports, balance of trade deficits, overseas borrowings, and periodic devaluations. The Germans and Japanese reconstructed their economies with modern advanced technology. In the 1950s and 1960s the deutschmark and the yen were undervalued, resulting in immense trade surpluses in each country.

As long as the dollar remained strong the system held. The Asian wars caused the United States to run balance of payments deficits. At first this was acceptable as there was a scarcity of dollars in the world. Indeed, CTT (the Irish Export Board) was established in the 1950s to develop exports to dollar areas, as Ireland had little or no dollar reserves.

During the early 1960s a glut of dollars appeared. In theory, central banks could submit their dollar holdings to the United States Treasury and obtain gold at the rate of $35:1 oz. In practice, most countries did not wish to offend the mighty United States, so they held their dollar assets in the form of United States treasury bills. One group of institutions decided to loan dollars among themselves. This led to the development of the Eurodollar market (see below).

The fixed rate system continued to show stress. In 1968 a two-tier gold pricing system was developed. This system allowed for a private market in gold where the price could find an equilibrium level and a central bank market where the price was maintained at $35 per oz.

By the early 1970s the system was in shreds. The deutschmark had revalued and the French franc devalued in 1969. In August 1971 the United States decided that they would no longer convert dollars into gold. In effect this smashed the whole basis for the existing system. In December 1971, the Smithsonian agreement produced a revaluation of currencies against the dollar, a 10 per cent devaluation of the dollar against gold, and a widening of the bands around parities from 1 to $2\frac{1}{4}$ per cent.

By the end of 1973 the Smithsonian agreement had itself collapsed. The major world currencies were allowed to float against each other. The theory behind a floating system is simple. The value of a currency against any other currency is decided by the laws of supply and demand. In reality no country allows a 'clean float'. Central banks intervene in exchange rates to ensure an orderly market and also to moderate the effect of exchange rate changes on domestic policies. A system of managed floating rates in known as a 'dirty float'.

The last half of the 1970s was a period of unprecedented uncertainty in foreign exchange markets. The United States ran a series of horrendous balance of payments deficits—mainly due to oil imports. The United Kingdom, for long the weakest member of the reserve currency club, found new oil-based economic strength. Sterling, which had declined from $4.00:£1 in 1944 to $1.58:£1 in 1975, rose to over $2.30:£1 by 1980 and back to under $2.00:£1 by 1988 The deutschmark and yen rose against most currencies. Oil producers built up large surpluses. Throughout the decade the role of the International Monetary Fund grew but it was not capable of solving singlehandedly the financial problems facing the world currency system.

During the 1980s there was continuous upheaval in world currency markets. A dramatic reduction in oil prices led to elimination of the huge surpluses built up by the OPEC oil producing countries.

Third world countries found themselves totally unable to repay international loans. Brazil, Nigeria, Mexico, Argentina and Peru were among countries which had to restructure their obligations to international banks. There was a real possibility of massive defaults which would destroy the capital base of most large international banks and would lead to the collapse of the existing world monetary system. A third factor affecting the world monetary system was a sustained economic boom in the United States. This had two effects:

(a) The US became an attractive market for investors who bought billions of dollars worth of US assets, thus driving up the value of the dollar.

(b) The economic boom fueled imports which led to US balance of trade deficits of over $100 billion annually.

Certain countries, Japan, West Germany, Taiwan and Korea amassed vast reserves of US dollars.

The pressure on the system grew until the convulsion on world stock exchanges in October 1987. The dollar collapsed against the yen and the West German deutschmark. The US authorities belatedly moved to rectify a major budget deficit as a world economic recession loomed.

As the decade of the 1980s drew to a close there was growing unease with the world monetary system of floating exchange rates. The expectation that floating rates would lead to automatic and easy adjustments of economic policies did not materialise.

EUROPEAN MONETARY SYSTEM

In 1972 a group of European countries came together and produced an agreement to keep their currencies floating within a band of 2.25 per cent around a central parity. This system known as 'the snake' was an important step along the road to European Monetary Union. The idea was to create within Europe a zone of monetary stability. This system floundered in 1976. In 1978 a new attempt was made to bring together, in some co-operative format, the nine currencies of European Economic Community (EEC) members. In March 1979 the European Monetary System (EMS) was established. All EEC members with the exception of the United Kingdom were involved.

On the 30 March 1979 an event of major Irish economic significance took place. The Irish punt broke parity with the pound sterling, breaking a link over 150 years old. The break came because the pound sterling appreciated against the basket of EMS currencies, one of which was the Irish punt.

The ultimate objective of the EEC is political union. An essential part of a political union is a common currency. No-one could possibly envisage the United States of America with fifty differing currencies. As a first step on the road towards monetary union the European Commission proposed a system whereby a European Currency Unit would be established. This ECU represents a weighted average of the economic strength of EEC members. The initial weights and currency units as of March 1979 together with the revised position as of September 1984 are shown in Table 56.

Table 56 Composition of the ECU

		March 1979		September 1984	
		Weights	Currency Units	Weights	Currency Units
West Germany	Dm	27.3	0.828	34.93	0.719
France	FF	19.5	1.15	18.97	1.31
United Kingdom	£Stg	17.5	0.0885	11.87	0.0878
Italy	Lira	14.0	109.00	9.44	140.00
Netherlands	DG	9.0	0.286	11.04	0.256
Belgium/ Luxembourg	BF/LF	8.2	3.66/0.14	9.07	3.71/0.14
Denmark	DKr	3.0	0.217	2.79	0.219
Ireland	Ir£	1.5	0.00759	1.13	0.00871
Greece	Dra	—	—	0.76	1.15
		100%		100%	

Note that the Irish currency has a weight of only 1.13 per cent as of September 1984. Given that the values of the currencies change over time, so too do their weights. Further, a re-alignment of currency units takes place every five years or so, to take account of the movements in inter-community trade during that period. It is clear from the above table that the only movements likely to affect the overall value of the ECU are in the currencies of West Germany, France and the United Kingdom.

Members of the EMS, except Italy, have agreed to keep their currencies within a band of 2.25 per cent on either side of the central parity. Italy has a band of 6 per cent. In practice, if a currency crosses a divergent threshold, which is at 75 per cent of the maximum allowed spread, there is a presumption that the authorities concerned will correct this situation by adequate measures. When a currency reaches its maximum divergence, that is, it is at its limits with another currency, there is an automatic obligation on the two countries concerned to act. At the margins any or all of the following policies come into play:

(a) Intervention by a number of central banks.
(b) Monetary measures such as adjusting interest rates to relieve pressure on the exchange rate.
(c) Drawing on central credit facilities.
(d) Other external and domestic policy measures.

These four policies are the essence of the EMS. Their purpose is to buffer member economies from currency fluctuations. It is hoped that over time the 2.25 per cent bands can be reduced and finally eliminated.

The failure of the EMS to achieve currency stability is evidenced by the need for several realignments despite heavy central bank intervention. Relative to their positions in March 1979, the Deutsche mark and the Dutch guilder have soared, while the French franc and the Italian lira have nosedived. The gap has widened every year.

The basic reason for the apparent failure of the EMS is the demonstrated unwillingness of the major countries in the system to subordinate domestic political considerations to exchange rate considerations. This is demonstrated by the Germans, in response to an electorate's sensitivity to inflation, putting a premium on price stability, whilst the French have generally pursued a more expansive monetary policy in response to high domestic unemployment. The politicians who create fixed exchange rate systems are primarily pursuing broader sorts of unity such as political union, that is, the EEC. However fixed rate systems tend not to survive under the constant pressure of market forces towards 'purchasing power parity' and, in general, intervention to maintain a disequilibrium rate is either ineffective or injurious when pursued over lengthy periods of time. However, considering the turmoil and wide swings in rates between many currencies, the managed rates of the EMS have offered relative stability.

Ireland Within the European Monetary System

The major effect of the EMS on Irish business life was that parity with sterling could no longer be maintained. Apart from introducing a variable exchange rate with Ireland's major trading partner it also produced exchange controls between the two countries. This caused the loss of access to the London money market as a source of finance for Irish business, thus leading to higher domestic interest rates.

A second effect of the EMS was the discipline imposed on the Irish economy. Ireland is now a member of an economic grouping which has experienced much lower inflation than that usually in Ireland. If Ireland is to maintain membership of the EMS then her cost increases cannot get out of line. Stated simply, if one country has a rate of inflation 10 per cent higher than another then, assuming no productivity changes, the currency of the rapidly inflating country should devalue by 10 per cent. Because Ireland has accepted the discipline of a narrow band, domestic policies will have to bring inflation in line with that in other EMS member-states. There was evidence of this happening in the late 1980s.

MANAGING FOREIGN EXCHANGE RISK

From a business viewpoint the main effect of floating exchange rates is the problem of determining the local value of funds received from overseas sales. When a businessman sells abroad he expects a certain price in punts. In international trade the price set by the businessman might not equate with the funds actually received. Basically a business trading abroad faces three types of foreign exchange risk:

(1) Transaction Exposure.

This type of exposure occurs whenever a company imports or exports goods or services with another country and is invoicing them in the other country's currency. The company then has an exposure to that country's currency from the time they know how much currency is being charged, and not when the goods are delivered or warehoused. It is the most prevalent type of exposure in any company as it can be created by the day to day running of the company.

(2) Balance Sheet Exposure.

This type of exposure is of particular relevance in the case of multi-national companies operating foreign subsidiaries. The problem is that the foreign company's investment is the currency of the host country. When a foreign company sets up a plant in Ireland, they convert their own currency into Irish punts. From that moment they have an exposure against Irish punts. Notwithstanding their trading performance, the overall value of this investment if dollar based would have dropped by up to 35 per cent in the nine year period 1979 to 1987.

(3) Operational Risk.

This measures the impact of exchange fluctuations on all operational cash flows regardless of whether they require exchange transactions. It is conceptually a sound way of capturing the effects of exchange-rate changes on the value of a firm. However it is extremely difficult to measure and the various approaches used are outside the scope of this text.

A businessman selling abroad has a number of policy options available:

(1) He can sell in punts, thus leaving the currency problem to the buyer. This is an unsatisfactory method of overseas marketing as the buyer is likely to have many potential sources of supply. An Irish supplier pricing in punts is at an immediate disadvantage.

(2) He can price in the overseas currency, immediately borrow the sum of foreign currency and convert it into punts and repay the foreign currency loan when the overseas buyer pays. In this way the exporter protects the value of his sale. The cost of doing this is the cost of borrowing the funds less the interest profits earned in using the borrowed funds. The

principal difficulties attaching to this method are that banks may be unwilling to advance funds and the term of the loan is subject to the time of payment by the buyer.

(3) He can insure against currency changes by 'selling forward'. Some currencies have two exchange rates, the 'spot' rate, which is the current rate of exchange, and the forward rate, which is a rate of exchange projected 90, 180 or 360 days into the future. If a businessman expects to receive a sterling payment in ninety days time he can insure against any changes by selling sterling for punts with a delivery date ninety days hence. This system of insurance is known as 'hedging'.

In a perfect certain world there would be no difference between methods (2) and (3) above. The forward rate for a currency would represent the interest rate differentials between one currency and another. Interest rate differentials signify the difference in interest rates between similar financial instruments in different countries. If the annual interest rate on an Irish Exchequer bill was 15 per cent against a 10 per cent rate on United Kingdom Treasury bills then, other things being equal, the punt should be at a 5 per cent premium against sterling in the twelve-month forward market. Alas, other things are never equal, with the result that forward rates often deviate from the interest rate differential rate.

Hedging, as method (3) is known, is available only in widely traded currencies. Luckily the vast bulk of Irish exports are to countries which have forward currency markets.

An Irish importer who has to pay for goods at some future date is in a similar position to the exporter. He faces the uncertainty of not knowing how many punts will be required to pay the overseas supplier. The three methods outlined above apply, but in reverse, to this situation.

Managing foreign exchange requires not only a detailed knowledge of the exposure of the company over time on a currency-by-currency basis but also an understanding of the spot and forward exchange markets for the currencies involved. As Irish business grows and expands abroad this area will assume a significant importance in the profitability of the firm.

FOREIGN CURRENCY BORROWING

It is a measure of the growing sophistication of Irish business that the 1980s saw the evolution of overseas borrowings by companies other than state-sponsored enterprises. The resort to overseas sources was due in part to serious credit restrictions in the domestic economy and to a realisation by some companies that they could finance overseas interest and capital repayments out of their export revenue. The approval of the

Central Bank is necessary before a company can obtain foreign loans. Foreign borrowing is of four types:
- (a) Eurocurrency loans.
- (b) Borrowing foreign currencies from Irish institutions.
- (c) Borrowing foreign currencies from overseas institutions.
- (d) Swap loans.

Eurocurrencies

Many years ago the Eurocurrency market was called a 'transatlantic telephonic money market'. Over time the market developed to encompass long-term debt and equity instruments.

The Eurocurrency market evolved from the dollar glut. Some dollar holders, for various reasons, did not wish to invest their funds in the United States. They lodged them in European-based banks who agreed to open dollar denominated accounts. Interest in dollars was paid on their accounts and the deposits were repayable in dollars. There were many borrowers only too eager to borrow dollars who were willing and able to repay loans in dollars. In the 1980s the Eurocurrency market attracted other currencies such as the yen, the deutschmark, the Swiss frank and sterling. An Asia-currency market centred in Hong Kong also developed.

The Eurocurrency market is free of practically all regulation so that the rates of interest charged reflect supply and demand. This freedom from regulation has resulted in great flexibility. The sums involved are large, transaction costs are low and, because there are many lenders, loans of almost any maturity can be arranged. International banking markets helped recycle the so called 'petrodollars' but this has led to serious problems. Some countries borrowed large amounts to finance industrial development; Mexico, Brazil and Argentina being the three largest borrowers. These and other countries have experienced debt repayment and service problems, which has led to the need to reschedule debt repayments. Further problems in this area could create significant problems for the banking community.

The most significant development in Eurocurrency markets in recent years is the growing dominance of Japanese investors and bankers. In an attempt to offset their trade surpluses Japan has invested large sums overseas, often through the Eurocurrency markets. Japanese security houses and banks have bought into banks, stockbrokers and financial institutions in London and New York.

Few Irish companies are of such a size that they can borrow in the Eurocurrency markets. Part of the Alcan and Tara financing originated in the Eurocurrency markets; businesses borrowing dollars usually do so from this source. Interest rates are based on LIBOR—the London Inter Bank Ordinary Rate.

Foreign Currency Borrowing from Irish Institutions

The availability and cheapness of foreign currency loans makes them very attractive to borrowers. However, the danger of a devaluation of the punt against the borrowed currency creates a risk of severe capital loss. Consider the following example.

On the 12 March 1985 an Irish clothing manufacturer borrowed 369,000 deutschmarks at a 10 per cent interest rate with a four-year term. Interest was payable annually and the capital sum was repayable in full on the 11 March 1989. Assume an annual devaluation of the Irish punt against the deutschmark of 5 per cent. Table 57 shows the effect of changes in currency rates on the borrower's punt repayments.

Table 57   The Effect of Exchange Rate Changes

		Deutschmarks		Punts	
	Spot Rate	*Inflow*	*Outflow*	*Inflow*	*Outflow*
Year 0	3.69 DM:£1 IR	369,000		£100,000	
1	3.50 DM:£1 IR		36,900[1]		10,542
2	3.33 DM:£1 IR		36,900[1]		11,081
3	3.16 DM:£1 IR		36,900[1]		11,677
4	3.00 DM:£1 IR		36,900[1]		12,300
5	2.85 DM:£1 IR		405,900[2]		142,421

1. Interest at 10 per cent
2. Interest plus capital repayment

Note the outcome carefully. The Irish businessman borrows £100,000 in deutschmarks. He must pay his annual interest in deutschmarks but to do so each year he must set aside an ever increasing number of punts. The real crunch comes when the capital must be repaid. To purchase 369,000 deutschmarks in 1989 cost £129,473. The apparently cheap loan has increased to an annual rate of 15 per cent per annum. Imagine what would occur if the rate of devaluation was 15 per cent per annum. In four years the exchange rate would fall to 1.92 DM:£1 IR. The unfortunate Irish borrower would need to put up £192,188 to repay the 369,000 DM capital.

Borrowing a non EMS currency is even more risky. Certain Irish businesses have taken severe capital losses because of Swiss franc and yen boons. In the early part of the 1980s dollar loans caused losses which were reversed in 1987 and 1988 when dollar values declined.

Short-term borrowing is less risky, as short-term economic predictions can be made with some degree of assurance. Companies with revenues in overseas currencies can minimise the risk of exchange rate losses by borrowing only in those currencies in which they have revenues.

Because of the exchange rate risk banks make foreign currency loans only to financially strong businesses.

Foreign Currency Loans from Overseas Banks

An innovation in Irish lending has been the willingness of some European-based banks to provide foreign currency loans to Irish-based businesses. Ideally the foreign lenders receive a loan guarantee from an Irish institution but in certain cases where the Irish borrower is well known to the European lender such guarantees are not required.

Swap Loans

An Irish business may wish to borrow punts but due to a credit squeeze or to lack of collateral it is unable to do so. However, the Irish business has connections abroad such as a sister or parent company which has liquid funds. The overseas company agrees to deposit funds in an overseas bank. The Irish branch, or associate, of the overseas bank now makes a loan to the Irish borrower. The bank has a lien on the funds deposited abroad. The bank usually pays interest on the deposit and charges interest on the loan. The 'spread' between the two rates depends on numerous factors but can be as low as 1 per cent. Such loans are also known as back-to-back loans.

INTERNATIONAL FINANCIAL INSTITUTIONS

A growing number of international or supranational organisations affect the operations of modern business. A small proportion of such organisations are financially oriented and it is these which are examined in this chapter. The organisations examined are the European Regional Development Fund, the European Investment Bank, the International Monetary Fund and the World Bank.

The European Regional Development Fund

The European Regional Development Fund was established in 1975 by the Council of Ministers of the European Communities and was most recently amended by the Council in June 1984. Regulation (EEC) No. 1787/84 of 19 June 1984 now governs the operation of the Fund. The purpose of the ERDF is to contribute to the correction of the principal regional imbalances within the Community, by participating in the development and structural adjustment of regions whose development is lagging behind and in the conversion of declining industrial regions. For ERDF purposes, Ireland is regarded as one region.

ERDF resources are allocated to Member States on the basis of a range of upper and lower limits. Ireland's quota of the Fund ranges between a lower limit of 3.82 per cent to an upper limit of 4.61 per cent. The lower limit indicates the minimum amount of ERDF resources guaranteed to Ireland provided that an adequate volume of applications are submitted which satisfy the conditions of the Regulation.

The ERDF provides assistance on foot of investment in specific projects which cost in excess of 50,000 ECU (approx. IR£35,800) and which are of the following type:

(1) Investment projects in the industrial, craft or services sectors which relate to economically sound activities and which help to create or maintain permanent jobs.

(2) Infrastructure investment projects the cost of which are borne by public authorities or by other organisations designated as responsible for carrying out such projects and which contribute to the development of the region or area in which they are located.

The Fund may also assist in the provision of facilities to small and medium-sized enterprises (SMEs) which will enable them to expand their activities, obtain access to new technology and facilitate their access to the capital market.

Applications for ERDF assistance for the above investments may be made on the basis of individual projects or multiannual programmes of investment. All applications must be made through the State. To benefit from ERDF assistance, investments must fall within the framework of our regional development programme and must have national assistance already committed. The ERDF contribution in the case of projects in the industrial, craft or services sectors is 50 per cent of the aid granted to each project by the public authority under a regional aid scheme. In the case of infrastructural schemes, the contribution is 50 per cent of the total expenditure being met by a public authority where the investment is less than 15 million ECU and between 30 per cent and 50 per cent where the investment costs more than 15 million ECU. These rates may rise to 55 per cent in the case of projects of particular importance to the development of the. region or area in which they are located. In the case of assistance to SMEs, the amount of the ERDF contribution is decided by the Commission of the European Communities.

ERDF assistance to Ireland amounted to IR£557.6 million by end-1985 and covered all the main sectors of economic activity as shown in Figure 9. The sectoral breakdown of the grants is shown on an annual basis in Table 58.

Table 58 ERDF Net Commitments 1975-85 (IR£million)

	1975	1976	1977	1978	1979	1980	1981	1982	1983	1984	1985	Total	%
Industrial Grants	3.4	4.9	4.7	8.1	9.2	5.9	10.6	21.1	10.4	32.1	27.3	137.7	25
Telecommunications	—	3.4	2.5	1.3	7.8	26.0	31.4	19.1	12.0	30.0	—	133.5	24
Roads	0.3	1.2	0.6	5.7	3.4	2.8	7.4	11.8	20.8	29.7	30.3	114.0	20
Sanitary Services	1.3	4.2	2.0	5.4	6.2	8.0	8.1	14.2	17.3	12.9	31.0	110.6	20
Education/Training Centres	—	—	—	—	0.2	—	—	—	—	2.8	15.1	18.1	3
Tourism Infrastructure	—	—	0.2	—	—	—	—	—	—	0.2	—	0.4	⎱ 3
Airport Development	—	—	—	—	—	—	—	—	0.2	—	0.6	0.8	⎰
Arterial Drainage	—	—	—	—	—	2.5	3.0	7.8	—	—	—	13.3	
Harbours	—	—	1.1	—	3.0	—	1.8	0.2	0.2	0.1	5.1	11.5	2
Railways	—	—	—	—	—	5.5	—	—	5.8	—	—	11.3	2
Advance Factories	1.0	0.2	0.4	1.2	1.2	1.0	1.4	—	—	—	—	6.4	1
TOTAL	6.0	13.9	11.5	21.7	31.0	51.7	63.7	74.2	66.7	107.8	109.4	557.6	100

Figure 9   ERDF Grant Commitments (Net)
                              Sectoral Breakdown

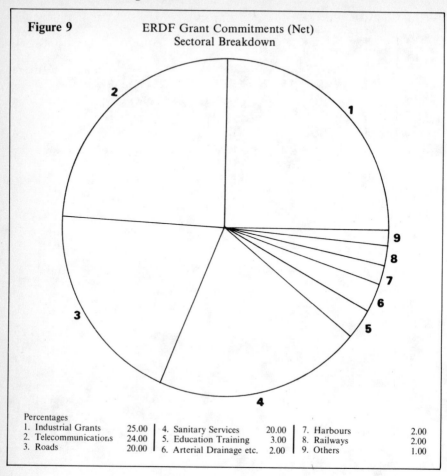

Percentages

1. Industrial Grants	25.00	4. Sanitary Services	20.00	7. Harbours	2.00
2. Telecommunications	24.00	5. Education Training	3.00	8. Railways	2.00
3. Roads	20.00	6. Arterial Drainage etc.	2.00	9. Others	1.00

The European Investment Bank

The European Investment Bank (EIB) was set up under the Treaty of Rome to contribute to the balanced and steady development of the Common Market in the interest of the Community. The Bank makes or guarantees loans for investment projects, principally in industry, energy and infrastructure which further:

(a) The economic development of the Community's less developed regions;

(b) Modernisation or conversion of undertakings, development or introduction of advanced technology to improve the competitiveness of Community industry, fostering of cooperation between undertakings in different Member Countries;

(c) The improvement of communications between Member States and other Community objectives such as energy policy and the protection of the environment.

The EIB finances capital investment which contributes directly or indirectly to an increase in economic productivity in general and which is economically and technically viable. Capital is subscribed by Member States; however the bulk of resources comes from borrowings on capital markets inside and outside the Community. The European Investment Bank also plays an important role in deploying development finance in the Mediterranean region and under the Third Lome Convention to African, Caribbean and Pacific countries.

In 1986, the Bank provided financing (including loans from the New Community Instrument for borrowing and lending) inside the European Community of over 7 billion ECUs (IR£5.4 billion). Of this, approx. IR£196 million was provided to Ireland.

The loans given were for four different categories of projects.

(1) Infrastructure projects financed by the Exchequer under the Public Capital Programme and for which the Exchequer borrows directly from the EIB.

(2) Projects undertaken by state-sponsored bodies for which they borrow on their own behalf from the EIB without any exchange risk cover from the Exchequer;

(3) Global loans from the EIB to the ICC and ACC for on-leading, for fixed asset investment to small and medium-sized manufacturing and agri-business firms as well as for tourism projects. Exchange risk cover is provided by the Exchequer where certain eligibility criteria are met;

(4) Direct loans for private sector industrial projects. Mainly because of exchange risk, there have been few direct loans to the private sector in Ireland.

Just over half (54 per cent) of these loans went directly to the Exchequer to finance investment in infrastructure. The sectoral breakdown of these loans is shown on an annual basis in Figure 10. It will be noted that telecommunications was relatively prominent until the early 1980s prior to the reorganisation of the telecommunications and postal services. More recently, roads and sanitary services have benefitted substantially from EEC loan finance while forestry has attracted substantial EEC loans for a programme of its size. The education/training sector is also noteworthy. The EIB is strictly confined to assisting infrastructure of a clearly economic (rather than social) nature. In recent years, Ireland has secured loans for AnCO (now part of FAS) and ACOT (now integrated into Teagasc) training centres, for regional technical colleges and for other institutions in the higher education sector such as NIHE Limerick, NIHE

Dublin, the Dublin Institute of Technology at Bolton Street and Kevin Street as well as for the National Microelectronics Research Centre in Cork. This provides clear recognition of the crucial role played by such institutions and centres in developing the Irish economy.

EIB lending to State sponsored bodies has been concentrated on the ESB's energy programme, mainly for the construction of the Moneypoint plant but also for the development of its transmission network. The telecommunications programme has also benefitted through loans to Irish Telecommunications Investments Limited. Industry and agriculture have been funded largely through the global loans to ICC and ACC. Other loans have been to CIE mainly for the DART project and to B and I for the purchase of car ferries.

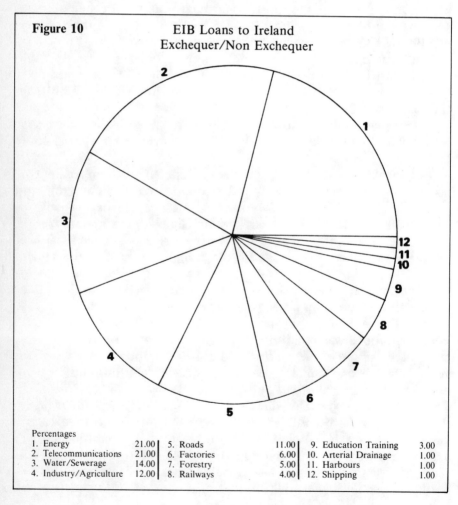

Figure 10   EIB Loans to Ireland
Exchequer/Non Exchequer

Percentages					
1. Energy	21.00	5. Roads	11.00	9. Education Training	3.00
2. Telecommunications	21.00	6. Factories	6.00	10. Arterial Drainage	1.00
3. Water/Sewerage	14.00	7. Forestry	5.00	11. Harbours	1.00
4. Industry/Agriculture	12.00	8. Railways	4.00	12. Shipping	1.00

The securing of EEC grants and loans requires a cooperative effort between the Department of Finance, the sponsoring Government departments/agencies and other bodies such as local authorities. The role of those bodies in charge of the actual implementation of the project is of particular importance. In many cases, EEC financing is made available only on foot of an in-depth project appraisal, including an on-the-spot investigation carried out by an EEC team. This is standard procedure for EIB financing. The cooperation of the sponsoring bodies is of paramount importance for such appraisal visits. Once projects are approved for EEC financing, the Government enter into contractual commitments regarding the implementation of the projects within a specified time scale and must provide appropriate annual allocations, on foot of the EEC finance thus made available, to ensure that their commitments are honoured. It is then the responsibility of the sponsoring bodies to ensure that these allocations from the Government are expended in the manner intended. Project implementation is closely monitored by the EEC institutions and, during the course of construction and/or on completion, on-the-spot checks may be carried out by a number of such institutions notably the Commission, the EIB and the European Court of Auditors. In addition, the Government are required to provide the European institutions with annual progress reports. Again the involvement of the sponsoring bodies is essential at all these stages. Clearly, therefore, the sponsoring bodies play an important role in securing the EEC grants and loans to finance the Government's capital investment programme. There is, of course, a clear advantage to the sponsoring body in having its project approved for EEC financing, since this guarantees that the funds will be provided by the Government, on foot of their contractual commitments to the EEC, to enable the project to be completed on schedule.

The International Monetary Fund

The IMF was first mooted in 1944 and commenced financial operations in 1947. The fund was set up with a reserve of currencies supplied by members. Its objectives are:

(a) To assist in the development of international prosperity by assisting members with balance of payments deficits.

(b) To implement guidelines for international monetary stability.

(c) To promote cooperation on international monetary matters.

The IMF acts internationally in a manner similar to that of a local commercial bank. The fund provides temporary or emergency currency reserves to countries in balance of payments difficulties just as a bank provides overdraft facilities to a company. A member's maximum access to the Fund's reserves is determined by its quota which is, effectively, its subscription to the Fund and which is subject to revision every five years or so.

A country running deficits can borrow from the IMF. As the level of borrowings increase so too do the restrictions imposed on the borrower. The objective is for the borrower to implement economic policies which will redress the adverse balance.

In the late 1960s the Fund membership agreed to the creation of Special Drawing Rights (SDRs). This was a major step towards the creation of a supranational central bank. SDRs are a form of international credit instrument. Countries can use them to cover deficits and/or they can be kept as reserves.

Ireland is an active member of the IMF. While we used the borrowing facility in the early years of our membership, we have not had recourse to it since 1970.

The World Bank

The World Bank was created at Bretton Woods as a new type of international investment institution to make or to guarantee loans for reconstruction and development projects. It was conceived originally to assist in the reconstruction of post-war Europe but evolved rapidly into an organisation to assist in developing third-world countries, by fostering economic development through financial, technical and advisory assistance.

It comprises a group of three affiliated institutions. The International Bank for Reconstruction and Development (also known as the World Bank), the International Development Association (IDA) and the International Finance Corporation (IFC).

The World Bank (IBRD) and IDA make loans for high priority projects and programmes in member countries to further their development plans. These loans are made to sovereign governments or to entities enjoying the full faith and credit of sovereign governments. In the case of the Bank, these loans are made on commercial terms. IDA's lending terms, on the other hand, are very generous or 'soft' as IDA was established to assist the poorest countries which could not afford to borrow money from the Bank on its normal terms. The purpose of the IFC is to assist developing countries in promoting private enterprise. The Corporation's investments take the form of both loan and equity financing of private sector projects in developing countries.

In the earlier years of its operations, the Bank concentrated its lending on capital infrastructure projects—mainly transportation, electric power, telecommunications and irrigation and flood control. In the 1970s, the requirements of such sectors as agriculture, education and industrialisation were recognised by the Bank and IDA to be crucial to social and economic progress and lending was extended to those sectors. In recent years the Bank has increased the amount of loan finance which is not tied to specific projects but is conditional on national policies being adjusted to cope with balance of payments difficulties and to promote growth. This lending is known as structural adjustment lending.

The Bank's finances are based on increases in capital subscriptions made from time to time by its members. At the end of June 1987 over 85 billion dollars had been subscribed but of this only about 8.75 per cent is paid-in. The Bank's lending programme is financed in part through the paid-in capital, but mainly through commercial borrowing on the international capital markets.

IDA's resources come predominantly from grant contributions, known as replenishments, from the richer countries among its membership. From its establishment to end June 1987 IDA had issued some 44 billion dollars in credits to member countries.

As in the case of the World Bank, member countries subscribe for capital in the IFC. Paid-in capital amounted to over 700 million dollars at end June 1987. These subscriptions, in conjunction with borrowings are used to fund the Corporation's investments.

Ireland is a member of all three World Bank affiliates. In the period 1969-75, eight loans were made by the Bank to Ireland to promote agriculture and small business development and to improve education and telecommunications facilities. Ireland no longer qualifies for World Bank loans because of our developed status of the economy.

CONCLUSION

The business environment facing Irish firms throughout the 1980s was the growing international aspect. No longer can a local firm rely on local markets, suppliers or financiers. As communications improve and as Ireland integrates further into the European Economic Community the opportunities and the threats posed by international business will grow.

From a financial management viewpoint there are two significant factors attaching to international business, the problem of exchange rate fluctuations and the possibility of raising finance from overseas sources. The foreign exchange market is complex but needs to be understood by businessmen. All over the world and particularly, in America, financial houses are coming up with new methods and techniques. The financial wizards on Wall Street have come up with a bevy of acronyms, to describe the new techniques which are now available. Not far behind the Americans in this field are the Japanese. Now the Irish financial specialists are trying to interest their Irish clients in these new methods.

This chapter indicated a number of ways in which the risks attaching to exchange rates can be reduced.

Overseas borrowing is relatively new to Irish borrowers but it is likely to expand rapidly in the coming years.

Further Reading
F. M. Wilkes & R. E. Brayshaw, *Company Finance and its Management,* Van Nostrand Reinhold (UK) 1986.
R. M. Rodriguez & E. E. Carter, *International Financial Management,* (3rd Ed.), Prentice Hall, Englewood Cliffs, New Jersey 1984.

Appendices

PRESENT VALUE TABLES (To be used in conjunction with Chapter 6)

APPENDIX A — Present Value of £1 Tables — Percentage

Year	5	6	7	8	9	10	11	12	13
1	.952	.943	.935	.926	.917	.909	.901	.893	.885
2	.907	.890	.873	.857	.842	.826	.812	.797	.783
3	.864	.840	.816	.794	.772	.751	.731	.712	.693
4	.823	.792	.763	.735	.708	.683	.659	.636	.613
5	.784	.747	.713	.681	.650	.621	.593	.567	.543
6	.746	.705	.666	.630	.596	.564	.535	.507	.480
7	.711	.665	.623	.583	.547	.513	.482	.452	.425
8	.677	.627	.582	.540	.502	.467	.434	.404	.376
9	.645	.592	.544	.500	.460	.424	.391	.361	.333
10	.614	.558	.508	.463	.422	.386	.352	.322	.295
11	.585	.527	.475	.429	.388	.350	.317	.287	.261
12	.557	.497	.444	.397	.356	.319	.286	.257	.231
13	.530	.469	.415	.368	.326	.290	.258	.229	.204
14	.505	.442	.388	.340	.299	.263	.232	.205	.181
15	.481	.417	.362	.315	.275	.239	.209	.183	.160

Year	14	15	16	17	18	19	20	21	22
1	.877	.870	.862	.855	.847	.840	.833	.826	.820
2	.769	.756	.743	.731	.718	.706	.694	.683	.672
3	.675	.658	.641	.624	.609	.593	.579	.564	.551
4	.592	.572	.552	.534	.516	.499	.482	.467	.451
5	.519	.497	.476	.456	.437	.419	.402	.386	.370
6	.456	.432	.410	.390	.370	.352	.335	.319	.303
7	.400	.376	.354	.333	.314	.296	.279	.263	.249
8	.351	.327	.305	.285	.266	.249	.233	.218	.204
9	.308	.284	.263	.243	.225	.209	.194	.180	.167
10	.270	.247	.227	.208	.191	.176	.162	.149	.137
11	.237	.215	.195	.178	.162	.148	.135	.123	.112
12	.208	.187	.168	.152	.137	.124	.112	.102	.092
13	.182	.163	.145	.130	.116	.104	.093	.084	.075
14	.160	.141	.125	.111	.099	.088	.078	.069	.062
15	.140	.123	.108	.095	.084	.074	.065	.057	.051

Year	23	24	25	26	27	28	29	30	
1	.813	.806	.800	.794	.787	.781	.775	.769	
2	.661	.650	.640	.630	.620	.610	.601	.592	
3	.537	.524	.512	.500	.488	.477	.466	.455	
4	.437	.423	.410	.397	.384	.373	.361	.350	
5	.355	.341	.328	.315	.303	.291	.280	.269	
6	.289	.275	.262	.250	.238	.227	.217	.207	
7	.235	.222	.210	.198	.188	.178	.168	.159	
8	.191	.179	.168	.157	.148	.139	.130	.123	
9	.155	.144	.134	.125	.116	.108	.101	.094	
10	.126	.116	.107	.099	.092	.085	.078	.073	
11	.103	.094	.086	.079	.072	.066	.061	.056	
12	.083	.076	.069	.062	.057	.052	.047	.043	
13	.068	.061	.055	.050	.045	.040	.037	.033	
14	.055	.049	.044	.039	.035	.032	.028	.025	
15	.045	.040	.035	.031	.028	.025	.022	.020	

APPENDIX B Present Value of £1 Receivable Annually
at the End of the Each Year

					Percentage					
Year	1	2	3	4	5	6	7	8	9	10
1	0.990	0.980	0.971	0.962	0.952	0.943	0.935	0.926	0.917	0.909
2	1.970	1.942	1.913	1.886	1.859	1.833	1.808	1.783	1.759	1.736
3	2.941·	2.884	2.829	2.775	2.723	2.673	2.624	2.577	2.531	2.487
4	3.902	3.808	3.717	3.630	3.546	3.465	3.387	3.312	3.240	3.170
5	4.853	4.713	4.580	4.452	4.329	4.212	4.100	2.993	3.890	3.791
6	5.795	5.601	5.417	5.242	5.076	4.917	4.767	4.623	4.486	4.355
7	6.728	6.472	6.230	6.002	5.786	5.582	5.389	5.206	5.033	4.868
8	7.652	7.325	7.020	6.733	6.463	6.210	5.971	5.747	5.535	5.335
9	8.566	8.162	7.786	7.435	7.108	6.802	6.515	6.247	5.995	5.759
10	9.471	8.983	8.530	8.111	7.722	7.360	7.024	6.710	6.418	6.145
11	10.368	9.787	9.253	8.760	8.306	7.887	7.499	7.139	6.805	6.495
12	11.255	10.575	9.954	9.385	8.863	8.384	7.943	7.536	7.161	6.814
13	12.134	11.348	10.635	9.986	9.394	8.853	8.358	7.904	7.487	7.103
14	13.004	12.106	11.296	10.563	9.899	9.295	8.745	8.244	7.786	7.367
15	13.865	12.849	11.938	11.118	10.380	9.712	9.108	8.559	8.061	7.606

Year	11	12	13	14	15	16	17	18	19	20
1	0.901	0.893	0.885	0.877	0.870	0.862	0.855	0.847	0.840	0.833
2	1.713	1.690	1.668	1.647	1.626	1.605	1.585	1.566	1.546	1.528
3	2.444	2.402	2.361	2.322	2.283	2.246	2.210	2.174	2.140	2.106
4	3.102	3.037	2.974	2.914	2.855	2.798	2.743	2.690	2.639	2.589
5	3.696	3.605	3.517	3.433	3.352	3.274	3.199	3.127	3.058	2.991
6	4.231	4.111	3.998	3.889	3.784	3.685	3.589	3.498	4.410	3.326
7	4.712	4.564	4.423	4.288	4.160	4.039	3.922	3.812	3.706	3.605
8	5.146	4.968	4.799	4.639	4.487	4.344	4.207	4.078	3.954	3.837
9	5.537	5.328	5.132	4.946	4.772	4.607	4.451	4.303	4.163	4.031
10	5.889	5.650	5.426	5.216	5.019	4.833	4.659	4.494	4.339	4.192
11	6.207	5.938	5.687	5.453	5.234	5.029	4.836	4.656	4.486	4.327
12	6.492	6.194	5.918	5.660	5.421	5.197	4.988	4.793	4.610	4.439
13	6.650	6.424	6.122	5.842	5.583	5.342	5.118	4.910	4.715	4.533
14	6.982	6.628	6.302	6.002	5.724	5.468	5.229	5.008	4.802	4.611
15	7.191	6.811	6.462	6.142	5.847	5.575	5.324	5.092	4.876	4.675

Year	21	22	23	24	25	26	27	28	29	30
1	0.826	0.820	0.813	0.806	0.800	0.794	0.787	0.781	0.775	0.769
2	1.509	1.492	1.474	1.457	1.440	1.424	1.407	1.392	1.376	1.361
3	2.074	2.042	2.011	1.981	1.952	1.923	1.896	1.868	1.842	1.816
4	2.540	2.494	2.448	2.404	2.362	2.320	2.280	2.241	2.203	2.166
5	2.926	2.864	2.803	2.745	2.689	2.635	2.583	2.532	2.483	2.436
6	3.245	3.167	3.092	3.020	2.951	2.885	2.821	2.759	2.700	2.643
7	3.508	3.416	3.327	3.242	3.161	3.083	3.009	2.937	2.868	2.802
8	3.726	3.619	3.518	3.421	3.329	3.241	3.156	3.076	2.999	2.925
9	3.905	3.786	3.673	3.566	3.463	3.366	3.273	3.184	3.100	3.019
10	4.054	3.923	3.799	3.682	3.571	3.465	3.364	3.269	3.178	3.092
11	4.177	4.035	3.902	3.776	3.656	3.544	3.437	3.335	3.239	3.147
12	4.278	4.127	3.985	3.851	3.725	3.606	3.493	3.387	3.286	3.190
13	4.362	4.203	4.053	3.912	3.780	3.656	3.538	3.427	3.322	3.223
14	4.432	4.265	4.108	3.962	3.824	3.695	3.573	3.459	3.351	3.249
15	4.489	4.315	4.315	4.001	3.859	3.726	3.601	3.483	3.373	3.268